INDIA EMERGES

INDIA EMERGES

**A CONCISE HISTORY OF INDIA
FROM ITS ORIGIN TO THE PRESENT**

STEVEN WARSHAW

diablo press

PRINTING HISTORY
First edition as part of ASIA EMERGES

First Printing
1964

Second Printing
1966

Third Printing
1967

Revised and expanded as INDIA EMERGES
1974

Second printing as INDIA EMERGES
1974

Third printing as INDIA EMERGES
1979

Fourth printing as INDIA EMERGES
1985

Fifth printing as INDIA EMERGES
1987

Sixth printing as INDIA EMERGES
1988

Seventh printing as INDIA EMERGES
1989

Library of Congress Cataloging in Publication Data

Warshaw, Steven.
   India emerges.

   (The Asia emerges series, 4)
   First published in 1964 as part of Asia emerges, by
A. J. Tudisco; rev. and expanded.
   Bibliography: p.
   1. India–History. I. Bromwell, C. David, joint
author. II. Tudisco, A. J., joint author.
III. Tudisco, A. J. Asia emerges. IV. Title.
DS436.W36   954   73-93983

ISBN 0-87297-019-1 Paper Edition

CONTENTS

Contents

Contents

Contents

Political Development, 185-92
Early struggles: Pakistan. The restoration of martial law.
The Postwar Nations, 192-98
Pakistan: internal politics. Foreign relations.
The Future of Pakistan, 198
Bangladesh, 198-201
Problems and policies.

PREFACE AND ACKNOWLEDGMENTS

INDIA IS ONE OF THE WORLD'S oldest cultures and one of its newest nations. For centuries it struggled inconclusively with the problem of government. Lacking the centralized bureaucracy of China or the homogeneous, hierarchical society of Japan, its historical behavior has been less well focused than theirs. Now, having achieved independence by its own unique means, it can be expected to express its spiritual past in new terms. Measured by its size, population, raw materials, and momentum, it has suddenly become one of the world's major powers.

India's new problems are more critical than any it has faced before. They involve countless millions more people. Under the constant pressure of population growth, the Union of India races daily to avert mass starvation and epidemics, to educate, and to overcome ancient social barriers. Water, shelter, and clothing, as well as food, are in short supply. Yet, rising above these threats there is a new India. In it there are unrivaled dams, irrigation projects, and nuclear power. India, as always, is a kaleidoscope of life.

In recent years, India has become increasingly prominent in the American consciousness. Its philosophies and arts have attracted people who are aware that they will need more than technology to solve their spiritual problems. Despite this new awareness of Indian ideas, most Americans know little about the history from which those ideas spring. It was to help them gain an introductory knowledge of this history that *India Emerges* was written. The book, which is eclectic, offers no new scholarship to this vast field, but for many may serve as the beginning of a study which English-speaking peoples can no longer afford to postpone.

It is unlikely that the revision would ever have taken place without the specific encouragement of the members of two faculties: Sister M. Naomi Schreiner O.S.U., of Cleveland's Villa Angela Academy; and John Szablewicz, Social Studies Chair at Connecticut's Fairfield College Preparatory School. Their persistence in calling for a new edition and their willingness to read the manuscripts in advance of publication inspired changes which, it is to be hoped, will live for another eight printings. Their suggestions, and those of David Driscoll, long a teacher of Asian history, also of Fairfield, resulted in many helpful additions.

In the same generous spirit Tom Koberna, a distinguished author and the editor of many texts, analyzed the material. His incisive questions concerning data and his penchant for plain English improved all four books. Other readers, of course, chiefly focused on the one manuscript of the four in whose subject they are noted and so put the books to severe texts for accuracy and clarity. The material was presented to readers who reviewed it with the precision that is characteristic of the best scholars in the field. They included:

J. V. Bondurant, Associate Research Political Scientist, Institute of International Studies, University of California, Berkeley; Leo E. Rose, Assistant Research Political Scientist, University of California, Berkeley; and Mary-Leela Rao, Asia Foundation, San Francisco. The book was revised in its fourth printing and was significantly improved by the contributions of Professor Eugene F. Irschick, a specialist in Indian studies at the University of California, Berkeley, as well as by Mr. Koberna, who at that time was a consultant to a division of the Macmillan Company.

The illustrations for *India Emerges* were drawn from many sources, in particular: Frank Huggins, Associate Editor, *The Asian Student*, a publication of the Asia Foundation; Dr. Elizabeth Huff, Dr. Richard G. Irwin, and Chang-Soo Swanson, of the East Asiatic Library, University of California, Berkeley; the Consulate-General of India, San Francisco; and the India Travel Service, San Francisco. Rand-McNally and the U.S. Government Printing Office, publisher of the Area Handbooks of the American University, supplied the maps.

Finally, it is unlikely that the initial printings of the book would have been as well accepted if not for the work of C. David Bromwell and A. J. Tudisco, both of whose contributions were made to the first eight chapters.

SW
Berkeley, California

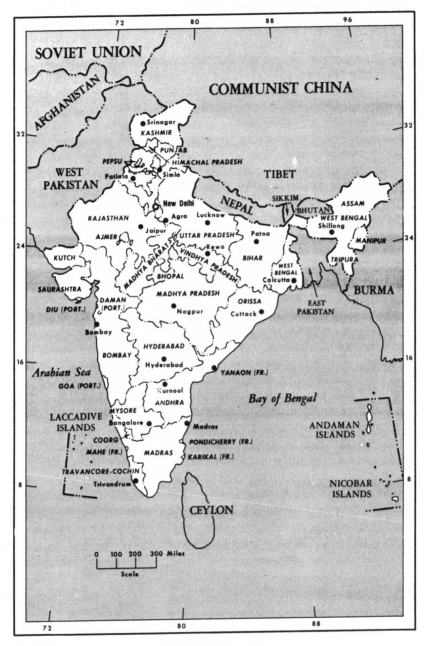

India after independence.

As India builds industrial power, traditional and modern ways are vividly contrasted. The women above are carrying ore in a great new steel plant.

नत्वेवाहं जातु नासं न त्वं नेमे जनाधिपाः ।
न चैव नभविष्यामः सर्वे वयमतः परम् ॥१२॥

*"Never was there a time when I did not exist, nor
you, nor all these kings; nor in the future shall
any of us cease to be."*

The Bhagavad-Gita

CHAPTER 1

INDIA IN PERSPECTIVE

THE INDIAN SUBCONTINENT is a vast, wedge-shaped peninsula, roughly triangular, which juts south from the mainland of Asia into the Indian Ocean. Along the northern base of the triangle, in the temperate zone, rise some of the world's loftiest mountains—the majestic Hindu Kush, Pamir, and Himalaya ranges. Nearly 2,000 miles to the south, at Cape Cormorin, the tip of the peninsula extends down through the tropical zone almost to the equator. The whole enormous area lies between the 8th and 37th degrees of north latitude, and stretches laterally nearly 2,000 miles from east to west, from Calcutta to Bombay.

This huge and diverse natural setting has profoundly influenced Indian history and culture. In the past, the high, rugged mountain barrier in the north cut the subcontinent off from the rest of Asia and offered some protection against invaders. And for centuries, the broad Indian Ocean, touching the peninsula on two sides, kept the region comparatively isolated from the outside world. This relative isolation allowed the development of a unique culture, distinct from that of Western Europe or China.

India's climate is predominantly hot and dry. This has a pervasive influence on the life of the subcontinent. Agriculture, for example, depends for success upon the warm, rain-laden monsoon winds, which sweep up every June from the Indian Ocean. If the monsoons are late or the rainfall is inadequate, there is famine in the land. India has often experienced disastrous famines, plagues, and epidemics because of lack of rainfall.

For although India includes about 1,262,000 square miles, its region is desperately overpopulated. Lured by the rich soil and an ample rainfall, much of the population has crowded into the Ganges River Valley and the eastern and western coastal regions. Of diverse racial types and speaking almost 200 different languages and 630 dialects, the population of the Indian subcontinent today numbers more than 768 million. It is increasing at the explosive rate of 2.2 percent, or almost 17 million people, each year. In the slums of Calcutta, Bombay, and other large cities, thousands die of malnutrition and disease each year. Under the relentless pressure of population increases, economic, political, and social life is increasingly strained.

Today the situation in the region is further complicated by the forces of religion and nationalism. The peoples of the subcontinent are deeply divided by the Hindu and Muslim faiths. Their loyalties are split between the nation-states of India, Pakistan, and Bangladesh, which share the subcontinent. In many instances, the age-old geographical divisions of nature have been ignored by the political actions of men who created these nations. This has caused grave new problems for the governments of the three countries.

Land

The part of the subcontinent called India has a dramatically varied topography, ranging from arid deserts to snow-capped mountains, and from lush river valleys to barren plateaus. Some regions receive less than 10 inches of rainfall a year, while others wallow in more than 200 inches. Yet for all its bewildering diversity, India can be viewed as a single geographic entity. The peninsula falls into three distinct areas: the northern mountain ranges, the river plains, the southern plateau.

India is dominated by the spectacular mountain ranges of the Himalaya, the Pamir, and the Hindu Kush. These ranges give the northern region the name "roof of the earth." Here are the world's highest peaks, Mount Everest (29,141 feet) and K2 (28,250 feet).

A wall of mountains extends across the north of the Indian subcontinent. Descending from it, melting snow streams into the broad plains at its base.

Life is crowded along the banks of India's rivers. Here on the Ganges, in Benaras, buildings line the shore. Many of them have bathing stairs or ghats.

From the snow beds of these northern ranges flow the life-giving river systems that water the plains to the south.

South of the mountain foothills lie the all-important lowlands drained by the Indus, Ganges, and Brahmaputra rivers. Along the banks of these rivers are fertile croplands and large cities. Here the population is densely concentrated, and millions make their living. Historically, this whole broad lowland has been a center of the Hindu culture.

Farther south, in the region running to the southern tip of the peninsula, is a smaller triangular-shaped tableland—the plateau of the Deccan. This region is bounded on the north by the Vindhya Hills. The remaining two sides of the elevated triangle are bounded by the Eastern and Western Ghats, which are steep outcroppings, resembling steps. The Ghats make up a mountain wall separating the plateau from the coastal plains. The Deccan has considerable mineral resources, but the Ghats prevent the plateau from receiving sufficient rainfall. Thus, although it occupies the largest part of the subcontinent, its population is relatively sparse.

The three main geographical areas can be broken down into a number of sub-regions:

Northwestern Frontier. The northwestern boundary of Pakistan is known by this name. On the west, running along the borders of Afghanistan and Iran down almost to the Gulf of Oman, stretch the bare, rugged mountains of Baluchistan. Farther north, the peaks of the mighty Hindu Kush separate Pakistan from northern Afghanistan. The nomadic peoples of this vast, desolate region are tied to the Pakistan government by a loose alliance. The Northwestern Frontier has historically been the weak spot of the sub-continent. Several of its mountain passes, notably the Khyber, have served as avenues for invaders from Central Asia and the Mediterranean world.

Bengal-Orissa lowland. This area consists of the huge delta formed by the mouths of the Brahmaputra and Ganges rivers. Farther south, in West Bengal, a smaller delta is formed by the Brahmani and Mahanadi rivers. More than 70,000,000 people live in the vicinity of the delta. The major city is the thriving port of Calcutta (population approximately 6,800,000), the commercial and financial center of eastern India. The main crops of the region are rice and jute.

Though the peoples of the delta were closely bound by language, common history, and economic ties, communal strife finally tore them apart. When the area gained independence from Britain in 1947, the Muslim majority living there chose to become a section of Pakistan. They formed the eastern part of this country, which was divided in two. The Hindus of Orissa and the western part of Bengal came under the political authority of India. But this political victory turned out to be an economic tragedy. Most of the jute was produced in East Pakistan, while the processing plants were located in West Bengal, an Indian state. This situation has been remedied by the growing of jute in West Bengal and the building of necessary factories in East Pakistan, which in 1971 became the independent country of Bangladesh. The cost of this duplicated effort, however, has been great on both sides of the border.

Ganges Valley. This also is part of the river plains. From its source high in the Himalayas, the mighty Ganges River runs more than 1,500 miles down to its delta at the Bay of Bengal. In this great valley lives most of India's population. The silt deposited by the Ganges has created a rich, alluvial plain, which provides a livelihood for more than 90,000,000 people.

In the western part of the Ganges Valley, the river water is channeled for irrigation. The eastern plain, however, enjoys a heavy rainfall because of the seasonal monsoon winds. The valley produces many foods, primarily rice during the wet season and wheat during the dry season.

New Delhi, the capital of the Indian Union, is situated on the Jumna River, a tributary of the Ganges. Other important cities in this area are Agra, site of the famous building called the Taj Mahal; Kanpur, the chief industrial city of northern India; Allahabad, located at the confluence of the Ganges and Jumna rivers; and Benaras, a great religious center of the Hindus.

Indus Valley. This is a third sub-region of the river plains. The Indus River rises in remote Tibet, near Mount Kailash. It runs a course of more than 1,000 miles, curving west and south into the Arabian Sea at Karachi. The valley of the Indus was the cradle of Indian civilization. On its banks arose the ancient cultures of Harappa and Mohenjo-Daro.

Today more than 41,000,000 people live in the Indus Valley, most of them in its northern region, called the Punjab. The western Punjab, including the large city of Lahore, is now politically part of Pakistan. The eastern Punjab, including Amritsar and two-thirds of the region of Kashmir, is controlled by India. Pakistan holds the rest of Kashmir.

The Punjab region is drained by five important tributaries of the Indus and is the focal point of a vast irrigation system. The rain-bearing monsoons, which move westward from the Bay of

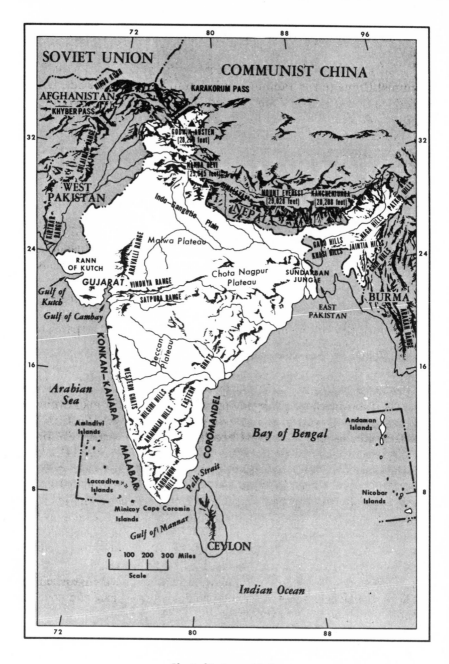

Physical features of India.

Bengal, are usually dried out by the time they reach the Indus region. Thus the farmers of the area cultivate wheat, which grows well in dry areas, rather than rice.

Western Coast. This is part of the southern plateau. The region runs like a sliver between the Arabian Sea and the Western Ghats, which separate it from the interior Deccan plateau. The high Western Ghats trap the monsoon winds, causing heavy rainfall up and down the coast. Thanks to the moist climate and favorable terrain, the region produces most of India's spices (cloves, ginger, pepper), copra, tea, and coconut oil.

Although the coastline is long, there are few good harbors. The outstanding exception is the giant metropolis of Bombay, a huge seaport which ranks second only to Calcutta in foreign trade. Bombay is also a financial center and a leader in cotton textile manufacturing. About halfway down the coast is the former Portuguese colony of Goa. South of Goa to the tip of the peninsula runs the Malabar coast. Its major cities are Mangalore, Cochin, and Trivandrum, the capital of the state of Travancore. Just inland from the coast stretch the so-called Malabar backwaters, a lush expanse of canals, lagoons, banana groves, and rice fields.

The entire southern coast has suffered from lack of contact with the rest of India. Because of the mountains, good communications and transportation facilities have developed slowly.

Southern Peninsula. The southern plateau also extends to the Southern Peninsula. This area includes the Deccan plateau and the southeastern coast. On the plateau itself, the most important cities are historic Mysore and Bangalore, a fast-growing city with aircraft and electronics industries. Farther south, on the eastern coast plain, is the state of Madras, with its chief city and port of the same name. This region, famed for its beautiful textiles, has a population of more than 50,000,000. Madras City is on a coastal plain that broadens into Tamil Land.

Culturally, the southern peninsula differs markedly from the areas to the north. Here Hindu culture is predominant, with fewer admixtures of alien elements. Until recent times, the Vindhya Hills and the rugged plateau of the Deccan isolated the region from foreigners. The people resemble the earliest inhabitants of India, the Dravidians. They are generally shorter and darker than the people of the north. Historically they escaped prolonged domination by invading Arabs, Turks, or Europeans. Thus they show far less evidence of racial blending than people in northern India.

CLIMATE

The Indian subcontinent has three seasons. The wet season occurs during the period of the monsoons, when temperatures average 90 degrees. The cool, dry season begins in December, when the sun is at the southern equinox. Brisk northeasterly winds sweep down from the Himalayas, and in Kashmir it is cold enough to ski. A hot, humid season begins in March, and the temperatures rise above 100 degrees. In the Rajasthan desert the thermometer may reach 115 degrees in

At Cochin, coconut trees shade this marketplace from the hot sun. Tropical plants grow along the Malabar Coast, where the monsoon arrives in summer.

the shade. This sweltering period lasts until June, when the arrival of the monsoons completes the cycle.

The monsoon is a powerful rain-bearing wind that sweeps landward in summer and seaward in winter. Its exact causes, whether wind currents, movements of the earth and sun, or other factors, remain mysterious. It is thought to be caused, however, by the vacuum created when warm air rises from a land mass. Winds rush in to fill the vacuum. Rolling up from the southwest across the Indian Ocean, the warm, rain-bearing monsoon wind arrives off the coast of Ceylon each year in early June. Soon it divides into an eastern and western current. The western current moves along the western coast and arrives at Bombay approximately on June 5. Laden with water vapor, the Bombay monsoon strikes the ridge of the Western Ghats, discharging its moisture on the coast in torrential downpours. One branch of the current continues up across Rajasthan. Another moves westward over the Arabian Sea.

The eastern current, known as the Bengal monsoon, reaches the coast of Burma and Calcutta around June 15. Swirling over the coast, it drenches the Ganges Delta, moves inland, and arrives in the Punjab area on about July 1. Another more easterly current swings up to Assam, an area to the north of Bengal at the base of the Himalaya Range. In late September, the force of the monsoon falls off sharply. Cool, gentle winds again spring up from the mountains in the northeast.

Throughout the subcontinent, millions of people are at the mercy of the monsoon for sustenance. Thus the period preceding the monsoon's coming is always charged with anxious expectancy. Any significant variation in the arrival time, intensity, distribution, and duration of the monsoon, with its precious rainfall, means disaster for the population. If the monsoon is late, the rice seedlings may burn up in the fields under the intense sun. If the monsoon is early, it can drown the seedlings before they have had time to grow. Either event means famine.

The regions in the direct path of the monsoon receive the heaviest rainfall. Assam records a yearly deluge of more than 450 inches. (Compare this with California, which averages 14 inches in the southern part of the state and 18 inches in the northern section around San Francisco.) But outside the path of the monsoon it does not rain. As noted earlier, the Western Ghats catch most of the rain along the Bombay coast, so that a wide strip along the Deccan plateau is chronically drought stricken. A number of other areas are similarly afflicted.

AGRICULTURE

For thousands of years, the peoples of India have wrested a living from the land. In spite of recent strides in industrialization, agriculture continues to be the chief economic activity. In fact, nearly three-quarters of the population is still directly or indirectly engaged in it.

Villages are the keystone of Indian agriculture. The subcontinent is dotted by more than 600,000 of them. Many are tiny places with fewer than 100 families. Most are isolated because of poor transportation and communications. Before the arrival of the British, in the 18th century, many villages were self-sufficient and enjoyed a high degree of political autonomy. They were usually governed by a *panchayat*, a council of elders whose responsibility to the central government was the collection of taxes and the maintenance of law and order. Most present-day villages remain primitive places, without electricity, sewage disposal, or other elementary conveniences.

The productivity of the soil is affected by both climate and the conditions of village life. In the regions in the path of the monsoon and on the alluvial floodlands of the river valleys, two crops can be grown per year. But these regions account for only a little more than one-seventh of the total acreage. Vast areas of the Indian subcontinent are not productive because farmers do not have the tools, funds, or conditions to cultivate them adequately. More than 70 percent of India's total labor force is engaged in farming, yet it creates less than half of the country's gross national product. Consequently, the average yield per acre in India is far below the world's average.

The subcontinent has more than 75,000 miles of irrigation canals, many of which date back to antiquity. About 23 percent of the farm lands are watered through these systems. However, techniques are generally primitive. Usually, the water is brought out of wells by the use of the ancient "Persian wheel," an ox-drawn apparatus. The water may also be taken from "tanks" which are nothing more than dug-out ponds built to catch the heavy monsoon rains. In many villages, these tanks are the only source of water and are used for cooking, bathing, and washing, as well as for irrigation purposes. These stagnant ponds become breeding grounds of malaria, typhus, dysentery, and other diseases. They are therefore a major concern to the health departments of India, Pakistan, and Bangladesh.

The modern governments of India and Pakistan have instituted programs to educate the peasants in up-to-date farming techniques. However, their efforts have run up against the formidable obstacles of superstition and religious belief. The Indian farmer traditionally

Villagers of Hangala Pura (pop. 500), sixty miles south of Mysore, store grain fifteen feet beneath the street, in a place invisible to strangers.

tills his field with a wooden plow harnessed to a bullock. He may harvest the grain with a stone sickle or grind sugar cane at a hand mill. Suspicious of new ideas and techniques, he also lacks the purchasing power to improve himself. The typical poverty-stricken peasant, chronically in debt to the *bania,* or moneylender, cannot afford expensive farm machinery or chemical fertilizers to rejuvenate his exhausted soil. Even the use of cow manure for fertilizer is restricted. Because of the limited supply and high cost of wood, peasants use dried-out "cow-dung patties" for cooking fuel.

The principal beasts of burden are buffaloes, camels, oxen, and elephants. In India the cow is considered sacred by the Hindus and therefore is not used for beef. A sacred cow may often share the same hut with the peasant family. Although India has more than one-half of the world's cattle, the cows are of limited use to people. A large percentage of these cattle suffer from disease. The cow's sacred status

Calcutta women draw their water from neighboring wells. With more than 7.1 million people, Calcutta is short 75 million gallons of water a day.

has hindered farming and governmental efforts to give medical treatment to these animals.

The cow has caused bitter conflict between the Hindu and Muslim communities. While Muslims are forbidden to eat pork, they are allowed to eat beef. On ceremonial occasions, they have led cows to the slaughter under the anguished and horrified eyes of devout Hindus who have religious love for them. The Hindus, in turn, have frequently gathered outside Muslim mosques during the reading of prayers, and have sung and played musical instruments—a grave offense to Muslim belief. Riots often followed.

INDUSTRY

For the vast majority of the peoples of the subcontinent, life is extremely hard. This fact can be grasped from a few tragic statistics. The average life expectancy of males is 52 years, about the same as in the People's Republic of China. By contrast, the life expectancy of males in the United States and Japan is about 71 years. In India the

A village boy studies while his mother prepares dinner and his father tills their small field outside the house. These devout Hindus are vegetarians.

rate of infant mortality is an appalling 145 per thousand births, more than seven times the rates in the United States and Japan. Only 26 percent of the Indian population is literate, by contrast to 98 percent in the United States. The standard of living of the peoples of the continent is among the lowest in the world.

India and Pakistan are striving to raise their low standards of living by creating new industry. While Pakistan is handicapped by a lack of natural resources such as iron and coal, India has these basic materials. It also has rich deposits of limestone, copper, and three-fourths of the world's known deposits of manganese and mica. However, there are a number of serious obstacles to India's industrial ambitions. These include: poor transportation facilities, a lack of capital, shortages of experienced managers and technicians, and the lack of skilled labor.

India's transportation system suffers from a deficiency of good road-building materials. The torrential monsoon rains also create havoc, washing out roads, railroad embankments, and bridges. Unfortunately, India's minerals, raw materials, industrial plants, and markets are not in a common vicinity. To tie them together, a good system of roads is essential, but the cost has so far been prohibitively high. The railroad system, however, is one of the longest in the world.

India is a political democracy whose economic philosophy is socialism. Most basic industries are owned and operated by the government. In addition, the government controls private industries. After gaining independence in 1947, the Indian government, fearful of Western economic power, required that at least 51 percent of the stock of any company formed in India would have to be Indian-owned. This restriction hindered foreign investors in India. The government, desperate for capital to build industry, had to change this policy. Then investments by foreigners increased.

The problem of severe shortages of skilled technicians and managers can be traced to conditions that prevailed under British rule. The British increased the production of raw materials for export, including coal, jute, hides and skins, tea, vegetable oils, spices, and cotton. Cotton was shipped in large quantities to the British Isles, manufactured into cloth, then resold on the vast Indian market. Though a number of local factories were established, industrial activity was not encouraged on a large scale. Thus, after the British departed, there were relatively few technicians trained to build a modern industrial economy.

The government is meeting this shortage through extensive education programs. Universities and technical schools now teach essential scientific, technical, and agricultural skills. Hundreds of young Indians and Pakistanis attend universities in Europe and the United States, as well as the Soviet Union. On the other hand, foreign nations have sent their own technicians and scientists to the subcontinent. From its foreign aid programs to the Peace Corps, the United States has helped. International agencies such as the United Nations and the World Bank as well as private organizations such as CARE, have also furnished expert assistance and advice.

The shortage of skilled labor for industry has its roots in the system of village agriculture described earlier. The great masses of peasants, superstitious and unwilling to seek new ways, have been slow to leave their villages for the uncertain opportunities of the large industrial cities. Those who have left have often found themselves the victims of miserably low wages, long hours, and sweatshop conditions. In recent years, the growth of the Indian labor union movement has resulted in the correction of the worst abuses and the improvement of the living standards and education of factory workers.

More general problems stem from widespread illiteracy, provincialism, language differences, and the malnutrition, disease, and despair which accompany poverty. More profound difficulties derive from the tendency of most Indians to accept their miseries. The Hindu caste system, to be fully described later, prevents the intermingling of peoples at different levels of society and limits the full use of human resources. Another obstacle to progress is the inferior status traditionally accorded women.

As it gropes for ways to reconcile its history with its present needs, India increasingly is becoming a nation of contrasts. Its industry is arising in the midst of what basically remains an agricultural economy. Near plants fueled with nuclear power farmers struggle to produce rice in ways that have not changed for thousands of years. Near factories run with the help of computers there are laborers who cannot speak the principal language in their communities.

In response to public needs, the government has concentrated on increasing consumer goods, such as shoes and radios, rather than producer goods, such as machine tools. India is one of the ten largest producers of goods in the world. Yet it is one of the ten poorest in per capita income. With its massive labor force, vast supply of raw materials, and governmental abilities, India is a country of enormous potential. But it is a complex nation, a giant struggling to overcome a troubled past, and it has begun to realize this potential only in recent years.

CHAPTER 2

ANCIENT INDIA: CIVILIZATION AND INSTITUTIONS

INDUS VALLEY CULTURES: HARAPPA AND MOHENJO-DARO

IN THE 1920's AND 1930's, archeologists discovered the remains of ancient cities along the Indus River, at Harappa in the North Punjab and at Mohenjo-Daro in the province of Sind. (Mohenjo-Daro, where many skeletons were found, literally means Mound of the Dead.) Scientific methods dated the sites back to 2500 B.C. The society, however, was at least as old as the most ancient Egyptian civilization of the Nile Valley. Hundreds of stone seals inscribed with pictographs have been found at the Indus Valley sites, but no archeological clue, similar to Egypt's "Rosetta Stone," has yet been unearthed to aid in deciphering the ancient writings. Still, artifacts uncovered to date make it possible to piece together at least a rough picture of this earliest known culture.

Large sections of the sites at Harappa and Mohenjo-Daro have been excavated. The two cities were the largest of more than 40 settlements which comprised an empire. At Mohenjo-Daro, nine separate strata of buildings were unearthed. Both cities gave evidence of the existence of highly organized societies. Their people used a hieroglyphic script containing 270 characters. The city streets were laid out in rectangular patterns, and houses were made of standardized, kiln-fired bricks. The inhabitants lived in sturdy two-story houses, with bathrooms which drained into central sewers. Other discoveries show that the people used standard weights and measures and were ruled by a strong central government. There is also evidence that they had developed a complex religion based on the worship of a "Mother Goddess" and animals. The discovery of a large bathing pool with cells for worship set off to one side indicates that they practiced ritual purification with water.

The Indus Valley dwellers were primarily farmers who grew wheat, barley, and cotton. No evidence of rice culture has been uncovered. The arts were well developed. Beautiful cups and vases of bronze, silver, copper, and lead, in addition to exquisite pieces of jewelry and coins, have been turned up. Similar coins found in Persia and Egypt indicate that the Harappa people traded with the Middle East.

15

Ruins at Mohenjo-Daro, in the province of Sind, date from 2500 B.C, proving that one of the oldest civilizations arose on the subcontinent.

About 1750 B.C., a great disaster befell the Harappa civilization, which suddenly and mysteriously collapsed. Some historians believe that the Indus River flooded, weakening the government. Later, invaders came down through the passes of the Hindu Kush, destroyed the culture, and subjugated the peoples of the Indus Valley. Fragmentary evidence supports this theory, for soon after the Harappa culture vanished, warriors called Aryans arrived.

Indo-Aryan Civilization: The Vedic Period

For unknown reasons, nomads living above the Black Sea in Central Asia began to migrate about 2000 B.C. One branch of this migration moved westward, overrunning Greece and Western Europe. Another moved southeast, penetrated the passes of the Hindu Kush, and streamed down into the Indus Valley. These Aryan nomads were tall, light-skinned, and fierce fighters. Throughout northwestern India, they rapidly subdued the short, dark-skinned natives, the Dravidians. The remnants of the Dravidian peoples took refuge in the south of the peninsula. The Aryans had iron weapons to use against the wood and bronze of the Dravidians. They were skillful horsemen and charioteers, while the Dravidians could supply only foot soldiers. The Aryans took full control of the north.

Our knowledge of the Aryans and their institutions comes from a collection of religious hymns, chants, and incantations known as the

Vedas. (In Sanskrit, the Aryan language, Veda means "Divine Knowledge.") This body of popular wisdom, of natural lore, and religious belief, composed between 1200 and 600 B.C., is thought to have originated with gods. The authors of another body of Vedic literature, developed between 600 and 400 B.C., are also thought to have been divine.

The Vedas consist of four sacred books, the first and most important of which is the Rig-Veda. This text tells of gods who live among men and affect them. The other Vedas are: 1) the Yajur-Veda, which includes sacrificial prayers and religious doctrine; 2) the Sama-Veda, which contains chanting verses; and 3) the Atharva-Veda, a collection of blessings, curses, and prayers designed to cause good or harm. While the messages of the Rig-Veda often were memorized by the priestly groups, the charms, blessings, curses, and spells in the Artharva-Veda were favored by the broad masses of India's people. Because of their influence, the name of the Vedas has been given to the thousand-year period of Indian history between about 1500 B.C. and 500 B.C. This time, when Aryan institutions and religious beliefs were dominant, is known as the Vedic Period.

Social and political institutions. Before their arrival in the Indus Valley, the Aryans were divided into three classes: the warriors, the priests, and the "cultivators." By the time they reached the valley, the fair-skinned conquerors wished to set themselves apart from the darker Dravidian subjects whom they called *dasyu*, or slaves. To preserve their distinctive ethnic traits they prohibited intermarriage of Aryans and Dravidians. Skin color thus became a mark of privileged social position. This idea helped to lay the foundations of the rigid Hindu caste system which later evolved. Although some historians question the Aryan origins of the Indian caste system, others see a direct cause and effect.

Politically, the Aryans were loosely organized into *rashtras*, states ruled by *rajas*, or kings. In their early stages of development the rashtras were governed not only by the kings, but also by councils, the sabhas (literally, "people") and samitis ("councils"). The word sabha appears to have referred to groups of noblemen, while the samitis were evidently meetings of free tribesmen. The sabhas and samitis limited the power of the rajas and in some cases were able to govern their regions without monarchs. In time, however, the position of the rajas became hereditary; the sabhas and samitis persisted, but with less authority. One major function of the raja was the administration of justice. Crimes were severely punished, but never by death.

The patriarchal family was the basic unit of Aryan society. The husband's (or patriarch's) authority was supreme and the wife's secondary. Often men kept more than one wife. Economic conditions, however, made the single husband-wife union the more general

Indra, the daring god of the Aryans, appears (left) with his mate, Indrani, in a temple of Khajuraho. He was god of war and, later, of climate.

pattern. Marriages were established by abduction, purchase, or mutual consent; they were sanctified by religion.

Another important concept brought to India by the Aryans concerned the sense of time. They burned their dead. Through this gesture they hoped to release the individual spirit for union with an all pervading one. The act suggested to them the existence of a timeless presence in which all Aryans shared. It was to have a profound impact upon the thinking of the Dravidians. After centuries of subjugation, the conquered people adopted the practice of cremation. Burial, which suggests a continuity of ancestors and the linear progression of time, was thus abandoned for a new custom which blurred time and ancestry.

The Aryans were originally hunters and herdsmen. Wealth was determined by the number of cattle a family owned; the horse was important mainly for military purposes. The dog, however, was highly valued for its usefulness in shepherding the flock. Many Aryan myths involve the divine she-dog *Sarama*. India, perhaps more than any other nation in the world, has expressed itself in stories about the worship of animals.

Following further expansion eastward into the Ganges Valley, the Aryan nomads gradually turned to a more settled life. From the steady intermingling with the agricultural peoples of the subcontinent, called the Aryan-Dravidian Synthesis, new values and political institutions developed. The central government was strengthened, and laws protecting property were then passed. Artists who had delighted in depicting war and the hunt turned to more peaceful agricultural themes. New words and concepts related to farming crept into the language. The word *sindu*, applied to a river which the Aryans encountered in the northwest, was later evolved into the words Indus, Hindu, and Sind, for example. It is also the source of the word India; Hindus preferred to call their country Bharat Varsha ("The Land of Bharat"), after a monarch who ruled during the early stages of the Aryan invasion. Throughout the Aryan-Dravidian Synthesis, new gods of rain, the harvest, and the hearth were needed and created.

With the end of military expansion, the power of the warrior class declined, and the priests began to assert their authority. As the priest's role loomed larger, Aryan religion gradually expanded into a whole new way of life—the way of Brahmanism.

We shall later examine the essential concepts of this religious and social philosophy. Here it must be stressed that as it crystallized in the Vedic Period, it gave rise to a new social structure—the origins of the caste system. The Rig-Veda proclaimed that four distinct castes of mankind had sprung from the body of the first man, Purusha.

> *When they divided Purusha, in how many different portions did they arrange him? . . . His mouth became a* Brahman; *his two arms were made into* Kshatriya; *his two thighs were* Vaisya; *from his two feet the* Sudra *were born.*

Thus the four major castes of Indian society were formulated: *Brahmans* (priests), *Kshatriyas* (warriors), *Vaisyas* (merchants and bureaucrats and free farmers), and *Sudras* (menial workers). This early Aryan caste structure, called *Varna*, meaning color, was later greatly elaborated to include subclass groups called *jati*, meaning birth. Its early basis, however, was skin color.

RELIGION: THE RISE OF BRAHMANISM AND CLASSICAL HINDUISM

The ancient Dravidian peoples had evolved a complex religion, based on the worship of female fertility figures, including a moon goddess. Their religion suited the needs of an agricultural society; it appealed to nature to help them survive. The warlike Aryan invaders, on the other hand, worshipped strong, patriarchal male deities. They imposed their religion on the conquered *dasyu*. But in the course of the so-called Aryan-Dravidian Synthesis, the Aryan gods took on many of the gentler attributes of the Dravidian deities—such as watching over the hearth and insuring a good harvest.

The chief god of the Aryans was Indra. Originally, Indra was worshipped as a war god. His symbol of authority, like that of Zeus, his counterpart in Greek mythology, was the thunderbolt. And like Zeus and Thor, the Teutonic god, Indra was known for his daring amorous exploits: when not engaged in warlike pursuits, he devoted his energies to women. After the Aryans settled down to farming, Indra became identified with the god of weather. According to one myth, every year he slew with his thunderbolt a snake that was keeping back the rains in the mountains of heaven. This mythological act symbolized the first clap of thunder which announced the coming of the monsoon.

Second to Indra ranked Varuna. This god was responsible for *dharma*, the laws of the Aryan cosmos. As the guardian of morality, he punished all transgressions. Agni, the god of fire, was the chief deity of the Brahmans. He was looked up to as the high priest of the gods. The Aryan cattle herders worshipped Agni as the god of the hearth.

For centuries, the sacred Vedas were the basic scriptures of Aryan religion. Their wisdom, comprising hymns, prayers, and liturgy from the period 1500 to 500 B.C., provided a guide through which the rulers of the subcontinent set themselves apart from their subject people. Aryan cattle herders as well as noblemen relied upon them for religious instruction. But as society developed, simple religious rites gave way to rituals performed by priests. The use of written records had almost disappeared with the conquest of Harappa and Mohenjo-Daro. In their absence, great value was placed on the memory. Certain Brahman families undertook to memorize the Vedas and so to assume priestly status. Because they were able to marry and to will their positions to their children, they perpetuated their status within certain families. They maintained that without continuous sacrifices, the gods would desert mankind and the universe would collapse into chaos. The priestly class thus assumed a dominant role.

The Brahmanas and the Upanishads. As guides to the rituals in the Vedas, the Brahmans introduced liturgical texts called *Brahmanas*. A

Brahmana was attached to each Veda. Moreover, between 800 and 600 B.C., the Brahmanas were enriched with new elements of speculative thought. Mere ritualism could not allay a growing concern about graver questions—the nature of the universe, the fact of death, the hope of an afterlife. Answers to these more sophisticated questions were provided by new philosophical texts, called *Upanishads*. In Sanskrit, the word Upanishad literally means "sitting down next to." This name was given to the texts because they were physically and intellectually placed next to the Brahmanas. Perhaps it also refers to the fact that the wisdom of the Upanishads generally was explained to students when they sat down next to their teachers. While India has comparatively few records for Vedic times, it was during this period that the country developed its long tradition of communicating beliefs through wandering teachers. It is a tradition encouraged by the Upanishads, which said:

> *To many it is not given to hear of the Self. Many, though they hear of it, do not understand it. Wonderful is he who speaks of it. Intelligent is he who learns of it. Blessed is he who, taught by a good teacher, is able to understand it.*

The Upanishads were to have a far-reaching effect upon the nature of Indian life. They did not teach one faith, but six, which are called *darshanas*. Theoretically, they permitted any or all of these philosophies within the framework of the new Brahmanism: monism, dualism, theism, atheism, empiricism, and rationalism. In a sense, the Upanishads countered the tendency of the Brahmanas to make religion a formal body of rituals, known chiefly to the priestly caste. They were evidence of the unity within diversity that has characterized India throughout its history.

Instead of ritual, the Upanishads stressed right knowledge, or *jnana*, as the means of identifying the individual soul (*atman*) with the universal soul (*Brahman*). The material world and its goals were considered irrelevant to the broader search for the "Ultimate Reality" —the Brahman. To this extent the physical world was an illusion (*maya*). For the individual, the only enduring reality was his atman, his "soul" or "essence," caged in the prison of his body. But this individual soul shared the very essence of the world soul, the greater Atman which was Brahman. The paramount objective of every soul was to escape from the shell of the flesh and to return to its source, in short, to achieve union with Brahman. But the road to this union, or *Nirvana*, was strewn with difficulties. On its way to Nirvana, the soul must first endure a painful wandering—a transmigration.

The most significant concept introduced in the Upanishads is that of the transmigration of the soul. The Upanishads said that:

. . . the souls of those who have lived lives of sacrifice, charity, and austerity, pass to the World of the Fathers, the paradise of Yama . . . while the unrighteous are reincarnated as worms, birds, insects.

According to this doctrine, only those who lived irreproachable lives would reach Nirvana. Those who did not would accumulate around their atman, or soul, a shell-like matter called *karma*, the moral consequences of action. Above all, karma is a disinterested consequence. That is, in the course of transmigration, the individual suffers reverses or achieves advances according to his ability to express devotion, or *bhakti*, to the Ultimate Reality. Thus the accumulation of karma would prevent the achievement of union with Brahman. Whoever suffers this consequence must therefore start a new life in order to reduce the amount of shell. The deeds of his past would determine whether reincarnation would be to a higher station in life or to a lower one. The entire cycle of birth, death, and reincarnation was represented symbolically as a wheel (*chakra*). The universe, like the individual, undergoes this change. The basic turn of the chakra of the universe is thought to be four billion years, during which there is a cycle of growth, decay, and destruction.

The time in which the Upanishads were developed predates the spread of Hinduism in India. Yet it included significant changes from Brahmanism and was a step toward Hinduism. It is therefore called the period of Classical Hinduism. No founder or prophet led the way to this system of thought. Hinduism was born among the Indian people through the general consent of its followers, aided by many teachers. No event or force caused them to agree upon its elements. They appear to have done so out of their common history. The all-encompassing demands which they made upon themselves are revealed in this passage from the Upanishads, uttered by a mysterious figure called "The King of Death":

Know that the Self is the rider, and the body the chariot; that the intellect is the charioteer, and the mind the reins.

The senses, say the wise, are the horses; the roads they travel are the mazes of desire. The wise call the Self the enjoyer when he is united with the body, the senses, and the mind.

When a man lacks discrimination and his mind is uncontrolled, his senses are unmanageable, like the restive horse of a charioteer. But when a man has discrimination and his mind is controlled, his senses, like the well-broken horses of a charioteer, lightly obey the rein.

He who lacks discrimination, whose mind is unsteady and whose heart is impure, never reaches the goal, but is born again and again. But he who has discrimination, whose mind is steady and whose heart is pure, reaches the goal, and having reached it is born no more.

The development of Hinduism. Hindus agreed upon a philosophy rather than upon a doctrine. Although they built magnificent temples, they developed no church. Their priesthood was hereditary and could be achieved only through reincarnation. Of the few beliefs shared by all Hindus, respect for priests is among the foremost. Since priests are closer to Nirvana than others, Indians generally think it important to protect and support them with charity. All priests are drawn from the Brahman caste, although not all Brahmans are priests.

Another belief shared by Hindus is veneration of life, especially the cow, which is thought to embody fertility. Although rivers, trees, and other forms of life are regarded as sacred too, the cow is the holiest form. Indians have forbidden its killing from the period of Classical Hinduism onward, and perhaps before that.

As we will see, early Hindus were united in other philosophical respects. The transmigration of the soul represented one essential element of their faith. In the backward or forward movement of the soul there was an underlying cause: moral responsibility (*dharma*). It was dharma (which may also be translated as law, religion, virtue, morality, or custom) which obliged each member of society to maintain the role that he was given at birth. On the individual level, dharma required the pursuit of Nirvana in ways which were defined by the priests.

The doctrine of reincarnation, of which transmigration is a part, provided a vital link between the religion of Brahmanism and the social order in which it was practiced. The religion claimed a divine mandate to separate people by color, the Varna system. At the same time, it suggested to members of the toiling lower castes that they might become reincarnated at a higher level in another life. To win advancement in the next life, it was said, the individual must fulfill his moral obligations in the present one. Thus the doctrine of reincarnation persuaded members of the lower castes to be dutiful. The ultimate bliss of final union with Brahman was a dim and distant, but realizable goal. While this union might be achieved through correct actions, the nature of action was limited by each caste.

Effects of religious trends. At least from the time that Aryan kingdoms crushed their early clans, the people of India have been markedly pessimistic in their world view. The doctrine of reincarnation, together with the Varna and caste systems, further encouraged this tendency.

There were other political, social, and psychological consequences associated with Brahmanism and Classical Hinduism. To hold power it was necessary for the king to be confirmed by the priests, who with their advisers, the astrologers, claimed to know the will of the gods. Once installed, therefore, the king was considered to be divine. His authority was totally respected, reinforced by the caste system which granted increasing prestige to each succeeding caste. Dharma required every individual to respect the rules of his caste and the power of castes above him. Whoever failed to heed this duty might become an outcaste. To reject authority, moreover, might increase the shell of karma, thus bringing punishment in the next life.

These perceptions tended to restrict disobedience in India. Children were trained to respect authority, especially in their fathers, the heads of their jati and caste, and their king. However, the power of the king was subject to his own ability to perform according to dharma. Like the masses of people whose dharma was made known through their castes, he had the duty to uphold the sacred law and could be removed from office if he failed to do so. We have seen how, during the Vedic Period, sabhas and samitis tended to limit the power of the kings until the kings gained enough power to become autocrats. Even when the kings had gained absolute power, the masses of people governed themselves through local councils called *panchayats* (literally, "Councils of Five"). The panchayats enabled the people to check the despotism of their kings. Nevertheless, the Indian social structure tended to cause most people to act in groups rather than as individuals, especially in situations requiring disobedience. Thus if a king were resisted it was generally through collective, not individual action.

The Post-Vedic Period (ca.500–327 b.c.)

Throughout the civilized world, the period from the seventh to the fourth centuries b.c. was, in a broad sense, an era of spiritual change. Reacting to the increasing sterility of formal, priest-dominated religions, new movements and sects sprang up. They offered simpler messages aimed at the individual—messages of personal salvation and self-knowledge. In the Mediterranean world, this phase was marked by the emergence of Greek philosophy, as well as the prophecies of Judaism. China responded to the new doctrines of Confucius and Lao-tzu, Persia to the teachings of Zoroaster. In India, a parallel development took place with the rise of Jainism and Buddhism.

Jainism. One early, great leader of the Jain sect was Vardharnana Mahavira. He is said to have been the son of a Kshatriya (member of the warrior class), who ruled in the region of modern Bihar around 500 b.c. According to the tradition, Mahavira renounced his earthly possessions, deserted his family, and became a monk. He was the greatest saint of the Jain movement which spread throughout north and northwestern India.

Jainism is a creed founded on rigorous asceticism. Like the priestly Brahmans, the Jains held the material world to be an illusion. The goal of man was release from the cycle of birth and rebirth, the long transmigration of the soul. But the difference was in the method by which the soul was to be freed of its encrusting karma. Rejecting rituals and incantations, the Jains held that the karmic matter could be removed only through a life of strict self-denial, penance, and discipline. So, like the saintly Mahavira, the Jain monks renounced every earthly comfort, often even to the wearing of clothing. Only through such penance, they believed, would the soul escape reincarnation and instead become a *jina*, or conqueror (from which the sect takes its name).

Indian thought gained important ideas from the Jains, (pronounced "jines"). Among the most enduring of them were the doctrines of manysidedness and of nonviolence. The protest technique of "sitting dharna" can also be traced to Jainism.

The doctrine of manysidedness was illustrated by a famous parable. As an experiment, an Indian prince once ordered six blind men to touch various parts of an elephant and then describe their sensations. One man thought the elephant's leg was a tree, another that its trunk was a snake, another that its ear was a large winnowing fan, and so on, but, of course, none imagined the whole elephant. Through this parable, the Jains emphasized that all knowledge was relative and subject to varying points of view. The whole truth was a mystery for which men groped blindly. In India, this doctrine resulted in a growing tolerance for the opinions of others.

The Jains believed that every living creature possessed a soul. Their doctrine of *ahimsa* forbade doing violence to any creature,

Believing in the denial of the world in order to esteem things of the soul, members of the Jain sect built temples in such remote places as this.

down to the lowest insect, since these, too, possessed souls. In order not to hurt any insects, the Jains swept the ground before their feet when walking. Jain houses were kept scrupulously clean; vermin could be taken from the premises but never killed. In extreme practice, even water had to be strained before drinking, and the air purified by a mask worn over the nose and mouth. The doctrine of nonviolence had a considerable impact on later Indian thought. It played an important part in the independence movement led by Gandhi in the twentieth century.

"Sitting dharna" was the practice of a hunger fast. When a man believed that he had been morally wronged, he sat cross-legged upon the ground and fasted—often until death. If, as a result of "sitting dharna," a man died without the wrong being righted, the guilty party was doomed to be reincarnated as a member of the lowest order of living creatures. "Sitting dharna" later became a common practice among the Indians.

Jainism as an organized movement was never able to gain a large following on the subcontinent. Yet, its doctrines had an important influence on the values of Indian society. Many of its beliefs were shared by and later incorporated into the teachings of Buddhism.

Buddhism. A more far-reaching reaction to the arid ritualism of the Brahmans developed in the sixth century B.C. Its great leader was Prince Siddhartha Gautama, whose perceptions were to affect the history of the world.

Prince Gautama was a member of a rich and noble family of the Kshatriya caste. As the son of a chief in the Shakya tribe he experienced every earthly pleasure. But he was troubled by the sorrow that he saw in others. According to tradition, at the age of twenty-nine he abruptly renounced all worldly things in order to seek the cause of human suffering. Leaving his splendid palace, Gautama wandered for six years in search of enlightenment. During that period he gained five companions and with them adopted a philosophy of self-sacrifice. They begged for food or fasted. One day in the sixth year the band of travelers approached the village of Bodhgaya, near Benares. There, to the dismay of his friends, Gautama announced that he was abandoning the principle of self-sacrifice. He sat down beneath a fig tree (called a peepul, pipul, or "bo" tree; this particular one has been known as the sacred *bodhi* tree since Gautama's visit) and meditated for forty-nine days. This period of meditation brought a vision of enlightenment to Gautama. Rising, he sought out his former companions and found them in the deer park known as Iwipatana, at the city of Sarnath. He is said to have spoken to them quietly, and his words comprise the first sermon of the man who afterwards became known as the Buddha, or "Enlightened One." At

Buddha is said to have sat cross-legged, in complete repose, when offering his first sermon, as this elaborate statue of him at Sarnath Museum shows.

the heart of his speech, called his great "Sermon of the Turning of the Wheel of Law," was this statement:

There are two ends which the seeker must avoid. What are they? The pursuit of desires and of the pleasure which springs from desire, which is base, common, leading to rebirth, ignoble, and unprofitable; and the pursuit of pain and hardship, which is grievous, ignoble, and unprofitable . . . .

The Buddha proposed a "Middle Way" between self-sacrifice and self-indulgence. Humanity's torments, he said, arise from craving. He summarized this view in the *Four Noble Truths* that were stated in his first sermon:

And this is the Noble Truth of Sorrow. Birth is sorrow, age is sorrow, disease is sorrow, death is sorrow; contact with the unpleasant is sorrow, separation from the pleasant is sorrow, every wish unfulfilled is sorrow—in short all the . . . components of individuality are sorrow.

And this is the Noble Truth of the Arising of Sorrow. It arises from craving, which leads to rebirth, which brings delight and passion, and seeks pleasure now here, now there—the craving for sensual pleasure, the craving for continued life, the craving for power.

And this is the Noble Truth of the Stopping of Sorrow. It is the complete stopping of that craving, so that no passion remains, leaving it, being emancipated from it, being released from it, giving no place to it.

And this is the Noble Truth of the Way which leads to the stopping of Sorrow. It is the Noble Eightfold Path—Right Views, Right Resolve, Right Speech, Right Conduct, Right Livelihood, Right Effort, Right Mindfulness, and Right Concentration.

The *Eightfold Path,* that part of the Four Noble Truths which leads to enlightenment, may be defined as follows: Right Belief is the renunciation of worldly things and the dedication to a humanitarian faith. Right Resolve is the means by which the individual dedicates himself to the achievement of Nirvana. Right Speech enables the individual to serve as a model for others to follow. Right Conduct acknowledges the sanctity of life. Right Livelihood is a life of service rather than selfishness. Through Right Effort the individual keeps his inner self free of evil thoughts. Right Mindfulness is constant awareness that craving is pointless. Right Concentration enables the individual to be selfless in his mind and overt acts.

In each of the Eightfold Paths there was an underlying idea: human misery could be dispelled through a life of moderation and detachment, both achieved through effort. The Eightfold Path, in effect, was a moral code lying between self-indulgence, the asceticism of Jainism, and the aloofness of Brahmanism. Like Jainism, it stressed the principle of nonviolence. The necessity of rituals, prayers, and sacrifices was, however, emphatically denied. Enlightenment could be achieved only through the individual's control of himself. Finally, one more radical departure from earlier beliefs was that salvation was open to all, regardless of caste status.

In the view of Hinduism, rebirth and the transmigration of the soul was an expression of humanity's blind life-force. The processes of life continued despite anything that humans might accomplish. In opposition to this blindness, the Buddha proposed self-mastery. Since all forms of life inevitably decay, rendering power, possessions, and other expressions of individuality meaningless, he offered a new ethic, one based on the annihilation of craving. He declared the great objects of life to be forms of humanitarianism—to one's self and to others: universal love, friendliness, joy (based upon the pursuit of knowledge), and equanimity (based upon contemplation).

As stated in the First Noble Truth, life is sorrowful by its nature because individuality is made up of constantly shifting components. The Buddha identified these components as form and matter (what can be sensed), sensations (what can be experienced), perceptions (what can be thought of experience), psychic constructions (the unique character through which every individual sees the world), and conscious thought (the product of the first four components). This composite necessarily changes as any of its parts change. Any action that is taken, and any thoughts, perceptions, or deeds that are experienced, alter the whole personality by affecting one or more of the components. Therefore the individual at the end of his life is not the same individual who began it. Time erodes all things; at death nothing of the individual, not even a soul, is left.

Yet, the Buddha noted in the Second Noble Truth, most people live in the illusion that they can seize and retain some form of life. They seek conquests. It is through this illusion that the individual causes sorrow in himself and in others. The last two Noble Paths describe how craving may be eliminated.

Although he rejected many of the concepts of Hinduism, the Buddha and his followers incorporated the principle of transmigration in their philosophy. In a famous parable a Buddhist monk explained to a skeptical king how, if there were no souls, transmigration could take place. "Suppose, your Majesty," he said, "a man lights one lamp from another—does the one lamp transmigrate to the other?" The king's admission that it did seemed to verify the Buddhist principle that all things are part of all other things, that parts of every individual, after death, will become parts of other individuals.

The Buddha saw the process of life as a Chain of Causation. Through craving the individual causes his life to proceed along a chain of events which may be called aging. Unenlightened, the dead will be reborn in other forms. Enlightened and fully in control of life, the individual may break the chain and achieve Nirvana, which in one sense means "blowing out," as a candle. He will have eliminated the one part of himself which can cause him sorrows when it is reborn in others.

As he lay dying in the hill town of Kusinara at the age of 80, the Buddha's last words were said to have been, "All composite things must pass away. Strive onward vigilantly."

Like Jesus, the Buddha taught in parables known as *sutras* (literally "threads"). His principles were recorded by generations of his followers in a collection of writings called the *Tripitaka* (literally "Three Baskets"). The name refers to the collection's three parts, Conduct, Discourses, and Supplementary Doctrines.

Buddhism had a profound impact throughout Asia, spreading to Ceylon, Southeast Asia, Tibet, China, and Japan. Later, as we shall see, a schism developed among its followers: some looked upon Gautama as a great, but human, teacher; others regarded him as a god. Yet both groups accepted his essential message. Their elaborations on it were a part of its growth.

Mythological Brahmanism: The Mahabharata and the Ramayana

The rise of Jainism and, more especially, of Buddhism, threatened the Brahmans. The Buddhist doctrines of love and charity challenged the cold concepts of the Upanishads. For Gautama offered a code of behavior for all. The lower castes found hope in his doctrine.

It was, however, during this period that Brahmanism breathed new life. Its sacred literature was enriched by two great epic poems, or folk tales: the *Mahabharata* and the *Ramayana*.

The *Mahabharata* and the *Ramayana* were to ancient India what the Homeric epics were to the world of Greece and Rome. The *Mahabharata* gives us a vivid picture of the nomadic, war-oriented Aryan society in its early vigor. The *Ramayana*, showing the eventual triumph of peaceful, domestic virtues, suggests the transition to a civilization based upon agriculture.

The *Mahabharata* is mankind's longest poem, with 100,000 couplets. It is a passionate work dealing with heroic conflict between two royal families. Military might, courage, obedience, and loyalty are the virtues it extols. The hero of the poem is Arjuna, a member of the Kshatriya caste and in many ways a counterpart of the Greek Achilles. At one point in the poem the god Krishna, disguised as a chariot driver, appears to Arjuna on the field of battle. The account of their meeting is known as the *Bhagavad-Gita*, or Lord's Song. Not only is it a poetic masterpiece, one of the finest passages in world literature. Also, the viewpoint it embodied was, as we shall see, a vital ingredient in the later development of the religion of Hinduism.

The *Ramayana* tells of the ultimate triumph of good over evil. Sita, the wife of Prince Rama, is carried off by the king of the demons while her husband is away hunting a white stag. To rescue his wife, who was held captive on the southern island of Ceylon, Rama appeals to the king of the monkeys. The monkey king answers his plea by having subjects build a bridge from the tip of India to the island. After many ordeals and adventures, Rama triumphs, and Sita is reunited with her husband. The poem, which stressed the virtues of loyalty, obedience, and conjugal fidelity, became a guide to conduct between husband and wife.

Historically, the *Mahabharata* and the *Ramayana* greatly enhanced the appeal of Brahmanism. They translated Brahmanism into human terms, offering fascinating human characters as models of conduct. They made Brahman, the vague "Ultimate Reality," more concrete and personal. As we shall discover, it was an easy transition from mythological Brahmanism, with its anthropomorphic human-like gods, to Hinduism.

As great works of literature, the *Mahabharata* and the *Ramayana* live to this day. Like the poems of Homer or the plays of Shakespeare in Western countries, the great Indian epics are still read and enjoyed. The personalities and events of the Indian tales have long been favorite themes of Indian painters and sculptors.

Important religious festivals also derive from the epics. In Mysore the triumph of Rama is celebrated each year by a ten-day holiday. The festivities culminate in a colorful parade of the palace guards, followed by the royal camels and elephants. The Maharajah of Mysore himself rides an elephant at the head of the procession. The most famous Hindu festival is that of Dewali, which also celebrates Rama's victory. It is performed each December on the longest night of the year. In villages and cities candles are kept burning as a sacred vigil. In some villages the faithful dress up in elaborate costumes and dance out scenes from the *Ramayana*, to the accompaniment of frenzied drumming. At last dawn comes, symbolizing the triumph of light (Rama) over darkness, of good over evil.

CHAPTER 3

THE MAURYA ERA (322–185 B.C.)

Since ancient times, India had carried on trade with the Middle East and the Mediterranean. The first Western people to make political inroads in the Indian subcontinent were the Persians. In the sixth century B.C. they seized the Punjab and made it a *satrapy*, or province, of their empire. More extensive penetration did not take place until the fourth century B.C., during the reign of the celebrated Macedonian conqueror, Alexander the Great.

After bringing the Greek city-states under his sway, Alexander advanced against the Persians. In a series of brilliant campaigns, he crushed the armies of Darius III at the battles of Issus and Arbella (333–331 B.C.). Then his powerful war machine, with irresistible momentum, rolled on across the Iranian plateau into Bactria, west of India. From Bactria, Alexander's armies continued their epic march, penetrated the passes of the Hindu Kush, and entered the Indus Valley. There they easily overran the small kingdoms of the region. Alexander dreamed of building a great Hellenic empire in the East; his immediate goal was the conquest of the populous Magadha Kingdom of the Ganges Valley. But Alexander's great scheme never materialized. Homesickness among his troops, together with the threat of a mutiny, forced him to turn back.

Upon Alexander's death in 323 B.C., three of his generals divided his empire. Bactria and northeast India fell to Seleucus, who immediately dispatched an army to the Indus Valley to establish his authority. But his forces were defeated by a new Indian army under a brilliant young commander—Chandragupta Maurya. A peace treaty was concluded between Chandragupta and Seleucus. For many years, Bactria remained under Greek control and was an outpost from which Hellenistic thought and art spread to India. Seleucus, however, surrendered all political claims to the Indus Valley. The authority of Chandragupta Maurya was soon established throughout northwestern India.

THE RULE OF CHANDRAGUPTA MAURYA: THE ARTHASASTRA

Chandragupta, the first Indian ruler to establish a strong centralized government in the subcontinent, next conquered the Magadha

Kingdom of the Ganges Valley. He rapidly extended his empire eastward to the Bay of Bengal. In the south, he marched far down into the region of the Deccan. From his capital at Paliputra, he exercised absolute power. Then he followed a noble Indian tradition, that of responding to a powerful sense of conscience. After a reign of twenty-four years, Chandragupta relinquished his throne and donned the humble robes of a Jainist monk.

During his despotic reign, Chandragupta was greatly aided by his chief counselor, the brilliant but unscrupulous Kautilya. Kautilya is credited with the authorship of a memorable treatise on statecraft called the *Arthasastra*. Like a similar treatise, *The Prince*, written by the fourteenth-century Italian Renaissance statesman, Niccolo Machiavelli, the *Arthasastra* was intended as a practical guidebook for authoritarian rulers. But in its sheer, cynical realism, Kautilya's work is really more all-encompassing than its Western counterpart.

In foreign affairs, the *Arthasastra* advocates a policy of ruthless expansion at the expense of one's neighbors. Kautilya believed the state to be a living organism which had to expand in order to survive. To gain additional territory, the ruler should seek to make alliances and treaties with neighboring states. Treaties, however, were to be considered mere scraps of paper, made to be broken when it served the state's best interests. If negotiations failed, war was justified as the ultimate weapon of state policy.

The *Arthasastra,* as well as other works of its time, reflected the militarism that was inherently part of a region of many kingdoms that lacked any unifying principle. In contrast to medieval Europe, where the Roman Catholic Church could moderate disputes, India had no continent-wide institution that could restrain its many kings. Huge armies were maintained. Battles were incessant. The Mauryas considered peace to be only one of "six instruments of policy" for the state. The others were war, waiting for the enemy to strike, attack, forming alliances, and forming alliances while attacking.

The last of the six strategies was a complicated form of statecraft. It brought about an analogy known as the Doctrine of Circles. According to this doctrine, any king might draw a series of concentric circles on a map to learn who were his friends and who were his enemies. The enemies were adjacent to him while his friends were in alternate circles beyond them. All of the other circles contained his enemies' potential allies.

From the time of the Aryan conquest Indian literature had listed three types of warfare. The first was righteous and was an important part of the Aryan tradition. The second was for acquisition, and the third for destruction. The *Mahabharata* condoned only the first: "A king should not attempt to gain the earth unrighteously, for who reveres the king who wins unrighteous victory? Unrighteous conquest is impermanent and does not lead to heaven." In the south of India Dravidian kingdoms were less restrained by this precept and often fought to the death. The *Arthasastra*, however, did not encourage this tactic. Its central objective was an expanding empire in which conquered people could be persuaded to accept their defeat.

Basing his arguments on the *Mahabharata*, Kautilya declared the state to be the result of divine authority, delegated to protect the people and their property. This Indian concept of contract was marked by elements of religious mysticism. For, although the people had the right to revoke the contract when it was violated by the ruler, violation was limited to the ruler's failure to preserve the divinely ordered laws of the Varna system. As for abuses of power, such as censorship or brutality, the subjects were completely at the ruler's mercy.

In the *Arthasastra*, the point that foreign policy should be based on considerations of expediency was illustrated with a famous parable: A rat discovered his natural enemy, the cat, trapped in a net of ropes. The rat was delighted at the cat's plight. However, his joy was short-lived, for an owl appeared and perched over the rat's hole. This was a new threat to the security of the rat, since the owl no longer feared the ensnared cat. This situation forced the rat to reconsider his relationship to the cat. An agreement was reached between the rat and the cat. In return for the rat's chewing away the rope, the cat agreed to drive away the owl. The grateful cat suggested that a permanent alliance be concluded between the rat and himself. But the rat scampered back to his hole. He refused the cat's proposal, pointing out that the former alliance was merely a temporary arrangement based on expediency—that by nature they were destined to be enemies.

THE PHILOSOPHER-KING ASOKA (273–232 B.C.)

In 273 B.C. Asoka, the grandson of Chandragupta, succeeded to the throne after a brief struggle with his brothers for the succession. He thus gained control of an empire which included all of north India, with the exception of the southern tip of the subcontinent. The legend of his career, although only partly true, reveals an important aspect of the Indian mind. It goes this way:

Early in his reign, the young king was bent on military glory. Then, in 261 B.C., he made war against the small kingdom of Kalinga. The armies of Kalinga succumbed to Asoka's forces only after a long, bloody, and valiant defense. Watching the battle, Asoka was suddenly overcome with revulsion and grief at the terrible loss of life. He resolved from that moment to renounce war and became a

India's first Buddhist emperor, Asoka (273–232 B.C.), caused round-domed stupas to be built throughout the land, as memorials to saints.

convert to Buddhism. Thereupon he drastically reduced the size of his armies, retaining forces only to guard the borders of the kingdom. And in accordance with the Buddhist principle of nonviolence, he gave up not only war but hunting, the eating of meat, and animal sacrifices. He forbade the slaughtering of animals for the palace kitchens.

Asoka's historic conversion to Buddhism ushered in a new era of peace and prosperity. Under his benevolent reign, policies based on the principles of equality and brotherhood were introduced. In keeping with the Buddhist doctrine of tolerance, religious freedom was allowed. Asoka's humane concern for his subjects led to large-scale public-works projects. Hospitals and resting places were built throughout the empire, and shade trees were planted along the public roads. The arts, especially architecture, flourished as never before. For the first time in India, stone as well as brick was used in palaces and public buildings. Asoka's edicts, by which he spread the teachings of Buddhism, were carved at the tops, or capitals, of sandstone pillars, some of which were forty feet high and weighed up to fifty tons. The most famous of them, announcing the Wheel of Law, was supported by the statues of four lions. This so-called "lion capital" at Sarnath and other pillars now in ruins are reminders of the magnificence of Asokan architecture. Also surviving throughout India are round, dome-roofed structures called *stupas* which he built as memorials to Buddhist saints.

Thanks to Asoka's efforts, Buddhism left its mark upon Indian society. The emperor also fostered the spread of Buddhism throughout Asia, sending missionaries to Burma, Tibet, Ceylon, and other regions. These missionaries took with them not only the ethical concepts of Gautama, but also the arts of writing, painting, sculpture, handicrafts, irrigation, and other skills. Buddhism thus performed an important civilizing mission.

Although he fostered peace, Asoka could not always achieve it. He reminded his people that in a single war over the territory of Kalinga 100,000 were killed and 150,000 taken captive. "When an unconquered country is conquered," he wrote, "people are killed, they die, or are made captive. That the Beloved of the Gods (Asoka) finds very pitiful and grievous . . . . If anyone does him wrong it will be forgiven as far as it can be forgiven."

Asoka even offered to forgive the forest tribes that continually harassed his empire. But he was not prepared to forego all violence where they were concerned. "The Beloved of the Gods is not only compassionate, he is also powerful, and he tells them (the forest tribes) to repent, lest they be slain," he wrote. "For the Beloved of the Gods desires safety, self-control, justice, and happiness for all beings."

While he was unable to accept nonviolence completely, Asoka encouraged respect for humans and animals. Thus, although he maintained his army and continued to resist the forest tribes, Asoka was preaching and practicing love, charity, and humility two centuries before the birth of Christ. Unfortunately, after his death in 232 B.C., his example was not followed by his successors. In 185 B.C., after a period characterized by corruption, ineptness, palace intrigues and insurrection, the Maurya Empire collapsed.

The spread of Buddhism, nonviolence and vegetarianism were among Asoka's legacies. Another was the doctrine of the Universal Emperor (*chakravartin*). The Maurya Empire was the first which had the prospect of extending from western to eastern oceans since Mohenjo-Daro and Harappa. With Asoka, it was evident that a benevolent ruler might unify the entire subcontinent and perhaps the world. The idea of the Universal Emperor was not an aggressive concept, but a wholly religious one. It became part of Hinduism and Buddhism. These two major Indian faiths each suggested, in time, that fate would deliver a Universal Emperor to earth. Thus Asoka called himself "Beloved of the Gods" and took the modest title Rajah, or ruler. Later rulers were to call themselves "Great King," "Son of Gods," and "Great King of Kings, Supreme Lord."

BRAHMAN REACTION IN THE POST-ASOKAN PERIOD: THE CODE OF MANU

Though all religions were tolerated during Asoka's reign, Buddhism thrived, largely as a result of the emperor's inspiring personal example. Because he respected them, the Brahmans remained secure during his lifetime. After he died, they attempted to increase their power further by appealing to the many petty rulers who emerged from the crumbling empire.

To strengthen their position, the priests developed a greatly elaborated version of Brahmanism—the Code of Manu. This code, which was attributed to the deity Manu, who was said to have once ruled over the earth, consisted of a body of rigid regulations governing the caste system. It formalized the basic caste lines which, as we saw, had divided ancient Aryan society. Returning to the ancient beliefs of the Aryans, the priests revived the story of the first man, Purusha, from whose body had emerged the four main castes of Indo-Aryan society. Besides accepting the structure of four castes, the Code of Manu also defined the exact duties and obligations of all members of society in minute detail. Its rules covered all areas of Indian political, social and economic life. Although it was not used everywhere in India, four other codes, all resembling it, were developed to accomplish the same ends.

Let us examine this formalized structure in detail. The Code of Manu described the four main castes. They were called *varnas* for their distinguishing varna, or color of skin. These Varna castes were:

1. *Brahmans.* The priest caste was to occupy the highest position of prestige and influence. The distinguishing color of the Brahmans was white. To the white-robed priests was reserved the performance of rituals and all scholarly pursuits. The Brahmans were primarily scholars, not priests in the sense of clergy in the West. Brahmanism (and its successor, Hinduism) has never been a church-going creed. While the priests were called upon to perform some temple services, worship was usually practiced by the individual or family group.

2. *Kshatriyas.* The warriors, who in ancient times had been at the head of society, now were ranked second to the priests. The color of their dress was red to symbolize their work of providing military and political leadership. Warfare was considered a duty of the Kshat-

riyas, and any hesitancy to fight, even against one's own kin, was considered a violation of the dharma, or law, of the caste. Politically, the Kshatriya king was judged according to the well-being of his subjects. A famine-stricken populace, for example, was considered a sign of an incompetent ruler, even when he could not prevent the famine.

3. *Vaisyas.* This was the large commercial caste, whose ritual color was yellow. The Code of Manu delegated to this caste the more mundane tasks of raising cattle, tilling the soil, shopkeeping, and lending money. The Vaisyas lacked the social, ritualistic, and political privileges associated with the Brahmans and the Kshatriyas. But ultimately, as a mercantile order, they gained great power and wealth.

4. *Sudras.* The ritual color of this lower caste was black. According to the Code of Manu, the function of the Sudras was to perform menial tasks for the three higher groups. Most of the members of this caste were poor tenant farmers and artisans.

The Code had little sympathy for the Sudras. Their lot was an unhappy one. Violation of the group dharma called for terrible penalties: "If a Sudra listens to a recital of the Veda, his ears are to be filled with molten wax; if he repeats them, his tongue is to be cut out; if he remembers them, his body is to be torn asunder." The most the Sudras could hope for was that they would be reborn in a higher caste. Revolts or other signs of discontent were held in check by fear of

The Vaisya, or merchant class rose to power early in Indian history and took a dominant position in trade throughout Asia. Many Vaisyas kept fleets. This 19th century lithograph shows wealthy Vaisyas in Calcutta.

being reincarnated into a lower form of life as a punishment for violating caste dharma; for dissatisfaction was a sin which would add to the karma of the soul. Seeking escape from their hard lot, numbers of Sudras became Buddhists or Jains.

As a general rule, the Brahmans (and in some areas, the Kshatriyas) were considered to be "twice-born"—once at their natural birth and the second time through an elaborate ritual whereby they received the "sacred thread" which they wore over their left shoulder. This made them intrinsically superior. The Vaisyas and the Sudras, on the other hand, were denied this privilege.

5. *The Untouchables.* The four principal castes described above do not complete the picture of Indian society. Still lower than the lowly Sudras was a vast "underclass"—the Untouchables, or outcastes. These were originally made up of the Dravidians and other subject populations conquered by the Aryans.

The main group of the Untouchables was the *candala.* They were not allowed to live within the boundaries of a community or to have access to the village well. They had to perform those duties which were considered "unclean," such as tanning leather, cremating the dead, and executing criminals. The candala were restricted in their movements. In various parts of India, they were obliged to clap pieces of wood together to warn the inhabitants of a village of their coming. No members of higher social castes were allowed to have direct contact with the Untouchables.

In time, as society became more complex, the four major social castes prescribed by the Code of Manu (the Untouchables were considered outside the pale of society) developed subgroups called *jati.* Jatis were ranked in a social hierarchy within each caste and based on birth and occupation. The dharma, or laws, which governed each caste, also regulated the life and role of the jati member. Born into a particular jati, the Indian was trained to perform the duties of his group. Each jati developed strict regulations for its members. We will consider some of these regulations later.

Historically, the elaborate and rigid caste system had furnished the continuing thread of Indian culture. It became part of the religion of Hinduism, which evolved from Brahmanism. And it has endured through almost two thousand years of political turmoil and foreign domination.

The Code of Manu elaborated on the concept of the Universal Emperor. Despite roots in the Aryan and Brahman past, it concurred in this point with Buddhists. The widespread violence following the collapse of the Maurya Empire caused the Brahman authors of the Code to yearn for the arrival of the Universal Emperor. The Code proclaimed the divinity of the king:

He (the Lord) made him (the. king) of eternal particles
  Of Indra and the Wind,
Yama, the Sun and Fire,
  Varuna, the Moon, and the Lord of Wealth.

And, because he has been formed
  of fragments of all those gods,
the king surpasses all other beings in splendor.

Even an infant king must not be despised,
  as though a mere mortal,
for he is a great god
  in human form.

CHAPTER 4

INDIAN CULTURE IN TRANSITION: KANISHKA AND THE GUPTA DYNASTY

FOLLOWING THE BREAKUP of the Maurya Empire, northern India lapsed into political anarchy. Waves of Central Asian nomads swept down into the region. Tribes struggled for power, but no stronger central government emerged. Meanwhile small but prosperous kingdoms were developing in southern Tamil Land. Based on a flourishing sea trade with the Mediterranean world, they attained considerable heights in architecture and the arts. Their influence, however, did not extend north of the Deccan.

After long turmoil, Central Asian nomads, called Kushans, succeeded in establishing their authority in the west and northwest of the subcontinent. Under the leadership of Kanishka (120–162 A.D.) the Kushan Empire extended beyond the Hindu Kush into modern Afghanistan and the Tarim Basin. This region was the site of oases that linked Central Asia to the Mediterranean world. It was during the reign of Kanishka that significant developments occurred in Buddhism.

REIGN OF KANISHKA: MAHAYANA BUDDHISM

The Kushans first felt the influence of Buddhism when missionaries sent north by Asoka reached the uplands of Central Asia. Kanishka, an enlightened ruler and patron of the arts, created his own personal religion which favored Buddhism but included elements of other Asian religions and of Greek philosophy.

About this time a dispute broke out among Buddhist missionaries over the correct interpretation of the teachings of Gautama. As Buddhism spread, its message was transformed to such a degree that some of the most pious followers began to protest. Transported by the missionaries across the mountain ranges of the Himalaya, Buddhism had been changed to appeal to the tribes of these remote areas. These missionaries realized that Gautama's philosophy, with its stress on self-enlightenment, would not touch the hearts of primitive nomads. To enhance Buddhism's appeal, the missionaries taught a more mystical, emotion-laden doctrine.

41

To resolve the ensuing controversy, the emperor Kanishka called a great council. The decisions of this council resulted in a deep division within the ranks of Buddhism. One group, the *Theravadists* ("Believers in The Teachings of the Elders"), insisted on close adherence to the original teachings of Gautama. The second group, which sought to humanize and emotionalize Buddhist ideas, identified themselves as *Mahayanists* (from *maha*, greater, and *yana*, way or vehicle). This latter group contemptuously referred to the Theravadists as *Hinayanists*—those who follow the *hina*, or lesser, way.

The Theravadists, or Hinayanists, refused to regard Gautama Buddha as supernatural. Rather, they saw him as a great teacher who, through arduous self-discipline, achieved enlightenment and Nirvana. Following Gautama's teachings, the Hinayanists stressed that enlightenment could be achieved only by the individual himself. Priests, rituals, and ceremonies were of no avail in the lonely quest for salvation.

In addition, the Hinayanists taught that man should seek to become *arhat*, or worthy, of enlightenment; he had then but to await his natural death. The man who was arhat could not directly assist others in attaining the same state of enlightenment. At best, in his life and behavior, he might serve as an example for others to follow. Later the Hinayanist did introduce rituals and ceremonies, but they still adhered in theory to the pure concepts of the arhat.

The Mahayanists, on the other hand, offered salvation to all. Rituals, ceremonies, incantations, liturgies, fasts, holy water, incense, and other devices were introduced as means of assuring the attainment of the state of Nirvana. These practices were regulated by new scriptures which, it was claimed, constituted the teachings of Gautama to his more spiritually advanced disciples.

The Mahayanists were able to explain their position in philosophical terms by stating that Gautama could only have become a Buddha through an evolution. He had gained Nirvana, they said, through a succession of previous lives. Thus, he was part of a cycle—an idea that recurs throughout Indian thought. There are four great periods in every cycle, ending with the appearance of a future Buddha, or Maitreya, on earth.

Thus at other times other lives are being prepared to become the Maitreya. The Mahayanists maintained that saints called *bodhisattvas* ("beings of wisdom") must exist to take this role. In time, through transmigration, they would come to resemble Gautama Buddha and one day join him beside an Immeasurable Radiance (*Amitabha*) in Heaven. The Buddhas were thought to occupy the World of the Fathers as disciples of Avalokiteshvara ("The Lord Who Looks Down").

Northern Indians were prepared for these ideas by the arrival of concepts from the Middle East which had been brought to them by the Greeks and Kushans. Mahayana Buddhism therefore became rooted in the north about the time of Christ and spread rapidly throughout India. Theravada Buddhism retreated to Ceylon, where the Tripitika was preserved verbatim. Although Theravada Buddhism was spread from Ceylon to Southeast Asia, where it still persists, it was overcome by the Mahayanists throughout India by the third century after Christ. To preserve their orthodox doctrine the Theravadists continued to utter the "Three Jewels" of Buddhism's early teachings: "I take refuge in the Buddha. I take refuge in the Doctrine. I take refuge in the Order." Countless bodhisattvas, meanwhile, were taking the vows which made Mahayana Buddhism so much more successful among the masses of Indians:

> *I take upon myself . . . the deeds of all beings, even of those in the hells, in other worlds, in the realms of punishment . . . I take their suffering upon me . . . I bear it, I do not draw back from it, I do not tremble at it . . . I have no fear of it . . . I do not lose heart . . . I must bear the burden of all beings, for I have vowed to save all things living, to bring them safe through the forest of birth, age, disease, death, and rebirth. I think not of my own salvation, but strive to bestow on all beings the royalty of supreme wisdom . . . .*

Buddhist monks of both major sects took similar vows to accept to refrain from "harming living beings . . . taking what is not given . . . evil behavior in passion . . . false speech . . . alcoholic drinks which cause carelessness . . . eating at forbidden times (afternoons) . . . dancing, singing, music, and dramatic performances . . . the use of garlands, perfumes, unguents, and jewelry . . . the use of a high or broad bed . . . the receiving of gold or silver."

Over the centuries, Mahayana Buddhism splintered into numerous sects, each emphasizing a particular Buddha or bodhisattva, each with its own ritual practices. Yet by converting Buddhism from a philosophical code of behavior into a formal religion, the Mahayanists greatly increased its popular appeal. Mahayana Buddhism gradually gained supremacy over the Hinayanists. It gained millions of converts in Central Asia, China, and Japan.

BUDDHIST ART: THE GANDHARA SCHOOL

Under the patronage of Kanishka, a new school of Buddhist art made its appearance. This school took its name from Gandhara, Kanishka's capital at the center of the Kushan Empire. Gandhara

Artists of Gandhara, a
northern city, were influenced
by Greeks and Romans
who came to trade. Their
Buddhas have "Grecian" hair.
This sample of Gandhara
art is at Sarnath.

was on a strategic trade-route—the famous Silk Road between China
and the Roman Empire. Like the other contemporary kingdoms in
the subcontinent in India, the Kushan Empire maintained friendly
trade and diplomatic relations with Rome. Because of this contact,
the Gandhara style of art reflects the influence of Greco-Roman
culture. This is why the faces of many of the images of Buddha bear a
Grecian form.

Gandhara art developed in response to a specific need. The triumphant Mahayanists needed icons, figures of the Buddha, to serve
as focal points for their religious services. The Hinayanists had denied
the deity of Gautama and never represented the Buddha in artistic
form. At best, representations of footprints or depressed cushions
served as symbols of his presence. But the Mahayanists wanted visible
symbols toward which the worshippers could direct their prayers.
This wish produced an outpouring of impressive sculpture.

Borrowing from Greco-Roman techniques, the Gandhara sculptors carved stately Buddhas garbed in Greek robes. Features were
stylized to suggest ideal attributes: curly hair indicated perfection;
long ear lobes symbolized nobility; a mark on the forehead, wisdom;
and signs on the palms and feet, luck. The sculptors also created

specific hand positions, or *mudras,* to symbolize Buddhist attitudes such as charity and meditation. In general, the Gandhara icons became standardized figures, stripped of individuality. The face of Buddha became a mask of serene meditation.

THE GOLDEN AGE OF THE GUPTAS (320–CA.544 A.D.)

After the death of Kanishka, the Kushans lost control of northern India. Governments emerged and collapsed. Finally, a single army led by a family called Gupta conquered most of the subcontinent. This family established a dynasty under the authority of Chandragupta II, who reigned from 380 to 413 A.D. The Gupta Empire reached across northern India.

The Gupta Era was to India what the Periclean Age was to ancient Athens: a golden age in which literature, science, religion and the arts flourished on an unprecedented scale. The truly creative work, however, was limited to a few fields. The easy-going life of the people was reported by a Chinese Buddhist monk, Fa Hsien:

> *The people are numerous and happy . . . . If they want to travel, they do so without molestation . . . . The king governs without decapitation or corporal punishment. Criminals are simply fined . . . . Throughout the empire people do not kill animals, nor eat onions or garlic . . . . There exist no dealers of intoxicating liquors . . . .*

Fa Hsien's record of his visit to the Gupta capital clearly shows the effects of Jainism and Buddhism upon the social ethics of the Indian population. Gupta India, at the height of its glory, was a relatively humane and gentle society, basking in peace and prosperity, although certainly violence was not wholly overcome.

Gupta literature. In this period, Sanskrit, the language of the Aryans, adopted by the Brahmans, was polished and perfected as a medium of written expression. The philosopher-king Asoka had preferred to ignore Sanskrit, using the various vernaculars in order to be better understood. But under the Guptas, Sanskrit was reestablished as the language of Indian literature.

One great writer was Kalidasa. Like most classical Indian poets, Kalidasa was not an innovator. He achieved his effects within the traditional framework of expression. Since the poetry of the period was written primarily for recitals at the court, emphasis was placed on the use of language rather than on content. A poem's delight came from the clever verbal manipulations and surprises. Consequently, some English translations make it seem more ornate than it would be in Sanskrit, as this Victorian one of a poem by Kalidasa shows:

On Naga Nadi's banks thy waters shed,
And raise the feeble jasmine's languid head;
Grant for a while thy imposing shroud,
To where those damsels woo the friendly cloud;
As while the garland's flowery stores they seek,
The scorching sunbeams tinge their tender cheeks,
The ear-hung lotus fades, and vain they chase,
Fatigued and faint, the drops that dew thy face.

The Indian classical poets lived highly sheltered lives. Under the Code of Manu, they were prohibited from mingling with the lower castes. Thus their works reflected little of the dark side of life. In fact, tragedy, as a separate medium, never developed at all, since any sign of discontent or disobedience to the gods was a violation of caste dharma. The main themes of Indian poetry were love, nature, and legends of the gods and their consorts. As Indian society placed a high value on *kama*, the pursuit of pleasure, love poetry often had distinctly sensuous overtones, as in these verses by Bharatrihari:

What is the use of idle speeches!
Only two things are worthy of man's attention:
The youth of woman . . .
And the forest.

Indian drama, or *nataka*, as perfected by Kalidasa and others, reached a high state of development. The drama had its roots in the Vedic period, when it fulfilled a religious function—like the "miracle play" of medieval Europe. Indian plays generally were performed for

The poets, dramatists and sculptors of the Gupta Period (320–ca. 544 A.D.) considered love their noblest theme. This sculpture is in Khajuraho.

the court or private groups; public performances took place periodically in the local temples. The Indian stage was very plain, with a curtain at the back through which the actors made their entrances. As no stage props were used, the audience had to rely upon its imagination. Symbolic hand gestures, or *mudras*, as well as dancing, were important in the productions.

Every drama began with a prayer, followed by a prologue in which the protagonist and the stage manager discussed the nature of the play. The dialogue was spoken on the stage. Violence might be referred to, but never acted out.

The plots of Indian drama usually revolved around love affairs, romantic mix-ups, Falstaffian blunders, and the inevitable happy endings. Kalidasa's play, *Shakuntala*, translated into English, was a great success when performed in London in the late eighteenth century and is still read with much interest today.

Besides poetry and drama, the Gupta era yielded a rich harvest of children's literature—fairy tales, fables, and animal stories. The *Panchatantra*, a well-loved collection of animal stories, has long been a source of material for Western authors, from Chaucer to Kipling.

Gupta science. The atmosphere of freedom of the Gupta period stimulated scientific inquiry. A university was established at Nalanda, which attracted scholars and pilgrims from all over Asia. Its libraries contained thousands of volumes.

Since ancient times, Indian scholars had believed that the universe was composed of five elements—fire, water, earth, air and ether. Most scholars assumed that the first four elements were the essence of all life. The Buddhists maintained that nothing was eternal and that atoms were destroyed and replaced by new ones. Indian science held that the atom had no distinguishing qualities—merely potentialities which came into play when it was brought into contact with other atoms. These combinations produced molecules which were the essential building blocks of the universe.

India's greatest scientific contribution was unquestionably its mathematics. Gupta mathematicians invented the all-important decimal system. They understood positive and negative quantities and devised systems for using square and cube roots. Lastly, India gave to the West the value of "pi" (3.1416) and the concepts of zero and infinity. In the Middle Ages, these vital concepts were carried to Europe by the Arabs.

Gupta medicine was also well-developed. Indian doctors understood the structure and function of the spinal cord and were aware of the complex nature of the nervous system. Bone-setting, plastic surgery, caesarean delivery, and other advanced medical techniques were practiced.

Gupta art. During this period, Buddhist sculpture reached its peak of development. It broke with the Greco-Roman style that was followed, to a degree, by the Gandhara school. In place of the swirling Roman or Grecian toga, Gupta sculptors draped the Buddha in tight monastic robes in order to dehumanize him. They sought to make sculpture conform to Buddhist ideals and so stripped away individuality, yielding a rigid mask-face with chiseled eyes, eyelids, and mouth. The effect of these innovations were one of magnificent serenity, of complete obliteration of self.

Buddhist painting also reached a high level of achievement. The best surviving examples of Buddhist paintings are the frescoes on the walls and ceiling of the Ajanta caves, about 200 miles northeast of Bombay. These frescoes portray the life and previous incarnations of Buddha in rich color and detail. (They also contain many paintings created after the Gupta Age.)

Artistic achievements were not, however, limited to Buddhist painting and statuary. Temple architecture also became highly complex. The typical large temple was (and is today) a huge honeycomb, with many outer and inner courtyards and shrines. The outer walls contained cells for visiting pilgrims, as well as stables for their horses. Temple walls were adorned with a fabulous array of sculptured figures. Columns and portals were decorated with semi-nude male and female forms, arranged in graceful tuliplike clusters. The effect was frankly sensuous. The flowering of this temple sculpture during the Gupta period was accompanied by the development of the Hindu religion.

Religion in the Gupta Era: The Emergence of Hinduism

Brahmanism, a product of the fusion of Aryan and Dravidian ideas, underwent constant changes throughout the early history of India. During the Gupta period, Indian religion entered a new phase. Over the two centuries of Gupta rule the popularity of Buddhism slowly declined and Hinduism was revived. In the Gupta court at Bihar, Brahmans, rather than Buddhists became predominant. As they regained influence they began to reinterpret the historical basis of Hinduism in order to revitalize it.

From its inception, every aspect of Hinduism has been amorphous. With neither founder, nor church, nor doctrine, it cannot be said to have begun at any precise time. Rather, it was developed, as we have seen, out of Brahmanism. Hinduism differed from Brahmanism in that it deemphasized the role of Brahman, the "Ultimate Reality." In a sense, it followed the pattern of "mythological Brahmanism" by introducing a greatly expanded cast of gods who took on human shapes. The two most important Hindu gods to appear were Vishnu and Siva. Together with Brahman, they made up a new Hindu "Triad": Brahman (Creator), Vishnu (Preserver), and Siva (Destroyer). Vishnu and Siva were still regarded as manifestations of the power of Brahman. But Vishnu and Siva were given human forms and a direct role in human affairs. They thus assumed greater importance in Hindu worship.

Vishnu. The followers of Vishnu consider him to be the source of the universe. According to Hindu thinking, Vishnu originally slept in the primeval sea upon a couch formed by the thousand-headed snake, Sesa. After the passage of eons of time, a lotus grew from Vishnu's navel; from the lotus emerged Brahman, who then created the universe. Once the universe was established, Vishnu awakened and ruled from the highest heaven with his consort Laksmi.

Vishnu is worshipped as the preserver of life, as a benevolent deity concerned with the well-being of man. He is believed to have made nine *avataras*, or descents, to serve mankind. As a fish, he rescued a sole survivor of the human race during the Great Deluge. As a turtle, he regained mankind's major possessions from the bottom of the ocean. Undoubtedly, his most import descent was in the form of Krishna, an event described in the *Bhagavad-Gita*, "Song of the Lord," a section of the *Mahabharata*. Composed during the Vedic period, this poem tells how Arjuna, a warrior, paused before the great battle of Kurukshetra to hold conversation with Krishna, who took the role of his charioteer. Among the enemy, Arjuna sees many relatives and friends, and he tells Krishna that he would rather die than kill them. Krishna replies that man's soul "neither kills nor is killed." That is, the soul (*atman*) is independent of the body, he says. Krishna advises Arjuna of various ways through which the soul can be saved from future misery. One is by taking selfless action appropriate to position in life. Another is by knowledge of the "Ultimate Reality." A third is by complete faith in a personal god, particularly Krishna. The wisdom imparted by Krishna in the *Bhagavad-Gita* formed the basis of the Hindu doctrine of deliverance, or *moksha*, which will be discussed later in this chapter. During the Gupta period it was recalled by Brahmans who employed the ancient literature in their efforts to revive Hinduism.

Siva. While Vishnu is worshipped out of love, Siva is worshipped mostly out of fear. This all-powerful god of destruction has in the middle of his forehead a third eye with which he can destroy the entire universe at a single glance. He is often pictured sitting in meditation upon the Himalayas, his body smeared with ashes and a string of skulls around his neck. Near him sits his consort, Parvati (also worshipped as Kali in some areas and as Durga in others).

Siva, like Vishnu, has the power to take on numerous forms and

Parvati, mate of the god
Siva, is in part
gentle and in part
fearsome.

shapes. Though feared as the god of destruction and death, he is also
worshipped as the deliverer, the god of reproduction. Hindus believe
that death without enlightenment results in automatic rebirth; thus
death and birth are usually the same. When worshipped as the god of
birth and reproduction, Siva is represented in Hindu iconography by
the *lingam*, or symbol of the male sex.

Siva's consort is also endowed with a two-fold nature. As Parvati,
she represents feminine beauty, gentleness, and fecundity. Parvati
receives homage from pregnant women and young brides. In iconography, she is represented by the *yoni*, symbol of the female repro-
ductive organ. But as Kali, she is feared as a destroyer, a fierce fury
who can only be appeased by offerings of blood. The worship of Kali
led to the formation of a secret society called *thuggee* (from which
comes our English word "thug"). Members of this society murdered
travelers and sacrificed their blood to a deity.

During the Gupta era, worship of Siva's consort became identified
with various cults of the "Mother Goddess." These cults, which dated
back to the ancient Harappa culture of the Indus Valley, revived
during the period. Female figures called *yakshis* were used as icons in
the temples of Siva and Parvati to symbolize fertility and sensuality.
Hindu artists also depicted the "Cosmic Mother" in horrible,
destructive forms. She was the womb from which all life emerged,
and the grave to which it returned. In some iconography, the Mother
Goddess was portrayed as Kali in the form of a wolf, lolling her
tongue to lap the life-blood of her children. As Durga, she was portrayed as an eighteen-armed figure subduing a gigantic bull in order
to preserve the universe.

The god Vishnu is called "The Preserver." This greatest of India's kindly gods is part of a cycle of births and rebirths which also includes Rama and Krishna.

Lesser deities. In addition to Vishnu and Siva and their consorts, Hindus worship a host of minor deities. Hindu mythology abounds with stories of lesser gods (*devas, suras*) and demons (*asuras*). Throughout the subcontinent, villages and families worship their own particular deity. In the daily lives of the common people, these semi-gods and goddesses play a more important role than the major deities of systematized Hinduism. Although Hinduism offers countless numbers of deities, it regards them all as manifestations of the "Ultimate Reality," Brahman.

Generally, the god or goddess is represented by an icon which serves as a focal point for devotional prayers and offerings. In the morning, the worshippers may draw the god's attention by ringing bells or playing musical instruments. The icon is washed and then offered water, flowers, betel quids or a cup of rice. A red paste may also be smeared on the idol. The god is said to consume the essence of the gifts. After a time, the sacrificed food is given to the poor. These devotions are performed by the villagers themselves. Only the essential ceremonies such as those at birth, marriage or burial require the presence of a Brahmanical priest.

Today in the larger towns and cities, Hindu temples are noisy, bustling places, as they were in the early days of the faith. At the shrine, worshippers may recite prayers aloud, or simply spend their time laughing and gossiping with friends. The air is full of the sound of excited voices and the smell of burning incense, sandalwood, marigolds, and rosewater. In the temple courtyards, merchants set up booths, and lively bartering takes place. Children scream and scamper about freely. The uproar and disorder is a shock to the

Western visitor, accustomed to the quiet of Christian churches. In India, however, the temple serves as a social center as well as a place of worship.

HINDU DOCTRINE: THE FOUR ENDS OF MAN

To the time-hallowed sacred literature of the Vedas, the Brahamanas, and the Upanishads, Hinduism added new doctrines derived from the epic poems (*Mahabharata* and *Ramayana*) and a new set of legends and religious instructions, the *Puranas*. Drawing upon this material, Hindu doctrine propounded the "Four Ends of Man."

1) *Dharma.* Man's first and most important end must be to observe dharma which is the all-encompassing concept requiring the consideration of religious duty, morality, and right conduct (mores, customs, codes or laws). Dharma also provides the precepts which allow the individual to secure material and spiritual sustenance. Without this regulating factor, man would carry himself to destruction in his pursuit of material gain and pleasure. The content of dharma provides for the needs of the individual and society by organizing the social life of the castes and the individual's status and role within the caste and subgroup. A model of devotion to dharma was Prince Rama, hero of the epic poem, who defended the ideals of his family and caste.

2) *Artha.* Although Hinduism considers the visible universe an illusion, it still allows for *artha*, the pursuit of material things, as a necessity of life. Artha, the second end of man, is permissible as long as it conforms to the dharma of each particular caste.

3) *Kama.* The third end of man is the pursuit of pleasure, especially the pursuit of sexual love despite anxieties, sufferings, and disappointments. Kama may also mean the pursuit of pleasure in the arts, singing, dancing and the theatre. The quest for pleasure and satisfaction is thought to prepare man for the ultimate spiritual union with Brahman.

4) *Moksha.* The fourth and final end of man is *moksha*, or deliverance from the wheel of rebirth. Through moksha, the individual attains reunion with the Ultimate Reality, or Brahman. As we have seen, the priests of the Gupta period recalled the words of the god Krishna in the *Bhagavad-Gita* to explain how moksha could be attained. Krishna tells the hero of the poem, Arjuna, that there are three main paths to moksha: right conduct (*karma*), knowledge, (*jnana*), and devotion (*bhakti*). Any or all of these paths can be used by the individual according to his personal needs.

The development of the doctrine of the Four Ends of Man popularized Hinduism, developing it well beyond its roots in Classical Brahmanism. Through this major development, supported by the ancient literature, Hinduism could be understood by all. The members of each of the castes knew that deliverance from the cycle of rebirth was essential to end human suffering. They believed in dharma, which it was every individual's fate to perform. Krishna's advice to Arjuna was that a man must act in the world to uphold the dharma of his caste, yet at the same time he must not attach any personal value to his actions. One widely known path to self-discipline, by which man is capable of "acting and yet not acting," is called *yoga*. The word is said to be derived from the word "yoke," meaning union with the Ultimate Reality.

The *Bhagavad-Gita* offered salvation to persons who followed dharma, practiced "involvement without attachment," and offered devotion to Krishna (Incarnate of Vishnu). This explains the enormous popularity of the Krishna cult among the lower castes and subgroups, the jatis. Traditional Brahmanism, as embodied in the Code of Manu, had offered salvation only to the upper caste. Hinduism, through the doctrine of moksha, broadened its appeal to those members of the lower orders who had previously found opportunities for salvation only in Buddhism.

HINDU SOCIETY: FAMILY AND CASTE PATTERNS

The history of Western civilization is in part the story of the individual's effort to protect himself against the unlimited power of the monarch or ruling group. As Western democracies developed, constitutions and laws increasingly protected the individual's rights. The history of Asia is different. India's philosophical and religious systems have long stressed the destruction of the selfhood. And until recent times, Indian social institutions have thwarted opportunities for individual expression. The emphasis was not on a person's legal rights, but on his duties and responsibilities to his family and caste.

In traditional India, the family was the basic social unit. The Hindu family was consolidated and defined by the religious ceremony of *sraddha* (commemorating one's ancestors) which linked the living with the dead. Inside the close-knit family, the father's authority was supreme; unquestioning obedience to one's elders was the rule. Individual privacy and opportunities of self-expression hardly existed. The welfare of the group was the prime concern of each family member. Income was pooled for the support of all and possessions were held in common. Although often restrained by the demands of the family, the individual enjoyed a comfortable feeling of identity. The intense pursuit of individualism which is a motivation in the West is altogether lacking in traditional Hindu society.

Hinduism outlines specific stages in a man's life. After childhood he enters a period of celibacy and study at the home of a teacher. He then returns home, marries, and raises a family. In middle age, after his children are married, he withdraws to the forest as a hermit. There, through meditation, he will seek to achieve moksha. In practice, however, few Hindus make this withdrawal. Most hope that by way of simple sacrifices and devotion moksha can be achieved.

Marriages were often contracted for economic reasons and thus were arranged by the parents. Many girls were married in formal ceremonies when still children. They remained with their parents until adolescence, then moved into the households of their spouses. In many instances of child marriages, the girl was considerably younger than her groom.

The status of women was determined by custom. A woman was regarded as simultaneously "goddess, slave, saint, and strumpet." She was expected to serve her husband with devotion. At the same time, religion demanded that she be cherished, provided for, well fed, and offered all the possible luxuries. She should not be beaten without cause. Divorce was not generally permitted, and unfaithful wives were severely punished. Among some Brahman and Kshatriya groups a wife was expected to commit *sati* (or *suttee*)—to throw herself upon her spouse's funeral pyre and perish with him in the flames when he died. Though in theory a voluntary act, suttee was usually carried out under strong social pressure. This practice was abolished by the British in the nineteenth century, but in remote areas it still persists.

Beyond the narrow circle of the Hindu family was the larger unit of the caste. We have already described the caste structure laid down in accordance with the Code of Manu. In Hindu society, the structure was further complicated by thousands of subcastes, or jatis, which developed within each major caste.

Membership in a caste was usually determined by birth and occupation. The son of a priest was born to be a Brahman, the son of a potter was born to be a potter, and so on. Caste members were traditionally restricted to marrying within their own group. However, occasional mixed marriages do occur. *Hypergamy* is the marriage in which the wife belongs to a lower caste than her husband. The offspring of a hypergamous marriage were despised bitterly. Tradition also required that caste members eat only with others of their same group, and even their food had to be prepared by a cook who was not of a lower rank. The diet also varied. Many Brahmanical priests practice vegetarianism.

Outside the family, the caste provided for the security and welfare of its members. In certain cases, the power of the caste exceeded that of the family. Thus if a man was ostracized by his caste for violating one of its laws, his family was held responsible. The family, too, was obliged to turn him out or suffer a similar fate. Once banished, a man was a social outcaste, reduced to the level of the Untouchables.

CHAPTER 5

THE IMPACT OF ISLAM

LATE IN THE FIFTH CENTURY A.D. the Gupta Empire, weakened by invasions of Huns from Central Asia, collapsed. After a chaotic century, temporary order was restored in the north by a single ruler, Harsha (606–647 A.D.). Gaining control of a state just north of modern Delhi, he extended his rule over most of the former Gupta dominions. Harsha was an enlightened ruler, a friend of Buddhism and a patron of arts and letters. However, the empire he founded broke up soon after his death. For the next four centuries, until about 1000 A.D., the rule of northern India was divided among a number of feuding dynasties and petty rival states.

Throughout this turbulent period Hinduism, the caste system, and family life remained relatively unaffected. Nevertheless, by the eleventh century A.D. a decline in Hindu culture was noticeable. Hindu culture proved unable to resist the new challenge which arose from a dynamic religion-oriented civilization called Islam.

HISTORIC ORIGINS OF ISLAM

According to Islamic tradition, in the year 610 A.D. Gabriel, the messenger of Allah (God) appeared to a merchant called Muhammad of the Arab city of Mecca. The messenger informed Muhammad that Allah had chosen him as his prophet to spread the new religion of Islam. (Islam means in Arabic "submission" to the will of Allah.) The holy instructions which Muhammad received were written down in the sacred scriptures of Islam—the *Quran*. Muhammad's own discourses were later collected in another work sacred to the Muslims—the *Sunna*.

In Mecca, Muhammad first proclaimed his message: "There is no god but Allah; Muhammad is the Prophet of Allah." Muhammad's teachings soon brought him into conflict with authorities of the city. Forced to flee for his life, he escaped from Mecca to the desert, taking refuge in the town of Medina. This flight to Medina, called the *Hegira*, took place in 622 A.D. which became the year 1 of the Islamic calendar. In Medina, Muhammad converted the desert tribesmen and formed a powerful army. He then returned to Mecca, drove out his enemies, and introduced the Islamic faith throughout the Arabian peninsula.

After Muhammad's death in 632 A.D., Islam spread east across the Iranian plateau and west across North Africa into Spain. At the Battle of Tours (732 A.D.) the Arab horsemen were finally halted and driven back across the Pyrenees by the Christian king, Charles Martel. At the very outset of this great expansion a conflict arose as to who should succeed Muhammad as *caliph*, or leader, of the Islamic community. One group insisted on Ali, the son-in-law of Muhammad, but the majority were opposed. Ali became caliph, but his opponents, known as the *Umayyads*, seized Egypt and Syria. Ali was later murdered, and the Umayyads established their own leader as caliph. A rebellion led by Ali's younger brother, Hussain, was ruthlessly suppressed.

This political struggle was paralleled by a religious schism. The Umayyads formed an orthodox group, called the *Sunni*, while the followers of Ali branched off into the dissident *Shi'a* sect. The Sunni recognized only the *Quran* and the *Sunna* as the authoritative works of Islam. The Shi'a, on the other hand, introduced the doctrine of the *Imam*—an infallible, sinless being (unlike Muhammad) who appears in every age as the interpreter of God's word in the Quran. In addition to these two groups, Islam produced a mystical movement, the *Sufists*. The Sufists advocated a life of strict asceticism and the suppression of passions and desires.

ISLAM VERSUS INDIAN FAITHS

Conflicts with Hinduism. The doctrines of Islam and Hinduism were sharply opposed to each other. While Hinduism was pantheistic, Islam was emphatically monotheistic, maintaining that: "There is no God, save Allah. He is the One, the Living, the Absolute Originator, the Knower, the Prevailer, the Tyrant. . . ." Moreover, while Hindus held that human existence was *maya*, an evil illusion, the Muslims looked upon life as a vital, pressing reality. Hindus thought that the soul passed through successive reincarnations; the Muslims believed that man lived only once. Every thought, word and deed in a Muslim's life was accountable to Allah on the Last Day of Judgment. And while the Hindus sought moksha, deliverance from this life, the Muslims considered life an opportunity to serve Allah, by combat if necessary.

The essential differences were complicated by further disagreements. Music and dancing were integral parts of Hindu worship, but Islam prohibited both during religious services. Hindus were forbidden to eat any beef, but Muslims were restricted only from eating pork, which was thought to be "unclean." The Hindus all worshipped icons of their gods in the temples. The Muslims denounced any form of idolatry. While no historical persons could represent Hinduism, the Muslims had proclaimed a series of prophets, culminating in Muhammad. In the perception of Islam, each succeeding prophet was said to have known more of the will of God. While Hinduism encouraged tolerance of all faiths, Islam propounded the concept of *jihad* ("exertion"), an ongoing effort to spread the Islamic faith. The Muslims imposed a special tax, called the *jizya*, on people of other faiths. Finally, while the Hindus accepted government passively, the Muslims actively sought to realize their religious beliefs through government.

The impact of Islam on Hindu society was jarring and profound. Islam was a classless creed, holding that all Muslims are brothers. This doctrine was at total variance with the Hindu caste system, which was based on a system of inequality at every level of society. There thus was little common ground between the two faiths. The clash between them led to much bitterness and bloodshed.

The annihilation of Buddhism. Buddhism had been steadily weakened in India since the ninth century, when it was contested by a group of Hindu priests. The priests were organized and led by Sankara, a religious leader from Tamil Land in South India. We have seen how Brahmans in the Gupta court succeeded in reviving Hinduism by expanding its pantheon and by making it more relevant to the masses of Indians. During the Gupta period, Hinduism began to absorb Buddhism. Buddha was regarded as one of the incarnations of the Hindu god Vishnu. Brahman priests were called upon to carry out ceremonies in Buddhist households.

Buddhist monks, however, persisted in their monasteries. They and much of what remained of Buddhism in India were finally destroyed by the Muslim invaders. Soon after the invasion began many monasteries and Buddhist libraries were destroyed. Buddhist monks were murdered or driven out of India. Some escaped to Tibet. Buddhism in India was gone, never to be revived.

THE DELHI SULTANATE (1211–1504 A.D.)

Arab invaders had seized the area of Sind in northwest India as early as the eighth century A.D. In succeeding centuries Muslims began raiding deeper into the subcontinent. These raids culminated around 1000 A.D. in the expeditions of the ferocious Turk, Amir Mahmud of Ghazni. Mahmud led seventeen plundering expeditions deep into India. The armies of the Hindu defenders were no match for this fanatical Muslim, whose swift horsemen easily ran circles around the lumbering Indian war elephants. Hindu temples and cities were pillaged throughout the land as Hindus resisted desperately. Women jumped into the flaming ruins rather than be captured by the Muslim warriors.

In the last quarter of the twelfth century A.D. another Muslim host, led by an Afghan, Muhammad Ghori, overran northern India. Unlike earlier raiders, Muhammad Ghori actually occupied the country, establishing a kingdom at Delhi. This Delhi Sultanate lasted almost three hundred years. It quickly extended its power across the Indo-Gangetic lowlands, south to the Deccan and along the Malabar coast. Everywhere Islam was ruthlessly imposed and unbelievers put to the sword. In the Deccan, however, the powerful Hindu kingdom of Vijaynagar withstood the attack. Its ornate, heavily-fortified capital at Hampi still stands. Later attempts of the Delhi Muslims to crush the southern kingdom proved equally unsuccessful.

Toward the end of the fourteenth century the Delhi Sultanate began to weaken. In 1398 the hordes of the terrible Amir Timur (known in English literature as Tamerlane) swept down from Central Asia and sacked Delhi. Though the sultanate temporarily recovered from the blow, its strength was further sapped by rebellions and court intrigues. For three centuries the Delhi sultans had ruled India. By about 1500 the Delhi Sultanate was exhausted and was no match for another invasion by Central Asian nomads.

THE MOGUL DYNASTY (1526–1740 A.D.)

As the Delhi Sultanate decayed, nomadic tribes resumed looting expeditions into the Indus Valley. Finally the Moguls, a fierce Turkish tribe under the leadership of Babur gained the upper hand. In 1524 Babur invaded India with a force of only twelve thousand men. They were well armed with muskets and artillery. Two years later, in 1526, he routed the army of the enfeebled sultanate at the battle of Panipat and made himself master of northern India. A descendant of Amir Timur, Babur was the founder of the great Mogul Dynasty which ruled India for more than two centuries.

The first Arab invaders of north India did not stay to live and rule. In the 17th century, however, later Muslims came and built Red Fort at Delhi.

The reign of Akbar (1556-1605 A. D.) Babur's death was followed by a period of instability, during which his sons struggled over the rights of succession. In 1556 Akbar, Babur's grandson, ascended the throne at the age of thirteen. Despite his youth, Akbar soon consolidated his power, leading his armies in a series of successful campaigns against the rebellious kingdoms of the south. More important was his creation of an efficient centralized administration, staffed with a competent civil service. The empire was divided into twelve provinces, each ruled by an administrator appointed by Akbar himself. Government officials were selected from all classes and ethnic groups solely on the basis of merit, and, in an effort to discourage graft, were given land from which they derived high land revenues.

Perhaps Akbar's greatest achievement was in conciliating his Hindu subjects. Hindus were given places in all ranks of the civil service, and some Brahmans and Kshatriyas were appointed to important administrative posts. Akbar also took steps to conciliate the group of haughty Hindu princes, the *Rajputs*. He himself married the daughter of a Rajput.

Although illiterate, Akbar was a great patron of learning. As emperor he surrounded himself with scholars who read to him from the noblest books of the ages. Akbar delighted in brilliant conversations, and scholars, theologians, mystics and poets from many nations flocked to the court for discussion and debate. During the reign of this enlightened Mogul, the arts flourished.

Unwilling to limit himself to the strict concepts of Islam, Akbar strove to create a universal religion, based on many faiths. To the delight of Hindus and Buddhists (and the horror of his Muslim advisers), he accepted the theory of the transmigration of the soul, abolished animal sacrifices, and became a vegetarian. He also did away with hunting parties and other violent sports. These reforms greatly pleased the gentle Jains. And when the Portuguese first set up their colony at Goa, the sovereign even agreed to have one of his sons educated by Christians. Akbar built a House of Worship and encouraged men of all faiths to use it to worship their god or gods in their own manner. To his court friends Akbar proclaimed his personal religion:

O God, in every temple I see people that seek Thee; in every language I hear spoken, people praise Thee; if it be a mosque, people murmur the holy prayer; if it be a Christian Church, they ring the bell for love of Thee. . . . But it is Thou whom I seek from temple to temple.

A mausoleum at Sikandra memorializes the tolerance of Akbar (1542–1605), the Moguls' greatest ruler during their long occupation of north India.

Thus, while Western Europe in the sixteenth century was suffering persecutions and the horrors of the Spanish Inquisition, Akbar's India was blessed with religious freedom. Sadly enough, Akbar's humane universal creed did not outlast him. Upon his death, he was quickly buried without religious rites. Soon his sons were plotting against each other for the throne.

Akbar's successors. Akbar was followed by his son Jahangir. The reign of Jahangir lasted until 1627, when that undistinguished monarch died a drunkard. After a bloody power struggle, Jahangir's son, Shah Jahan, gained the throne. His reign was even less noteworthy than that of his predecessor. He taxed his subjects heavily and, reversing Akbar's policy of toleration, launched a new persecution against the Hindus. Shah Jahan is remembered chiefly for the building of a huge tomb, the Taj Mahal, as a memorial to his favorite wife.

The age of the Moguls drew to a close with the long reign of Aurangzeb (1659–1707). The first twenty years of this monarch's rule witnessed savage religious persecutions. Hindus and Muslim heretics were cruelly put to death. Hindu temples were despoiled. Meanwhile the Mogul bureaucracy was purged of non-Muslims, and new taxes were imposed on the unbelievers. Wishing to restore the purity of orthodox Islam, Aurangzeb imposed a regime of austerity and frugality upon his court. Paintings and sculpture were removed from the royal household, and a ban was placed on singing and dancing.

Having purged his own empire, Aurangzeb embarked on conquest. In the tradition of the *ghazi,* the slayer of infidels, he wished to spread Islam to every corner of the subcontinent. Marching south into the Deccan, he managed to subdue the strong Hindu kingdom of the Marathas in the hills of the Western Ghats. By 1690, he had brought almost all India under his control. But this empire did not hold together for long. Rebellions by the Sikhs, the Rajput princes, and the indomitable Marathas kept Aurangzeb constantly on the alert. The small kingdoms of the Deccan formed a new alliance and turned the Muslim armies back. Meanwhile the vast wealth of the Mogul treasure was drained in fruitless campaigning.

Having devoted almost his entire life to battle, Aurangzeb finally died at the age of eighty-eight—India's most hated ruler. Near the end of his life he is supposed to have said:

> *I know not who I am, where I shall go . . . . My years have gone by profitless. God has been in my heart, yet my darkened eyes have not recognized His light . . . . There is no hope for me in the future. The fever is gone, but only the skin is left . . . . I have greatly sinned and know not what torment awaits me . . . .*

In the last analysis, Aurangzeb's policy of religious intolerance was a complete failure. By driving the Rajputs from the government, he alienated the powerful Kshatriya caste. His destruction of Hindu temples turned the Brahmans against him, while his heavy taxes earned the hatred of the masses. After the death of Aurangzeb in 1707, the Mogul Empire rapidly declined.

India's most hated Mogul king was Aurangzeb (1659–1707).

Mogul society and culture. During the Mogul period, Muslim influence in India was greatly strengthened. Proud and militant Muslim communities took root in many cities, and conflict between the Muslim and Hindu populations lasted until 1947. Despite steady friction, a number of Muslim institutions were adopted by Hindus. *Purdah,* the seclusion of women, was adopted in certain areas by upper Hindu castes; Hindu women, when appearing in public, were obliged to hide their faces behind a veil. At the same time the Hindustani language, formed of Persian and Sanskrit, became the dominant vernacular of northern India. (The newer languages, *Urdu,* which is spoken by Muslims, and *Hindi* which is spoken by northern Hindus, contain elements of Hindustani.) At the high levels of society, Mogul court manners were widely imitated by both Muslim and Hindu princely families.

Under the patronage of the Moguls, with the exception of Aurangzeb, the creative arts revived. Some of the greatest achievements were recorded in architecture. The Persian influence was marked by the use of onion-shaped domes, cupolas, narrow gateways, slender pillars, and intricate lattices in geometric and floral designs. Outstanding monuments survive in the mosque, palaces, and baths at Fathpur Sikri, a city built by Akbar. The emperor's palace in Delhi was famed for the value of precious gems and metals in the rightly named Peacock Throne. Also remarkable are the lake palaces at Udaipur and the great hilltop fortress of Jaipur. The latter was built in the eighteenth century by a Hindu maharajah, Jai Singh II. But the architecture is purely Islamic. The buildings, battlements, and watchtowers were constructed entirely from the local pink sandstone—giving the city a magical, fairy-tale quality.

Undoubtedly the crowning achievement of Mogul architecture was the Taj Mahal, the tomb built by Shah Jahan for one of his wives in the city of Agra. Over 20,000 laborers toiled for fifteen years to complete the vast structure in 1647. It was built of flawless white marble, inlaid with arabesques of semi-precious stones—agate, jasper, cornelian, and turquoise. At the center of the complex of buildings is the great mausoleum, set in the midst of gardens and fountains. At the four corners of the complex rise lofty minarets. The domes and spires are beautifully mirrored in a clear canal which borders the structure on all sides.

The Mogul era also saw the emergence of new schools of Indo-Persian painting. One was associated with the court and is aptly called the Mogul School. Its paintings were secular. It portrayed court life and such royal pastimes as hunting, riding, and falconry. The Rajput School, a related movement among the Kshatriya subgroup of Rajputs, catered to aristocratic tastes. It showed religious

The domed roof of the Taj Mahal—a white marble tomb built by a
sultan for his late wife—symbolizes the oneness of the universe
under Islam, and is a characteristic of most Mogul architecture.

motifs, especially scenes illustrating the loves of Krishna and his mate
Radha, and of Rama and his wife Sita. The Rajput School shows its
Persian influence in the two-dimensional treatment and the use of
black, wavy lines, and bright colors.

CHAPTER 6

THE RISE OF THE BRITISH IN INDIA

THE SPICES, SILKS, AND JEWELS OF Asia had been in demand in Europe since Roman times. For centuries, except during the Crusades, they had been delivered to this vast market by Arab traders who controlled overland routes. During the fifteenth century the Portuguese, inspired by their growing naval tradition, became determined to break the Arab monopoly of the "Far East" trade by finding an ocean route to Asia. In 1486-88 one of their explorers, Bartholomew Diaz, rounded the Cape of Good Hope. Plagued by storms, he returned to Portugal before reaching the Indian Ocean. Ten years later Vasco da Gama, in command of four ships containing 160 men, rounded the Cape again. At the island of Zanzibar he met an Arab navigator who agreed to help him. A year later, da Gama's ships were anchored off India's Malabar Coast. Indians there asked him why he had come. "For Christians and spices," he said.

A few Christians lived in India. The Portuguese wanted to protect them and to create new ones through the efforts of Dominican and Franciscan priests. For the most part the spices were not to be found in India, however. The Portuguese continued their search until they found the "Spice Islands of the East Indies," Indonesia. They regarded India as a trading station on route to the islands. Through the efforts of one of their most successful admirals, Alfonso d' Albuquerque, they gained bases in the Persian Gulf (1509), the Indian island of Goa (1510), and Malacca on the Malay Peninsula (1515). Other Portuguese bases were established in the areas of Bombay and Calcutta. This chain of trading posts enabled them to create an ocean-going monopoly over the spice trade throughout the sixteenth century. Meanwhile the Dominican and Franciscan missionaries, who had only slight success in converting Hindus to Christianity, were largely replaced by highly disciplined Jesuits. By learning Indian languages and culture, the Jesuits gained many friends among Brahmans. This tactic increased the number of converts among all of the Hindu castes. The Jesuits became the favorite conversationalists of the Mogul ruler, Akbar, and so were effective advocates of Christianity in the Muslim community, too.

In their pursuit of "Christians and spices," the Portuguese regarded themselves as instruments of God. Soon after arriving at

Goa their king, Manuel I, wrote to the Indian potentate at Malabar that he was determined to protect and spread Christianity there. "And if it should happen that . . . we find you in the contrary of this," he wrote, "our fixed purpose is to prosecute this affair and continue our navigation, trade, and intercourse which the Lord God wishes to be newly served by our hands." Portuguese missionaries spread the Holy Inquisition to Goa. They destroyed some Hindu temples and tried to make local customs conform to their own religious ideals.

Except for the relatively small amounts of land that they took for trading stations, the Portuguese made no effort to build colonies. When their trading stations came under repeated attacks by bandits, they asked the local rulers for permission to build forts. These forts guarded local communities as well as the Portuguese. Therefore, Indians began to contribute money to build and operate them. The Indian monarchs considered both the forts and the Portuguese to be under their ultimate authority. The Portuguese, on the other hand, began to think of their trading posts as permanent supply stations on the route to Indonesia. In time they discovered that India could also be a source of fabrics that they could buy cheaply for use as barter in Indonesia.

After 1600, Goa's wealth and influence began to decline. Portugal lost its monopoly of the spice trade to the Dutch who, early in the seventeenth century, took possession of Ceylon, Malacca, and much of Indonesia. Portugal was also weakened by the corruption of its colonial officials and by the growing hostility of Indians to its Catholic missionaries. Although the Portuguese were able to hold Goa until 1961, their role in Indian history after 1650 passed to the English as well as the Dutch.

ORIGINS OF BRITISH POWER

Early relations with Indians. England's East India Company was founded in 1600 under a charter granted by Elizabeth I to a group of London merchants. This private group was slow to seek a share of the spice trade. As the Dutch replaced the Portuguese in India, however, England became alarmed and prepared to enter the Asian trade. Efforts by the Portuguese to halt England were defeated in two decisive naval actions in 1612 and 1614. The English built their first trading station at Surat in 1613. This was accomplished with the permission of the Mogul king, Jahangir. As in almost all situations in which Europeans constructed bases in India during the early seventeenth century, the king issued a permit, called a *firman* or *perwannah*. The king considered the English trade helpful to local economies. The Europeans were entitled by their firmans to use part of local tax revenues to help build their bases.

By the end of the seventeenth century, the English had built a chain of bases on both coasts of India. The most prominent of them was Bombay. The Portuguese had founded Bombay as a headquarters for their nearby bases at Chaul, Bassein, Daman, and Diu Island. Recognizing that the Dutch had replaced them in Asia, they gave it to the English. It became part of a dowry accompanying a Portuguese princess who married Charles II of England. Soon after his marriage, King Charles sold Bombay to the East India Company.

As the Portuguese control of India deteriorated, many of their sailors in Asia became pirates. They attacked Indian ships and in Bengal captured Hindus for sale as slaves. The Portuguese government disclaimed responsibility for the pirates. The Mogul ruler, Shah Jahan, refused to accept the disclaimer and drove the Portuguese out of Bengal. They were replaced there by the English, French, and Dutch.

The Europeans were becoming active in India when the main local forces were:

1) The Mogul Empire, which began to disintegrate with the death of its last ruler, Aurengzeb, in 1707;

2) the Sikhs, a religious group founded in the Punjab in the early sixteenth century by Nanak, a teacher whose purpose was to fuse elements of Islam and Hinduism into a more casteless society;

3) the Marathas, Hindus of south-central India, whose organizer Sivaji, a tax collector, led a rebellion against the Moguls and was made a king by his followers in 1764;

4) the Rajputs, Hindu nobles who ruled small states in the northwest; and

5) the Nawabs, regional tax collectors for the Moguls who became sovereigns with the death of Aurengzeb.

The Mogul empire was crumbling rapidly. In 1739, a Persian army invaded the country and sacked Delhi. In the Deccan, the Maratha kingdom invaded north India and occupied Hindustan and Bengal the following year. The Marathas later clashed with Afghan forces invading from the north. In 1761, the Marathas were obliged to retreat to the south. To further confuse the picture, the militant brotherhood of Sikhs began to expand in the Punjab.

The many governments of India were incapable of imposing law over any large region. Kingdoms attacked each other often and without warning. In this chaotic period, governments found it difficult to finance themselves because local wars reduced the production of crops on which taxation was based. India, therefore, was in need of strong central rule.

British conflicts with the Dutch.   The Dutch formed their East India Company in 1602, just two years after the English company was begun. Like the English organization, it was made up of private investors who were franchised and supported by the government. Using the naval and military power permitted to it, the Dutch East India Company rapidly defeated the Portuguese in Southeast Asia, India, and Ceylon. By 1652, its competition with England was so severe that war broke out at sea and on the subcontinent. The Dutch were quickly defeated. Eliminated from the race for wealth in India, they began to concentrate on developing trade with Indonesia.

British-French conflicts. European wars and internal problems kept the French from forming their East India Company until 1664. Six years after doing so they began to establish trading posts, one of which, Pondicherry, on the east or Coromandel coast, became their headquarters for India. This base was to remain in French hands until 1954.

For years French resources were too heavily committed to Europe to permit expansion in India. Then, in 1742, her fortunes in India were placed under the control of the Marquis Joseph François Dupleix. This superb general and political strategist came to power in India at a time when Britain and France were at war in Europe and North America. He attacked the British and after two years was winning when the European conflict, the War of Austrian Succession, ended in 1748.

During this period, the French also fought a Mogul army in India. The battle was not part of the struggle between the two European powers. Nevertheless, it had immense significance for the future of colonialism in India. In it, a few French soldiers defeated the vastly more numerous troops led by a regional Mogul ruler, the Nawab Anwar-ud-din. The Mogul soldiers soon gave up the field to the highly disciplined French. Their defeat caused both Britain and France to recognize that India might be controlled with relatively few soldiers.

In his struggle with the British, Dupleix had little support from his government in France. He therefore sought to use his small but effective army in alliances with Indian powers. This tactic meant that a European power was intervening in Indian politics for the first time. In Hyderabad, Dupleix supported one of two rivals for the throne. His candidate won, causing French influence to grow in the area which included the British trading post of Madras. Soon afterward the French gained a similar victory in the north, near Bombay. The British reacted to this pressure by resuming the war against the French in 1751. Following the strategy introduced by their adversary, they began to form alliances with local monarchs. This new British-French struggle paralleled the Seven Years' War in Europe, North America, and the Philippine Islands (1756-63).

Struggling for control of the Punjab, the British found the Sikh troops there to be brilliant fighters who were not easily overcome.

Dupleix threatened to win a quick victory. With the help of their Indian allies the British turned him back, however. In 1761, they overran the French base at Pondicherry. Dupleix was recalled to France, and French power in India was lost forever.

The basis of empire. As early as 1669, the English governor at Bombay had written to the East India Company that "the times now require you to manage your general commerce with the sword in your hands." The English were still content to trade and had little thought of territorial expansion in India. However, they were increasingly called upon to defend their trading stations. By 1687, the philosophy of the Company had changed from one of self-defense to one of aggressive action. In that year it instructed its officials at Madras "to establish a polity of civil and military power, and create and secure such a large revenue to secure both . . . as may be the foundation of a large, well grounded, secure English dominion in India for all time to come."

The movement of goods from Asia to Europe brought the English into open conflict with Muslim powers in the Middle East. Hoping to resecure the trade that had been theirs for centuries, some Muslim governments attacked English ships. In further reaction against the westerners, a Mogul army sought to dislodge the English from Bengal in 1686. The English quickly formed an army and defeated the Moguls. This battle convinced the British that it would be necessary to build forts to defend all of their trading stations in Bengal. Within 25 years they were strong enough to make demands on the weakened Moguls. In 1716, they gained a firman enabling them to trade throughout Bengal without paying duty, to expand Calcutta, and to coin money for use throughout the country. This firman has been called the "Magna Carta" of British imperialism in India.

Following these negotiations, the British East India Company expanded rapidly. Madras, Bengal, and Bombay became the centers of its power. It had been a business; it became a government, equipped with an army, a judiciary, and tax collectors. In England, adventurous young men were encouraged to go to India to make their fortunes. Since their salaries were low, they were expected to gain whatever personal advantages they could from local conditions. Despite the discomforts of life in a remote country, many of them amassed fortunes through practices which in England would be considered unethical or illegal. Bribery and exploitation were common. Yet British efforts appeared useful to many Indians. Bandits were restrained and trade increased. By 1740, the population of Calcutta exceeded 100,000. All but a few of that number were Indians who had come to benefit from the activities of the British colony.

The assault on Calcutta. In 1756, the Nawab at Bengal, Siraj-ud-daula, was encouraged by the French to fight the British at Calcutta. He attacked and captured the base there. Then he imprisoned a number of British soldiers in the dungeon of the fort. In London, hysterical accounts of what took place in the dungeon raised demands that the Indians be punished. The dungeon, called the "Black Hole of Calcutta," was said to be a 20-foot-square room in which 123 prisoners suffocated one agonizing hot summer day. In fact, historians have since learned that 25 soldiers died in the "Black Hole." Nevertheless, the rumors were often told to make British soldiers more willing to fight. The Indians told atrocity stories about the British, too.

The next year, 1757, saw the decisive turning point—the Battle of Plassey. A small British force was led out of Madras by Robert Clive, a former clerk for the Company who had begun a brilliant military career against the French. Clive led his force to victory over a much larger army of French-led Indians. Then he installed a new Nawab, Mir Jafar, in Bengal. Later, Clive was accused of accepting an enormous bribe from Mir Jafar for giving his support. He was also accused of jeopardizing the British position in India by involving the Company in the complex business of collecting revenues from land. These accusations caused Clive's rapid fall from power. Ultimately they brought the British government into direct control of what had been the Company's affairs in India.

Government intervention. Under the Regulating Act of 1773, the British Parliament established the post of Governor-General for India. This job was to be filled by someone named by a Board of Control in London. Although the Governor-General was an employee of the Company, it was assumed that his selection by the Board would make him more aware of government's objectives than of the Company's. For the first time the government also required the Company to produce statements of its expenditures and income. A Supreme Court was established in Calcutta to supplement the judiciary that was provided by the Company. Finally, because of the Board of Review the Company was no longer completely free to make war and otherwise to upset India's political stability.

The Regulating Act affected, but did not completely change the purpose of the British in India. Trade was still their sole purpose. Although they had come into possession of large regions in Bombay, Madras, Bengal, and Bihar, they did not yet regard themselves as government in the fullest sense. To preserve trade they kept the peace. They also collected revenues to finance their police work. However, they were not concerned with public health, transportation, education, and other services ordinarily associated with government.

The first Governor-General appointed under the Regulating Act was Warren Hastings, who served from 1774 to 1785. Hastings had joined the East India Company as a young clerk at a salary of five pounds a year. Yet, because employees of the Company were permitted to have their own businesses in India, he had become an exceptionally wealthy man. As Governor-General he promptly undertook reforms that earned him a reputation for effective administration. He eliminated much of the bribery in tax collection, restricted some of the excesses of Company men who were seeking private fortunes, and ultimately unified the court system. These moves helped to establish a British tendency to expand government services in India. Under Hastings the British created administrative districts in Madras, Bengal, and Bombay. In these districts, officials were charged with the responsibility for seeing that taxes were collected and that trade was carried on efficiently. They were a training ground for the civil service.

Hastings was succeeded as Governor-General by Lords Charles Cornwallis (1786-93), Richard Wellesley (1798-1805), William Bentinck (1828-35), and James Dalhousie (1848-56). Increasingly these officials drew the British into the active task of more thorough government. Cornwallis strengthened the police and judiciary. As we will see, he affected the economy of all of India through new taxing and land policies. To the dismay of the people governed, Cornwallis would not permit Indians to rise into the highest ranks of the civil service. He thought that the experience might lead to independence and rebellion. During the administrations of Wellesley, Bentinck, and Dalhousie, Britain's view of its role in India changed completely.

After their defeat, the Sikhs became mercenaries for the British. This originally gentle brotherhood had been turned militant by persecutions.

By the mid-nineteenth century, the British regarded India as part of a vast empire which it was their duty to govern with traditional pride.

Expansion of British territory. In addition to the British during the late eighteenth century, major governments of India included the Marathas, Moguls, and two large southern monarchies, Hyderabad and Mysore. There were a number of smaller states ruled by princes. To the north the British used the state of Oudh as a buffer between their Bengali possessions and the fierce Maratha guerrillas.

The allied troops of Mysore and Maratha kingdoms defeated the British near Madras in 1780. However, Lord Cornwallis isolated and subdued Mysore. Afterwards the Marathas, who had formed a confederacy of their small kingdoms, began to fight among themselves. Lord Wellesley, brother of the Duke of Wellington, was then Governor-General. Wellesley decided to enter the Maratha wars in order to gain territory near Bombay, which the Maratha Confederacy adjoined. He also seized Oudh, expanding British territories in the northeast.

Full-scale war with the Marathas resumed in 1804. Meanwhile, Wellesley opened negotiations with the princes of smaller kingdoms. He offered noninterference in the princes' domestic affairs. In exchange, he obtained the right to handle foreign relations and to station garrisons in the territories at the princes' expense.

For both the Indians and the British, the consequences of the war were severe. Village life in central India was disrupted. Both sides lost many lives and supplies. The war with the Marathas dropped to a low level of action. It smoldered until 1817 when part of the Confederacy, in Pindar, attacked British stations in Bengali. Counter-attacking in force, the British compelled the rulers of the Confederacy to accept pensions, leaving them powerless.

The British next moved against the remote kingdom of Burma, to the east. Burma's rulers were isolated from the mainstream of Asian affairs. Their capital was an inland city, Ava. However, Burma became involved in a border conflict with Assam, an adjacent independent state. Britain, fearful that its possessions in nearby Bengal would be threatened, took Assam's side in the dispute. In 1824, it attacked Burma, won a brief war, and imposed the right to keep a resident in Ava who could help it to control the government there. In 1852, it annexed the southern provinces of Arakan, Pegu, and Tenasserim. Finally, Britain seized the rest of Burma in 1885.

At the same time, the British were fighting protracted border wars elsewhere. They defeated the Gurkas, a fierce mountain tribe of Nepal, in 1818. Gurkha units were later incorporated into the British Army. In 1840, the British were forced to contend with the strong Sikh kingdom in the Punjab. By 1849, after bloody battles, the Sikhs were beaten. Their territory at Sind was annexed in 1843 and later the Punjab also was annexed. The Sikhs, too, became British soldiers. Finally, the British feared that Russia might use local conflicts in Afghanistan, to the northwest, as an excuse to invade India. To thwart this possibility they sent troops to the remote, high passes of the northwest. They found it impossible to defeat the fierce Afghans, but managed to restrict them to the mountains.

One important means of expansion, the "Doctrine of Lapse," was conceived and administered by Lord Dalhousie. The Doctrine enabled Britain to seize any princely kingdom whose ruler died without leaving a son. It ignored the important Hindu tradition whereby a childless ruler could adopt an heir. This infuriated the Indian royalty. The British employed it, however, because it gained them more territory, usually without violence. By midcentury, most of India was in the hands of the British, who governed outright in Madras, Bengal, and Bombay, and exercised indirect sovereignty in the Princely or Native States.

RESENTMENT AGAINST THE BRITISH

Under Lord Bentinck, the British began to assert in India what had been a Puritan tradition in England—that of requiring conformity. Many Englishmen wanted India to become a more Christian country. Others wanted to change its laws so that it would become more like England socially, politically, and economically. To advance towards these goals, British administrators in India substituted English for Persian as the official language. European literature and technology were introduced through new Indian schools. Courts were made English in form. Customs which the British regarded as "barbaric" were suppressed. British missionaries discussed ways by which they could "uplift" Indians.

Early in the eighteenth century, Indians accepted their new role passively. One of their most influential leaders, Rammohun Roy (1772–1833), urged them to blend their ancient Hindu ideals with modern western technology. Roy's objective was to retain India's compassion and wisdom while leaving behind its social liabilities, such as the caste system and prejudices against women. Because of his efforts to pursue this dual premise he is called the "Father of Modern India." But not all Indians agreed with him. After 1833, the government's increasing authority in India enabled the British reformers to become more effective. Indians discovered that the education being given to them in British schools equipped them almost entirely for the civil service. Yet many educated Indians could find no work suitable to their training; there were few Indian activities in which their skills were needed when no civil service jobs were available. Finally, the British began to transport Indian soldiers for foreign wars. This violated the Hindu tradition which prohibited high-caste Indians from leaving their homeland.

Some of the social changes required by the British were no doubt helpful to India. For example, laws were passed against the murder of female infants, human sacrifices, and *suttee*, the practice in which widows threw themselves upon the burning funeral pyres made for their husbands. These practices were never as widespread as many Englishmen were led to believe, however. They grew out of ancient religious beliefs and were restricted to a relatively few areas. The more significant changes wrought by British administrators affected all of India. Two of the most important of these were in the area of tax collection and manufacturing.

Traditionally, land in India was not held by individuals. The state claimed it, even that land on which small farmers worked intensively. Farmers shared their crops with the state. Throughout history the governments of India had collected their share through appointed revenue agents, called *zamindars*. To pay the zamindars for their services, rulers allowed them to keep ten elevenths of the total that they had collected. During the Mogul period this amount was approximately 2.5 percent, while the state received between 25 and 33 percent. The farmers kept the rest. For the most part, the job of zamindar was an inherited one, held by an aristocracy whose members also served as local judges. The zamindars were known personally by the people from whom they collected taxes. These relationships restrained the zamindars from oppressing farmers. At all costs, the government sought to sustain the cooperation between the farmers and zamindars so that it could continue to finance itself.

From 1764, the British had been taking a share of public revenues to pay for its services. By this time, many of the zamindars were released from their obligations to the withering Mogul empire and considered themselves free agents. Because of the increasing power of the zamindars, in 1793 the British decided to combine the Indian revenue collecting system with the Western principle of private land ownership. This was accomplished under the leadership of Lord Cornwallis, who opposed public ownership of land. Cornwallis insitituted a policy called Permanent Settlement—which here meant the fixed share of revenue paid to the government. Under this policy, zamindars were permitted to become the owners of land whose farmers were unable to pay taxes.

The zamindars were encouraged by this policy to make demands for revenue which the farmers could not meet. The large sums owed to them often allowed them to seize land, which under the new policy they could own. It was to their advantage to collect increasingly larger amounts because they were paid a percentage of the total. In time, the zamindars began to remove themselves from the villages where their families had been known for centuries. They bought and sold the right to collect taxes at auctions. Zamindars gained rights in areas where they had little or no concern for the people. Often the rights were subleased as many as fifty times. That process further removed the revenue collectors from the source of the revenue, the farmers. While often living luxuriously in the cities, many zamindars strained the ability of the farmers to pay taxes to the limit. In further moves to encourage the principle of private land ownership in India, the British made grants of large tracts to Nawabs who gave them military aid.

Manufacturing was the second major area in which British policies caused major social changes during this period. When the British arrived on the subcontinent, the Indian economy was stable, balanced, and relatively wealthy. The village system was highly productive; the sale of products abroad brought substantial income. The monopoly granted by Parliament to the East India Company drastically affected India's foreign trade, however. By the end of the eighteenth century, most Indian materials were being shipped to England. There, they were used in machines that had been developed during the Industrial Revolution. The spinning jenny, the flying shuttle, and the power loom rapidly replaced the village weavers who had created Indian prosperity. Cheap products, manufactured by the new machines, were brought back to India to compete with the products made by the villagers. At the same time,

British tariffs restricted the sale of Indian products in British markets.

Faced with increasing competition from abroad, Indian farmers began to produce crops for the market rather than for their own needs. Their commodities were shipped on railroads constructed by the British. These same railroads brought back goods which, when sold in the villages, served to replace locally made goods. India's balanced village economy thus was turned into a more specialized one. Cities grew rapidly. Although India was not gaining the capital equipment that was a positive benefit of the Industrial Revolution, it began to suffer the same consequences that Western nations were experiencing during this period: poverty, dislocations, and unemployment at a time when population was rising.

The Sepoy Rebellion and Its Consequences

Causes of rebellion. In the spring of 1857, the long pent-up hostility of Hindus and Muslims was ignited by a single spark—the so-called "incident of the greased cartridges." Rumors spread among the Indian regiments of the British army, called "sepoys," that their cartridges, which were made of paper and filled with black powder and metal, had been coated with cow's fat and hog's lard—the former a sacrilege to the Hindus, the latter a grave offense to the Muslims. To use a cartridge it was necessary to bite off some of the

In 1857, Scottish reinforcements at Lucknow helped to save the British when Indian troops (Sepoys) rebelled.

paper. Muslim sepoys stationed in Bengal refused to accept the new cartridges and were given prison terms. Thereupon, revolts broke out in Bengal, and the uprising swiftly spread up the Ganges Valley. In the ensuing violence, atrocities were committed on both sides. The horror and bloodshed lasted twelve months before British reinforcements and allied troops quelled the rebellion.

Effects in government. The Sepoy Rebellion, which British historians called the Indian Mutiny, left a bitter aftermath. A major consequence was the British India Act of 1858, which stripped the East India Company of its political power and brought the country under the direct control of the Crown. A special agency, the India Office, was created to administer affairs. The India Office was headed by the Secretary for India, a cabinet official who was responsible directly to the British Parliament. The top-ranking official in India remained the Governor-General, who became known as the Viceroy and reported directly to the Secretary of India. The Viceroy's term of office was five years. He was assisted by an Executive Council, originally of five members, later more.

Under this stable system, the second half of the nineteenth century became the golden age of British imperialism. The British writer Rudyard Kipling proclaimed "the white man's burden"—to carry Western culture throughout the world. This offended educated Asians, who considered their civilizations at least the equal of Europe's. While the British, in their eagerness to bring the blessings of democracy, education, and science to "backward, naked peoples," often acted selfishly and betrayed their own principles, they gave India an effective, unified government at the higher levels.

British India was divided into administrative provinces, each headed by a governor, lieutenant-governor, and chief commissioner who were responsible to the Viceroy. The governors were assisted by provincial councils, whose decisions were subject to the governor's veto. Provinces were split into divisions which in turn were subdivided into districts. These districts, which totaled 250, were the key administrative units. To the District Officer fell the task of administering justice and collecting taxes. His job was by no means easy; often he had to cope with epidemics, floods, and revolts.

The mainstay of British administration continued to be the famous Indian Civil Service (I.C.S.). It was composed of highly competent officials, selected by careful examinations. Many Englishmen of distinction sought I.C.S. positions because of the high salaries and excellent retirement program. Many Indians served in the I.C.S., although they were not always permitted to compete for the higher positions.

The Indian armies were also placed under firm British control. To prevent possible rebellions among the troops, all officer ranks were reserved for non-Indians until 1917. This discrimination embittered the educated Indians, who felt they were equally entitled to positions of military leadership.

Outside the areas governed directly by the British Viceroy were the Princely, or Native States, which were ruled by Hindu maharajahs, or Muslim sultans or nizams and were allowed internal autonomy. Foreign relations of the Princely States were handled by the Viceroy, who could also intervene in domestic affairs if the native princes were unable to maintain order. This division between British India and the Princely States was in many ways unfortunate. While in the British-ruled regions democratic procedures were gradually introduced, including local self-rule, public education, industrialization, and urban planning, most of the Princely States remained static and backward under their despotic monarchs. Several of the larger states that escaped direct British domination, however, had very progressive governments. These included Mysore, Cochin, and Travancore. The latter two had higher literacy than those in the British provinces. When independence was gained in 1947, however, the Princely States generally lagged behind the rest of India in political, economic, and social development.

In sum, the Sepoy Rebellion caused government policies to become more conservative and cautious. Fearful of new uprisings, the British moved more slowly against such traditional practices as the seclusion of women (*purdah*) and suttee. While earlier Governor-Generals such as Bentinck had been intent on social reform, after 1858 the government was mainly interested in preserving peaceful conditions in which to develop India's economic resources.

The revolt also left psychological scars. Europeans tended to develop the "Indian complex"—to look down upon Indians as inferior. Indians were increasingly discriminated against in the allotment of government jobs. Segregation was practiced in the cities, where Europeans took to living apart in exclusive residential areas. This legacy of mutual fear, suspicion, and bitterness lasted until India and Pakistan achieved independence.

British Rule in Retrospect

During the twentieth century Great Britain was a country of about forty million, while India's population was about 300 million. Yet, the British controlled India thoroughly. Ignoring most local problems, they dealt with national and international ones with a civil service which in the 1930's contained less than 3,000 British officers. India, with its massive population and land area, remained a British colony when there were fewer than 117,000 Britons within its borders.

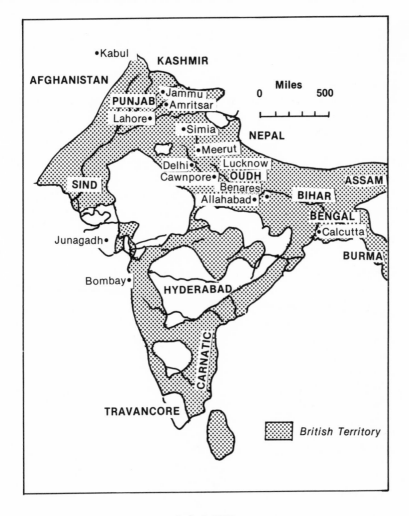

India in 1857

This achievement was made possible only because many Indians helped the British in the administration and because the general population accepted the government. Yet, British rule had both positive and negative effects. On the positive side were the benefits of a more systematized government than India had previously known. The people experienced more peace and order. Banditry, which before had been widespread, was virtually eliminated. Slavery was abolished in 1860. The British introduced a new legal code which, while not infringing on the basic beliefs of Hindus and Muslims, provided a more just treatment for all regardless of caste status.

The application of Western science and technology brought far-reaching improvement in transport and communications. By the early part of the twentieth century, India had 31,000 miles of railroads, ten times the number in China at that time. This railroad system was the fourth largest in the world. Where it was not possible to build extensive railroads, as in Kerala, networks of highways were constructed. British engineers supervised the construction of some major canals, such as the Buckingham, which joins the Krishna delta with lands more than 60 miles south of Madras city. They helped to develop major ports, including Bombay and Cochin on the west coast and Calcutta and Madras on the east coast. Enormous water diversion projects were undertaken, among them the Sirhind Canal, which irrigates 2.3 million acres with water from the Sutlej River; the Upper and Lower Ganges canals, which bring water to almost 3 million acres; and the Western Jumna Canal, which irrigates 1 million acres. Under the British, the government also enacted public health measures and took steps to combat the periodic famines that had plagued India for two centuries.

With these developments in law and technology, the British did much to heighten the political awareness of the Indians. Before the arrival of the British, Indian experience with self-rule was chiefly on the local level in the village councils. Although in the early stages of their occupation the British refused to allow Indians to gain key positions in the civil service, this policy was later changed. The Reform Act of 1909 authorized Indians to serve on the Executive Council, which advised the Viceroy. The admission of Indians to this level of administration was a major political step in the direction of complete self-rule.

Additional steps were taken by the British—always taken under the pressure of Indian demands, but taken, nevertheless—to establish parliamentary government in India. The Government of India Act of 1919 ("The Montagu-Chelmsford Reforms") allowed provincial administrations to establish their own legislatures. The concept of voting was introduced. It was extremely limited, however; only about 3 percent of the population owned the amount of property required to qualify for voting. In 1935, the British passed a second Government of India Act. It permitted the development of a federal constitution. Although the British Governor-General continued as the supreme authority in India, the concept of independent government became established during this period.

Generally speaking, the spread of British commerce and industry made possible the growth of an enlightened Indian middle class. This relatively well-to-do group benefited, in turn, from the education it received in British schools in India, as well as from opportunities to study abroad in such English universities as Oxford and Cambridge. Ironically, India's intellectuals—men like Gandhi, Nehru, and Bose—were first exposed to Western nationalistic concepts in British educational institutions. They learned and appreciated the Anglo-Saxon concept of free self-expression. At home this made them natural rebels.

Against these positive achievements of British rule, the negative effects must be weighed. Through their construction of railroads, highways, ports, and canals in India the British intended chiefly to benefit themselves rather than the Indians. They extracted more than one-third of India's annual production of raw materials from the earliest days of their occupation until World War II. At the same time they supplied up to 38 percent of India's imports—chiefly products made by machines financed through the profits of the empire. It was the Indians, not the British, who paid for the gains which were realized chiefly in Britain.

The amount of social damage caused by the British in India has often been overstated. Indian villages have been represented as idyllic, self-sustaining entities before the arrival of the British and as hovels afterwards. In fact they have changed, but not necessarily because of the British. Poverty in India is the result of overpopulation and the maldistribution of wealth. The British helped to cause both of these problems only indirectly, not for their own gain. The population was growing at the rate of .6 percent a year at the beginning of the twentieth century. There was almost no population growth because infant mortality was high. Aided by British public health and medical practices, India began to control famine and disease. The resulting reduction of the death rate caused the population growth rate to soar to 3 percent, or between 13 and 15 million people a year.

British policies contributed to the maldistribution of wealth by introducing the Western system of private land ownership through the Permanent Settlement Act of 1793. Previously, the land was owned by joint families; the government took a share of the crops for taxes. As the Act was increasingly enforced, the zamindars and other individuals became absentee landlords who drained farmers of their income. Farmers had to grow crops for distant markets rather than for themselves and their communities. Many small farmers had to quit agriculture and to move to cities. Some of India's wealthiest families began to buy the small farms or to foreclose mortgages and have developed some of the world's largest landholdings. But the failure of small farmers and the growth of cities in India were not solely a British responsibility. They were worldwide events. Despite the changes in population and in the distribution of wealth, India remains a relatively stable agricultural country.

The damage caused to India's culture by the British occupation was severe. The use of English as a national language, the introduction of Western education and law, and the efforts to convert Indians to Christianity all had a depressing effect. India needed a national language. Its schools before the arrival of the British mainly taught children of the rich to memorize the Vedas. Nevertheless, India had been one of the world's greatest sources of literature, music, and

The British required Indian princes to pour wealth into their treasury, as shown in this nineteenth-century painting.

science before the arrival of the British. Their mathematicians had been among the best in all history. They are said to have invented the concept of zero which, with other mathematical ideas, they taught the Arabs, who in turn taught it to the West. Indian culture stagnated throughout the British occupation until missionaries brought presses to publish religious tracts early in the twentieth century. As we will see, Indians began to use the presses to revive their own literature. One great writer, Rabindranath Tagore (1861–1941), a Bengali who was also an educator, inspired the entire country with his poems and dramas. As Tagore gained fame and won the Nobel Prize for Literature in 1913, many other Indians began to write and publish. Applying the ideas of nationalism and individualism they had learned from the British, they dealt with such social themes as the caste system and child marriage. Soon, a new spirit was stirring throughout India. The country's educated class began to think in terms of making the country aware of itself as a nation. By 1885, some of its members were able to join forces. They quickly made both their countrymen and the British aware that a nationalist movement was growing.

CHAPTER 7

THE TRIUMPH OF NATIONALISM

THE INDIAN NATIONALIST MOVEMENT faced seemingly insuperable obstacles. The foremost problem was the absence of real political unity. India's government structure included 532 semiautonomous Princely States, possessing approximately 45 percent of the population and ruled by autocrats who generally opposed any form of democratization. Besides, no national language could serve as a unifying element. The country was a linguistic Tower of Babel, with 15 major languages and more than 600 dialects. Religion appeared another grave handicap, for the Hindu caste system prevented the effective organization of the masses. Finally, the smouldering conflict between the Hindu and Muslim communities divided and weakened the nationalist movement.

Despite these obstacles, the forces of nationalism proved irresistible. The Princely States did not play an important part in the struggle. The lack of a national language was solved, ironically, by the use of English, which most educated Indians (about 1 percent of the population) could speak with ease. And, in spite of caste barriers and Hindu-Muslim conflict, religion became a driving force behind the movement for self-rule. A militant Hinduism, revived by nationalist leaders, served to rekindle the flames of Indian patriotism.

During its formative stages (1885–1919), Indian nationalism moved at a leisurely pace and concentrated on promoting limited reforms. As moderate action proved ineffective, more violent measures were employed and the campaign became a crusade. At length, under Mohandas K. Gandhi, the movement was transformed into a dynamic social force, supported by the mass of the Indian people.

INDIAN NATIONALISM BEFORE WORLD WAR I

At first the nationalist movement drew its support from the emerging intellectual middle class—journalists, lawyers, businessmen, and religious leaders. This class was fast acquiring a "social consciousness." In the latter part of the nineteenth century, wealthy Vaisya families sent their sons to study in Europe where they were exposed to democratic concepts. These young Indian students were stirred by the writings of Locke, Paine, Jefferson, and Mazzini, and inspired by the successful campaigns for national unity of Bismarck in Germany and Cavour in Italy. They also saw firsthand Europe's high standard of living, made possible by science and industrialism. In addition, modern medicine was demonstrating that malaria, cholera, and other terrible diseases could be conquered. Inspired by their European education, many Indian intellectuals returned home with the hope of elevating their country's economic and social life and of winning political freedom from British rule.

Meanwhile, in the late 1870's, Britain's Indian policy became harsher. Handicaps were placed upon Indian civil service applicants who were already denied the right to compete for high positions. Laws were also passed restricting the liberty of the Indian vernacular press and limiting freedom to bear arms. A final insult was the successful agitation of British imperialists against the Ilbert Bill, introduced in 1883, which was intended to give Indian jurists the right to try cases involving Europeans. These measures finally goaded the Indian nationalists to political action.

The Indian National Congress. In 1883, Allan Hume, an Englishman who had retired from the Indian Civil Service after thirty years of devoted effort, called upon educated Indians to organize an educational group. This led, in December, 1885, to the Indian National Congress, the seventy members of which met at Poona. The guiding spirits of the new organization were Western-educated intellectuals —chiefly Surandranath Benerjea and G. K. Gokhale. The delegates to the first and succeeding conferences were mostly Hindu lawyers, educators and journalists, with a few Muslim representatives.

The Indian National Congress was moderate in its objectives. It advocated social reforms, such as the betterment of the status of women and of the Untouchables, compulsory education, and improved employment opportunities for Indians in the civil service. Its ultimate goal was self-rule, but this was to be achieved by constitutional and peaceful means. Until the First World War, the Congress exerted a limited influence and succeeded in extracting some important reforms from the reluctant British administrators. The efforts of the moderates, however, were increasingly disrupted by the tactics of more militant groups.

The Hindu Renaissance. While Indian intellectuals were seeking to promote Western-type social reforms, in other circles there was a reaction against Western culture. The leaders of this reaction denounced Western philosophies as materialistic and inhuman, and called for a return to the spiritual values of traditional Hinduism. The Hindu revivalists glorified the ancient civilization of "Mother India" in an attempt to awaken a long-dormant popular patriotism. Nationalism was claimed to be a manifestation of the will of Brahman. This more militant Hindu nationalism alienated many Muslims and also some Hindus who could not identify with its objectives.

Another important Hindu revivalist was Sri Ramakrishna Paramahansa (1834-1886). Born to a poor Brahman family in Bengal, Ramakrishna set out to become a Hindu priest. Later he studied both Islam and Christianity. Ramakrishna considered all three religions to be paths to the realization of the Ultimate Reality and was convinced that none is superior to the others. Yet he was offended by the willingness of many Indian intellectuals to abandon Hinduism. They had apparently begun to turn to Christianity instead because they had identified it with the material progress of the West. Hinduism, he thought, more clearly reflected the spirit of the Indian people. He and his chief disciple, Swami Vivekananda, wanted to blend the compassion and tolerance that characterize Hinduism with the vitality that so many Christians seemed to have gained from their faith. "No religion on earth preaches the dignity of humanity in such a lofty strain as Hinduism," Vivekananda said, "and no religion on earth treads upon the necks of the poor and the low in such a fashion as Hinduism." In tours of the United States and Europe, Vivekananda attracted enormous crowds. His success elsewhere in the world brought prestige to the Hindu revival movement in India. "Rise, India," he proclaimed, "and conquer the world with your spirituality. Spirituality must conquer the West." To many of the tens of thousands of people who came to visit him and his disciple in the town of Dakshinesvar, Ramakrishna often raised the question, "Are you seeking God?" The advice that he gave seemed to represent a philosophy for the Hindu revival movement: "Then seek him in man," he said. "The divinity is manifest in man more than in any other object."

A less tolerant prophet of the Hindu revival movement was Dayanada Sarasvati. Born of a wealthy family, he rejected all Western ways and became an ascetic. Sarasvati wandered through India for fifteen years until he met a blind teacher with whom he studied intensively for two years. Afterwards he denounced all religions excepting Hinduism. The traditional toleration of other faiths in India, he said, violated the precepts of the Vedas. Sarasvati's powerful anti-Christian movement, known as the *Arya Samaj*, gained a large following.

Though Ramakrishna, Vivekananda, and Sarasvati limited themselves to religious appeals, other Hindu leaders resorted to political agitation. Like them, Aurobindo Ghose was profoundly mystical and was considered by many Indians to be a saint, but his writing was fiery in its nationalism. "Was India to deform herself from a temple of God into one vast inglorious suburb of English civilization?" he demanded. "India must save herself by ending the alien domination which had not only impoverished her body, but was also strangulating her soul." The British tried to prevent Ghose from writing and to keep his pamphlets out of circulation. They failed in this, but Ghose later voluntarily withdrew to a religious retreat at Pondicherry.

The firebrand of the Hindu revival movement was B. G. Tilak, "Father of Indian Unrest." Born a member of the Brahman caste, Tilak refused to enter the Indian Civil Service after receiving his education. Instead he organized a radical faction within the Indian National Congress and opposed the moderate position advocated by the dominant group led by Gokhale. In the region which was once part of the proud Maratha Confederacy he operated a newspaper and promoted the festival which honored the famous Maratha hero, Shivaji. Through this festival and others he began to foster among the people a sense of pride in the ancient history and religion. His hostility toward the foreigners was also directed towards the Muslims. His group also formed "cow-protection" societies.

Turning to the *Bhagavad-Gita*, Tilak argued that the sacred poem preached political as well as religious activity and implied that violence in a righteous cause such as independence was morally justified. His statement: "Freedom is my birthright and I will have it" gained him many supporters. He urged his followers to "Educate, agitate, and organize."

The Muslim League. Following the collapse of the Mogul Dynasty, the power and influence of the Muslim community drastically declined. Muslim sepoys were blamed for touching off the rebellion of 1857, and thereafter Muslims were looked upon suspiciously by the British. Muslims also fell behind the Hindus in commercial activities because of the Islamic law forbidding "usury."

B. G. Tilak (1856–1920) urged
the use of violence in the
struggle against the British.
They jailed him from 1908–14.

Consequently, no significant Muslim middle class developed under British rule. Islam dominated the lives of the believers. Few of the faithful received Western, secular educations which would qualify them for government jobs or the professions.

A few educated Muslims took a liberal attitude and wished to free the Islam community from restrictions. One such person was Sir Syed Ahmad Khan. He visited Europe and was impressed by the achievements of industrial civilization. He realized that the Muslims would have to adopt certain aspects of Western culture in order to survive in India. To educate his fellow believers, in 1877 he founded the Anglo-Oriental College at Aligarh.

Sir Syed was troubled by the effort of the Indian National Congress to build a representative government on the British model. He understood that if such a system were applied in India, the Muslims would become a permanent minority. He argued that Muslims should be given equal representation because they constituted a separate community. As the Indian National Congress came under the influence of Tilak and other Hindu militants, most Muslim delegates withdrew from the organization.

To counter the Indian National Congress, the Muslims, led by the Aga Khan, a landed prince, and Muhammad and Shankat Ali, wealthy brothers, created in 1906 the All-Indian Muslim League. The major goal of the League at that time was the preservation of the Muslim rights under any Hindu-inspired political reforms. But the formation of the League had a more far-reaching effect—it split the movement of Indian nationalism. Henceforth the fight for independence was weakened by conflicts between the Hindu and Muslim movements.

British reactions. How did the British authorities regard the upsurge of Indian nationalist feeling? At the outset, the Viceroy's government considered favorably the suggestions of the leaders of the Indian National Congress. But when the followers of Tilak began to stir up a more martial spirit, the attitude of the British turned unsympathetic and arrogant. The government welcomed the founding of the Muslim League, seeing in it a counterweight to Hindu nationalism.

At the turn of the century, droughts, famines, and plagues added fresh fuel to Indian discontents. Nationalist sentiment was also strengthened by developments on the international scene, where European imperialists appeared for the first time to be on the defensive. Ethiopia's defeat of Italy in 1896 and the shocking triumph of the Japanese over tsarist Russia in 1904–06 raised questions about the invincibility of Europeans. In addition, the stubborn defense of the Boers, who fought the British in Africa in 1899–1902, showed that resistance against Britain was not hopeless.

Revolutionary societies were formed, first in Bengal and then throughout India. They emphasized militaristic concepts that had been brought to India by the Aryans. Calling on the national pride that had been stirred by the Hindu revival movement, they proclaimed an Indian mission to unite the world, not through force, but in spirit. One of their most widely read revolutionary pamphlets, *Bhawani Mandir*, said to have been written by Aurobindo Ghose, said:

> *India cannot perish, our race cannot become extinct, because among all the divisions of mankind it is to India that is reserved the highest and most splendid destiny, the most essential to the human race. It is she who must send forth from herself the future religion of the entire world, the Eternal religion which is to harmonize all religion, science, and philosophies and make mankind one soul. . . .*

The revolutionaries carried out scattered bombings and assassinations. In Bengal they and more moderate forces promoted a movement that was to have immense importance to the colonial rulers, that of boycotting British goods in favor of Indian ones. This tactic had only lately been made possible by India's growing industrialization.

To cope with the growing unrest, Britain had in this period a highly competent Viceroy—Lord Curzon. Appointed in 1899, Curzon initially gained enormous popularity by undertaking land reforms, reducing taxes, and sponsoring irrigation projects. He also expanded India's railroad system and raised the standards of public education. Curzon was a dedicated student of Indian archeology and sponsored an act to protect the country's historic monuments.

By a single decision, however, Lord Curzon lost his popularity with the Indian Hindus. This was the decision to partition the Province of Bengal. The government of huge Bengal (population: 78,000,000) had become a breeding ground of provincial bureaucratic corruption. But while justified from the standpoint of administrative efficiency, the partition of Bengal was a political blunder. Bengal was the homeland of the Hindu Renaissance. Curzon's action was consequently interpreted as a deliberate blow at the nationalist cause, and it seemed to invite retaliation.

The partition law, passed in 1905, created two separate provinces. East Bengal, with its capital at Dacca, now had a predominantly Muslim population. West Bengal, with its capital at Calcutta, retained an overwhelming Hindu majority. But the Hindus, who had previously dominated the entire Bengal region, were extremely bitter. Hindu newspapers attacked the partition, street demonstrations took place in Calcutta, and British manufactured goods were boycotted. Finally Lord Curzon was forced to retire.

Because of resentment over partition, extremists were able to gain control of the National Congress. The rising nationalist fervor obliged Gokhale and the Congress to take a firmer stand. The moderates strongly condemned the partition of Bengal and called for Indian self-rule (*swaraj*) within the British Empire. Meanwhile, various extremist groups launched a campaign of terrorism. Trains were derailed, and bombs were hurled at British officials. Gokhale and his liberal wing of the Congress denounced these terrorist tactics, but the bombings continued and spread from Calcutta to other areas.

At the end of 1905, the British Conservatives were replaced in the government by the Liberal Party. Under the more progressive administration of John Morley, new secretary of state for India, and Lord Minto, the new governor-general, reforms were introduced. In 1909, the Morley-Minto Act was passed which allowed for greater control of local and provincial governments by the Indians, and for the seating of an Indian representative on the Viceroy's Executive Council. The British hoped that the Act would quiet the Hindu radicals. Despite these concessions, the Hindus keenly resented provisions which guaranteed Muslims seats on the provincial councils. Nor were they pacified when Britain annulled the partition of Bengal in 1911.

Agitation and terrorism continued until 1914. On the eve of World War I, however, the nationalist movement was still basically a middle-class effort, dominated by the intellectuals of the Congress group and lacking a broad popular base.

GANDHI'S CONTRIBUTION TO INDIAN NATIONALISM

World War I found colonial India fighting on the British side. Caught up in the war spirit, the Indian nationalists put aside for the time being their insistent demand for self-rule. For the most part, the Congress supported the war effort, but a small group of extremists living in exile abroad were plotting to provoke uprisings in the homeland. Before the outbreak of war, an Indian student of philosophy at the University of California, Har Dayal, organized the *Ghadr* ("Mutiny") group in Berkeley, California, which recruited Indians (mostly Sikhs) living in the United States and Canada. (A large colony of Sikhs settled in Northern California, particularly at Stockton and Marysville. They sent arms and money to their co-conspirators in India.) Dayal fled to Europe in 1914 and, during the war, conspired with the German High Command to spark a rebellion in India. His Ghadr subordinates in the United States also tried to smuggle agents and arms into India. Their efforts were foiled by British vigilance and because of their own ineptness.

After Gokhale's death in 1915, a change occurred in the policies of the Indian leaders. By the middle of 1916 the moderates were losing control of the Congress to the younger nationalists, led by Tilak, who revived cries for self-rule. The Hindus were joined in their demands by the Muslims, and a temporary alliance was formed between the Congress and the Muslim League. The pressure of this united front upon a war-weary England had its results. In 1919, the British Parliament passed a bill giving the Indians control of public works and education on provincial and local levels, as well as a majority position on the Viceroy's Legislative Council. The Viceroy still possessed the power of veto, however. These reforms, though welcomed by the Indian moderates, were unacceptable to the radical faction, and the breech in the nationalist ranks widened. It was at this critical time of the nationalist movement that Gandhi first rose to prominence.

Early career. In 1869, Mohandas Karamchand Gandhi was born to a prosperous Vaisya family. Gandhi's parents were devout Hindus, and the young man was brought up to revere the ancient traditions. Later his father sent him to England to study law. Gandhi found London a strange, alien world, and he led a secluded life in the slum area of the city. He applied himself to his law books and also studied the *Bhagavad-Gita* and the New Testament, as well as the writings of Tolstoy and later, Thoreau. In 1893, he returned to India and set up a law firm, which subsequently failed. Gandhi thereupon accepted an assignment from another law firm to go to South Africa.

In South Africa thousands of poor Indian laborers had been duped into signing contracts to work in the gold and diamond mines. Bound by their contracts to stay, these Indian "coolies" led a miserable life. Gandhi worked for years to better their position, in the face of unremitting South African hostility and bigotry. It was in Durban and other South African cities that Gandhi first organized nonviolent protest demonstrations. The tactics recalled the ancient principle of *ahimsa*. He called his new nonviolent movement *satyagraha* ("Truth Force") because it called for a "stubborn adherence to the truth."

When Gandhi returned to India in 1915, his reputation preceded him. His followers spoke of him as the Mahatma, meaning the "Holy One" or "Great Teacher." From his home Gandhi began to preach his message of love and truth: "My uniform experience has convinced me that there is no other God but Truth . . . and the only realization of Truth is ahimsa."

Anti-British activities. At the close of World War I, another wave of nationalist terrorism swept over India. Britain responded with the harsh Rowlatt Acts. These two acts authorized the government to

Bombay was a center of activity against the British. Here a crowd of Indians is being dispersed by baton-swinging British and local police.

arrest suspected terrorists and to hold secret trials for them without the right of counsel. More than any other legislation, they infuriated and united all India. They were called "the parents of the nonviolent movement." Gandhi, who previously had sympathy for Britain's effort to restrain terrorists, said the acts changed him from Britain's friend to its foe. As a protest, he urged all Indians to join in a great satyagraha campaign, with work stoppages, closing of shops, nonviolent demonstrations, fasts, and prayers. But when riots broke out during demonstrations in Delhi, Bombay, and other large cities, Gandhi, disappointed, called his satyagraha to a halt.

Famine, unemployment, and bubonic plague were tormenting the country. In the winter of 1918–19, influenza took about 13 million lives. In the aftermath of Gandhi's satyagraha campaign riots broke out in Delhi, causing the British to arrest Gandhi. Distressed by these events, crowds in Amritsar, a city of about 150,000 in the Punjab, killed several Europeans and blew up buildings. On April 13, 1919, four days after this riot, a British general, Reginald Dyer, suspended the right to public meetings in Amritsar. On the following morning, General Dyer, leading fifty soldiers, saw crowds flocking to an enclosed square to pray and to listen to speeches. Without warning, the British troops opened fire on the entrapped congregation, killing 400 and wounding about a thousand. The Indian reaction was fierce. They halted trains and destroyed communications systems. Attempts by Gandhi to organize another satyagraha proved futile. The Mahatma was deeply discouraged. Released from prison by the British, he returned home convinced that the Indians were not ready for nonviolence.

Gandhi realized that the nationalist movement had to broaden its base by appealing to the lower castes and to the millions of Indian peasants. To reach the people, Gandhi visited villages throughout the land. He taught the illiterate farmers and other menial workers the power of nonviolence and love by examples with the *Mahabharata* and the *Ramayana,* as well as myths and folk tales with which the common people were familiar. Gandhi's understanding of peasant psychology was his greatest strength. One of his chief concerns was to better the lot of the Untouchables. He renamed them the *harijan*— the Children of God. This name is still widely used.

By identifying with the poor, the Mahatma helped to break down caste barriers and unify the country behind his cause. In addition, he succeeded in establishing a temporary accord between Hindus and Muslims. He visited Muslim communities and sympathized with their problems. For the next twenty years, nonviolent demonstrations found Hindus and Muslims walking side by side.

During the 1920's and 1930's, Gandhi was the undisputed leader of the Indian nationalist movement. The Mahatma spent years in and out of British prisons or under house arrest. Numerous satyagrahas were carried out. The Mahatma periodically fasted for weeks. Crowds loved to follow the strange bespectacled figure with the warm, toothy smile. Many heeded his teachings. Gradually the image of Gandhi captured the imagination and sympathy of the world.

At the annual meeting of the Congress in 1929, pictures and other symbols of Gandhi were everywhere among the tents put up for the delegates in Lahore. The world's press was on hand to watch as Gandhi succeeded in persuading the Congress to adopt this resolution calling for complete independence:

> *We believe that it is the inalienable right of the Indian people, as of any other people, to have freedom and to enjoy the fruits of their toil and have the necessities of life. We believe also that if any government deprives a people of these rights and oppresses them the people have a further right to alter it or abolish it. . . . We will therefore prepare ourselves by withdrawing, so far as we can, all voluntary association from the British government, and will prepare for civil disobedience, including nonpayment of taxes.*

Gandhi was authorized to proceed with his satyagraha campaign. He made a number of demands upon the Viceroy, Lord Irwin. Among them were the abolition of the salt tax, the reduction of the land tax by 50 percent, reduction in the military budget and in the salaries of British administrators, and amnesty for political prisoners. When Irwin replied that he was unable or unwilling to meet these demands, Gandhi proclaimed that his campaign of civil disobedience would begin immediately.

On March 12, 1930, Gandhi led 79 Indians on what has since become known as the "Great Salt March" to the sea. To dramatize his defiance of the British tax, he and his companions walked 170 miles. Along the way, he was cheered by tens of thousands of supporters and observed by members of the world's press. When he reached the Gujarat coast near Dandi he waded into the water, recovered some of it, and extracted salt from it by boiling it. Thus he avoided the tax, which all Indians thought unjust, and set an example that his countrymen heeded. Millions of Indians promptly followed him in disobedience. They closed shops and businesses, resigned from government, and blocked the sale of British goods. Everywhere people took to the streets waving the flag of the Congress Party.

The British at first gave a moderate response, requesting that the leaders of the Congress meet with government officials in London. When this plea failed, there were mass arrests. By summer, the British had arrested more than 60,000 members of the Congress. Yet the disobedience campaign lasted through fall, when it was halted because of rising violence and the economic hardship that it caused. The British held all of their prisoners until January, when they released some of the Congress leaders, including Gandhi. A month later, Lord Irwin invited Gandhi to meet with him in the Viceroy's palace. The two men announced the Delhi Pact, under which both sides made compromises. The government reduced the salt tax in some areas and permitted Indians greater freedom of speech and organization. Except for those who had committed crimes of violence, all political prisoners were released. For his part, Gandhi agreed not to resume the civil disobedience campaign and to attend the next meeting of Indian and British leaders.

In London, conservatives called Irwin's bargaining with Gandhi "humiliating" for the empire. Within a month, he was replaced as Viceroy. More liberal Englishmen, however, had come to realize, with Irwin, that India's drive towards independence was irrepressible. In India Gandhi, having won a significant victory, was a national hero.

Tactics. The salt protest shows Gandhi at his wisest—as a brilliant political realist. He understood that Indian nationalism could best achieve its purposes by winning the sympathy of the world, because Britain, a democracy, was sensitive to public opinion. He knew that violence, on the other hand, would only hurt India's cause in the eyes of other nations. Gandhi also realized that India could not afford to buy arms, and that armed resistance against the might of Britain was foolhardy. The tactics he adopted cost nothing yet brought enormous rewards.

"... it is sinful for anyone to serve this government," Gandhi said. His nonviolence and non-cooperation damaged the British. Imprisoned, he gained the support of millions by fasting "... to reform those who love me."

Gandhi used many tactics in the fight, including: 1) *Satyagraha*—peaceful demonstrations in which police brutality would be met by "offering the other cheek," 2) *Swadeshi*—boycott of British manufactured goods, which had severe adverse effects upon England's economy, 3) *Sitting dharna*—fasting until death unless an injustice is remedied (usually practiced by Gandhi himself against Hindus as well as the British), and 4) *Hartal*—a day set aside for prayer in which all activities are brought to a complete standstill.

Gandhi also introduced *khaddar*, the spinning of one's own cotton cloth. He was able to persuade millions of Indians to use their simply-structured spinning wheels and make their own coarse cloth rather than purchase the finer-spun British cotton threads. The wooden spinning wheel became a symbol of the Indian nationalist movement.

The foundation of all the Mahatma's tactics was his faith in ahimsa—the principle of nonviolence. Gandhi's satyagrahas were often disrupted by rioting, and time after time he warned the Congress leaders that he would leave the movement if they condoned the use of force. He said:

> *History teaches us that those who have no doubt with honest motives, ousted the greedy by using brute force against them, have in their turn become prey to the disease of the conquered . . . . My interest in India's freedom will cease if she adopts violent means. For their fruit will not be freedom, but slavery.*

Gandhi had critics and enemies within the Congress who were impatient with the Mahatma's methods and preferred to fight British fire with Indian fire. The Mahatma, however, never lost his hold on the common people's imagination. No other leader had such power to move the Indian masses. And yet, this power never corrupted him. When not teaching or demonstrating against the British, he and his family lived quietly in a mud house in his native village. Many Congress leaders adopted Western clothes and manners, but Gandhi dressed and ate according to Hindu custom.

Traditionalism. All his life Gandhi gave new strength to the philosophy of Hinduism. He loved Hindu customs and used to quote from the *Bhagavad-Gita:* "Do your alloted work, but renounce its fruits. Be detached and work . . . . Have no desire for reward, and work." When reproached for concentrating on political rather than social problems, he would reply: "If I seem to take a part in politics, it is because politics encircles us today like the coil of a snake from which one cannot get out . . . . I wish therefore to wrestle with the snake."

Gandhi dreamed that after independence was won, India would build her own unique civilization, based on her glorious past. Gandhi feared the potential destructiveness of modern science, technology, and industries. While he accepted machines when they alleviated human drudgery or ended slavery, he was at times forced to oppose them. He acknowledged their use in cottage industries. But concentrated in factories, he believed, they would ultimately create unemployment and a new type of slavery. Gandhi hoped that India, once she achieved her independence, would return to a decentralized family of self-sufficient villages. *Swadeshi* and *khaddar* were thus means of rediscovering a long-lost spirit of individual self-sufficiency and independence. Gandhi considered urban industrialism the greatest threat to the family and the cause of the exploitation of man by man. Machines, he believed, often made slaves of the individual.

Steps Toward Self-Rule

The increasing pressure of Indian nationalism forced the British to permit more self-government in their prime colony. The first major change in this direction took place in 1919 with the passage of the Government of India Act. Under it, the central government's power to administer the nation's health, education, and agriculture was given to ministries situated in each province. Each province was given the right to elect a unicameral assembly that helped to oversee the ministries. But the Government of India Act was less democratic than it appeared. First, the electorate choosing the assemblies totalled less than 3 percent of the population because property and literacy restrictions were placed on the right to vote. Second, the assemblies did not have final authority in government. Ultimately their decisions could be overruled by the Viceroy, who also continued to control India's judiciary, police, and revenue systems.

Despite its shortcomings, the Government of India Act encouraged Indians to believe that they were participating in self-rule. The system by which they and the British shared power, however unequally, became known as Dyarchy, in contrast to Monarchy. Confronted with the effects of the World Depression in the 1930's, Indians became increasingly impatient with the limits that Dyarchy imposed upon them. They wanted more complete self-rule. During the 1930's, Britain was under the control of the Conservative Party, which had little sympathy for these demands, however. Then, in 1935, the British Parliament passed the India Act granting full self-government on the provincial level.

The India Act of 1935 had two parts, each of which became amendments to the Constitution. The first part, put into effect in 1937, gave the provincial assemblies and administrations full autonomy in government. The Viceroy retained the right to overrule them, however. The Act's second part attempted to establish a federal union combining the British-held territories with the more than 560 Princely States. The British-held territories by this time included Bengal, Assam, Punjab, Sind, Bihar, Orissa, Madras, North-West Frontier Provinces, Central Provinces, United Provinces, and Bombay.

To many Indians, the India Act of 1935 represented a sincere effort by the British to prepare their country for self-rule. Others, more embittered by the loss of national rights and culture, regarded it as a program for formally dividing the country. This latter group based its conclusion on Britain's attempt to create a representative government out of the diverse, often hostile religious groups in India. The India Act sought to guarantee that each minority would be represented in the assemblies through the assignment of a fixed number of legislative seats. Muslims, Christians, and Untouchables thus were assured spokesmen in every provincial assembly. A fixed number of seats also were reserved for other groups, including women, Sikhs, Europeans, laborers, and landlords. The quotas were based on the number of people in each group. Although still small in comparison with those in autonomous democracies, the electorate was greatly expanded to 18 percent of the population.

Britain's proposal for a federal union failed immediately because many of the Princely States refused to relinquish their sovereignty. The problem of reconciling minorities through government proved to be a more extended struggle. Among the Hindu leaders, Gandhi alone seemed to grasp the need for the unity of all Indians. With the end of his great satyagraha of 1934, he proclaimed a period in which all Indians must commit themselves to "nation building." But

Congress members were conscious of the poor showing by Muslims in the first elections held under the new India Act. While the Congress won majorities in five provinces and gained control through coalitions in three others, the Muslims gained victories only in Sind, Punjab, and Bengal. One nationalist leader, Jawaharlal Nehru, remarked after the election that "There are only two parties in the country—the Congress and the British." This and other statements by Hindu spokesmen caused Muslim leaders to fear that their community could not exist within the framework of a Hindu-dominated state. The Muslim leader, Muhammad Ali Jinnah, responded to them. "The majority community have clearly shown their hand that Hindustan is for the Hindus," he said.

M. A. Jinnah (1876–1948)

Jinnah, a lawyer, represented a group of Western-educated Muslims who were bitterly envious of their Hindu countrymen who had prospered in finance, industry, and other professions. He had been a follower of Gandhi's in the 1920's. He broke with the Mahatma because of a conviction that the Muslim League was in danger of being absorbed in the Hindu Congress. Fearing that in a future independent India the Islamic community could not survive he put forward a plan for Muslim self-determination—for a separate political state which would be created in areas with Muslim majorities after independence was won.

India during World War II. Britain's declaration of war on Hitler in 1939, and later, in 1941 on the Japanese, were both echoed by the British Viceroy in the name of India. Most Congress leaders supported the struggle against fascism. However, they criticized the British declarations, maintaining that India should not have been led into the conflict without first being consulted. The Congress angrily closed Indian ministries in eight provinces after the war began, thus dissolving the administration of the India Act of 1935. Jinnah urged his followers to celebrate the occasion as a "Day of Deliverance" from Hindu rule.

A substantial number of Indians considered the war against Hitler less urgent than their own struggle against the British. One of them, Subhas Chandra Bose, led a movement that regarded the Japanese as liberators of colonial Asia. Bose and his followers sought to sabotage the British in India. Arrested by them, he escaped and went to Germany, then to Singapore. There he organized the *Azad Hind* (Free India) movement of Indian soldiers who had been captured by the Japanese while fighting for the British. He offered its services to the Japanese.

Although Bose was regarded as a patriot by many Indians, the majority thought of him as a radical. His militant anti-British viewpoint gained prestige, however, when, early in the war, the Atlantic Charter was signed by Prime Minister Churchill and President Roosevelt in 1941. The Charter proclaimed the "right of all people to choose the form of government under which they will live." Churchill, however, later said that the Charter applied only to nations conquered by Nazi Germany, not India and Burma. Immediately after his remarks were made, Hindus throughout India began a new satyagraha campaign. About 1,400 of them were arrested, among them Jawaharlal Nehru.

Britain's policy of harshness was changed to conciliation as its position in the war worsened. After the fall of France to Hitler in 1940, the British became steadily more desperate. Further blows were rained upon them by the Japanese, who quickly overran their Asian territories. By early 1942, the Japanese had all of Burma and were threatening to advance into India. Seeking Indian help, the British sent an envoy well liked by Indian nationalists, Sir Stafford Cripps, to Delhi. He offered greater autonomy within the framework of the British Empire. But his plea was rejected.

The Congress called upon Gandhi to formulate its policy with respect to the war. He had withdrawn into semiretirement, relinquishing leadership of the National Congress to Nehru, his closest friend. Out of his commitment to nonviolence Gandhi denounced the war, though his sympathies were with the democratic countries. Next, he urged the Congress to pass a resolution calling upon Britain to leave India immediately in order to prevent a Japanese invasion.

This so-called "Quit India" resolution was combined with a renewed satyagraha campaign led by Gandhi. It shocked the British, who denounced the Congress leaders as disloyal to an essentially benevolent government. As the satyagraha campaign increased its efforts, they outlawed the Congress and arrested more than 60,000 of its members. During these arrests Gandhi became a British prisoner. British-Indian relations deteriorated still further when, in 1943, more than one million Bengalis died of famine. This catastrophe was blamed on British negligence.

Meanwhile, Indian resources were mobilized to meet the Japanese threat. A large Indian army was raised and war industries were established. Indian forces helped to turn back the Japanese attack from the northeast across the Burma frontier in the fall of 1943. To the embarrassment of Nehru and the Congress, the invaders included Indian contingents led by Subhas Chandra Bose. After the failure of the Japanese Burma campaign, however, Bose's movement disintegrated.

The Muslims, at the insistence of Jinnah, had remained in the British administration throughout the war. As the war drew to a close, Jinnah made public his demands for a separate Muslim state. He proclaimed that the Islamic community was a distinct nation, with every right to self-determination:

We are a nation of a hundred million, and what is more, we are a nation with our own distinctive culture and civilization, art, language, literature, architecture . . . laws, codes, customs, calendar, history, and tradition. . . . In short, we have our own distinctive outlook on life . . . .

In 1944, when Gandhi was released from prison, he immediately visited Jinnah and asked him to abandon his plan for a separate Muslim state. The Mahatma's efforts proved unsuccessful. He could not understand the Muslim's viewpoint and commented:

I can find no parallel in history for a body of converts and their descendants claiming to be a nation apart from the parent stock. If India was one nation before the advent of Islam, it must remain one in spite of a change in faith of a very large body of her children.

In the spirit of Hindu tolerance, Gandhi believed that "the true beauty of Hindu-Islamic Unity lies in each remaining true to his religion and yet being true to each other."

Independence achieved. In July, 1945, Churchill's government fell from power and was replaced by the Labor Party under Clement Attlee. The British Labor Party had long championed India's demand for independence. Its victory was hailed throughout the subcontinent. But while recognizing India's right to independence, the Laborites held that the conflict between the Congress and the Muslim

Lord Mountbatten, arriving to lead the British out of India, restored the land to the Hindu leader, Nehru (center), and to the Muslim, Ali Khan.

League must first be resolved. Attlee's government sent a Cabinet Mission to arrange details of the transfer of power.

The Cabinet Mission was prepared to grant India complete independence, with the option of remaining within the British Commonwealth of Nations. Attempts to reconcile Hindu demands for a strong central government with Muslim separatism proved futile, and in May, 1946, the British put forward a final compromise proposal. It called for a decentralized federal structure, with a Union at the highest level to conduct foreign affairs, defense, and internal communciations. The Union would be divided into three groups of provinces, Hindu, Muslim, and Native States, which would enjoy internal autonomy. This proposal, a last effort to conciliate the Muslims, was rejected by Jinnah and the League. In the summer of 1946, Hindu-Muslim tensions reached the boiling point, and in August, fierce fighting occurred in Calcutta. By February of the following year, Hindu-Muslim communal strife had taken 12,000 lives.

On February 20, 1947, Attlee told the British House of Commons that Britain would definitely quit India by June, 1948. If the Hindu and Muslim leaders could not agree among themselves by that date, the government would be turned over to two distinct "authorities," the British said. In March, Lord Louis Mountbatten was appointed Viceroy. He immediately took steps to speed up arrangements for the withdrawal of British forces. Despite this pressure, negotiations continued through the spring. In June the Indian Congress leaders, fearing a full-scale civil war after Britain's departure, finally agreed to partition. The British Parliament passed the Indian Independence Bill on July 4. At midnight on August 14, 1947, India officially became a sovereign, independent state. At the same time Muslims declared their new state, named Pakistan.

AFTERMATH OF INDEPENDENCE: GANDHI'S TRAGIC END

The independence celebrations were hardly over before the subcontinent was again engulfed by civil strife. Countless Hindus, afraid to remain as a minority in East and West Pakistan, the separate parts of the new Muslim state, began a great migration into India. Millions of Muslims, in turn, sought safety by crossing over into Pakistan. More than fifteen million people were involved in this mass migration, the largest in all human history. Most emigrants had never left their villages before setting out on the tragic trek. Government plans to direct the movement, or to provide shelter and food along the way, were inadequate.

The worst disasters occurred in the Punjab region near the West Pakistan border. Convoys of Sikhs, southward bound for India, clashed with Muslim columns moving northward toward Pakistan. All along the roads these foot convoys of men, women, and children, loaded with baggage and possessions, were attacked by marauders. Trains carrying emigrants were derailed, and everywhere fanatical Hindus attacked Muslims who decided to remain in India, while fanatical Muslims attacked Hindu families who wished to stay in Pakistan. So great were the disturbances that the two countries threatened to go to war. A British boundary commission sought to conciliate both sides by announcing lines of demarcation. Its conclusions only further infuriated both sides.

A similar upheaval almost took place in Bengal. But large-scale violence was avoided through the efforts of Gandhi. Fasts and appeals by the seventy-nine-year-old Mahatma brought both sides to their senses. Gandhi traveled to Hindu and Muslim villages in Bengal, calling for an end to bloodshed and preaching mutual tolerance. By December, 1947, the migration was slowing down and peace was returning.

Ultra-nationalistic groups such as the *Hindu Mahasabha* and the like continued to advocate the reconstituting of Indian unity, that is defeat of Pakistan. These organizations fed upon and nourished Hindu hostility toward Pakistan. In January, 1948, Gandhi began a fast for the cessation of communal hostility. A few days later, on January 30, 1948, on his way to a prayer meeting, Gandhi was assassinated by a fanatic.

Gandhi's assassination shocked India, and Nehru reflected the view of millions of Hindus and Muslims alike when he stated: "The light has gone out of our lives and there is darkness everywhere." This apostle of nonviolence died in the manner he most abhorred. Yet the Mahatma's sacrifice was not in vain, for it brought an end to a horrible episode in Indian history. In the spring of 1948, Hindu and Muslim leaders met, and conciliatory measures were agreed upon. India promised equal treatment and protection to her Muslim minority, and Pakistan promised the same to her Hindu minority.

The rise of Nehru. Gandhi's death left the Congress, and therefore India, under the leadership of Nehru. He was the son of Motilal Nehru, a distinguished leader of the nationalist movement. For generations his family had lived in Kashmir, but his parents moved to Allahabad shortly before he was born. Therefore, his early beliefs were shaped by Indian life. His education, however, took him to Harrow and Cambridge; then he traveled throughout Europe and Russia. More than any other Indian of his time, he was able to mingle Western and Asian ideas about government and society.

Nehru practiced law until 1919, when he heard of the massacre at Amritsar. Furious with the British, yet equipped with a better understanding of them than most of his colleagues, he committed himself to the nationalist movement. As a brilliant speechmaker and aide to Gandhi, he rose quickly in the Congress and became its president four times. After a satyagraha campaign in 1930, he was jailed by the British for six years—the first of two long prison terms in his life.

In prison, Nehru wrote two influential books, *Glimpses of World History* and *The Discovery of India,* which were to underscore his growing differences with Gandhi. While Gandhi wanted India to adapt its past to its contemporary needs, Nehru preferred to blend Western ideas into its society. A trip to Russia in 1927 persuaded him that the followers of Karl Marx were correct in their claims that Western economies depended in large measure upon their Asian colonies. Gandhi wanted India to gain freedom and to revive its ancient talent for self-sufficiency. Nehru joined the Mahatma in the quest for freedom. At the same time, he wanted India to become an industrial nation, capable of equalling the economy of any Western country.

Nehru helped Gandhi lead the Congress in its demand that Britain quit India as the price for Indian cooperation in World War II. Because of his nationalist activity during this period he was imprisoned from October, 1942 to June, 1945. When he was released he negotiated for India's independence and became the new nation's most powerful leader—Prime Minister, Minister of External Affairs, Minister of Defense, Chairman of the Atomic Energy Department, Chairman of the Planning Commission, and majority leader of both houses of Parliament. Throughout his rise to power he emphasized the need for economic as well as political democracy. His autobiography, *Toward Freedom*, written in prison in 1941, described the effects of his travels abroad:

> *My outlook was wider, and nationalism by itself seemed to me definitely a narrow and insufficient creed. Political freedom, independence, were no doubt essential, but they were steps only in the right direction; without social freedom and a socialistic structure of society and the State, neither country nor the individual could develop much.*

By 1947, Gandhi had been able to say of Nehru, "He is our king. But we should not be impressed by everything the king does or does not do. If he has devised something good for us, we should praise him. If he has not, then we shall say so." Less than a year later, the "king" was forced to rule without the benefit of Gandhi's wisdom.

CHAPTER 8

THE SEARCH FOR NATIONAL UNITY

D IVERSITY WAS THE CENTRAL PRINCIPLE upon which Indian society was based. With the British gone, the chief task of the new government was to develop a system for binding the country's many parts together—to create a nation out of chaos. There were two great problems confronting India's leaders. The first was that Indians had been trained to think and to act in terms of local rather than national interests. The second was that colonialism in India had come to an end during the time of crisis, when millions were threatened by starvation, fratricide, and disease. To understand the nature of these problems and the government's response to them, each must be explored in detail.

THE BURDEN OF THE PAST

Facets of Indian society. For centuries Indians had divided themselves by caste, by language, and by region. We have seen that the population had thought of itself as comprising four varnas ("colors") which become castes—the Brahman, or priestly caste; the Kshatriya, or warrior caste; the Vaisya, or trading and farming caste; and the Sudra, or artisan caste, which made up sixty percent of the population. Outside of these were the people called "Untouchables," whom Gandhi renamed the Harijans ("Children of God"). They were the handlers of meat, garbage, and the dead. While the members of the highest caste, the Brahmans, were regarded as "pure," those of the lowest, the Harijans, were thought of as polluted and defiled.

An intricate system of subcastes (*jati*) interlaced the four main varnas. In all, there were more than 3,000 jatis. An individual became a member of a caste at birth and thought that death alone could release him from it. He knew that he was not to marry outside of it, except in the rare possibility that he wanted a bride of a lower one. Nor, ordinarily, could hard work or the acquisition of property and education enable his children to leave it.

The members of the jati were closely united in their families, villages, and regions. In each community the jati lived side by side;

104

The central area of the town of Deli, in the state of Uttar Pradesh, shows something of the diversity that characterizes life in modern India.

related subcastes adjoined one another, and were organized into a hierarchy. A jati acknowledged to have more prestige gained greater rewards for its services than did others. Often the members of a jati would claim to have descended from a common ancestor, whether they had or not, as if to proclaim kinship with one another. They shared customs, traditions, and, usually, a dialect.

Based upon an occupation or a set of related occupations, the jati did not encourage their members to seek social relationships outside of the group. Tailors, sweepers, or moneylenders—some of the occupations which comprised jatis—did business with but maintained a social distance from one another. An individual might learn a new trade and so change his jati. However, he was confined to those trades, and therefore to that jati, which made up his caste.

The jati governed personal behavior as well as business and social relationships. The violation of its rules was normally punished by its council (*panchayat*). Policies of the group, such as working conditions, sales practices, or the disposition of goods held in common, were determined by its members. The panchayats functioned as courts and legislative bodies.

The existence of the jati created tens of thousands of local authorities to which Indians looked for guidance and regulation. The individual found this authority in his own village or community. Because his rank might not be accepted elsewhere, he was not inclined to leave it or to transfer his loyalty elsewhere.

Nor, if he moved, was it likely that his speech would be fully understood. Indians speak almost 200 different languages and 830 dialects. For instructional and official purposes the Indian Constitution recognized fifteen of these, in addition to English: Hindi, Telugu, Bengali, Marathi, Tamil, Urdu, Gujarati, Kannada, Malayalam, Oriya, Punjabi, Assamese, Kashmiri, Sindhi, and Sanskrit. The Indo-European group, including Hindi, is concentrated in the north and the Dravidian group, including Telugu, Tamil, Kannada, and Malayalam, is chiefly in the south.

The multiplicity of languages proved to be one of the most devisive forces in India. The different languages generally follow the lines of the country's seventeen political subdivisions. Only two of India's languages can be called national: Urdu, spoken by the Muslim minority, and English, which, though used generally, is regarded by nationalists as an unwelcome transplant. The regional languages all are influenced by Persian, European speech, and Sanskrit, the classical tongue of the Indian court which became a medium for literature. Hindi is the most widely used, yet it cannot be understood by more than one-third of the country. Most of the languages are intelligible only in their limited district. Local dialects further divide them. "Language changes after twelve villages," a Gujerati proverb cautioned.

Ethnic differences coincide with linguistic ones. Eighty-two percent of the population live in villages which mostly contain five hundred people or less. There are more than one-half million of these villages. Customs, dress, and behavior vary from one small district to the next. Thus while India had gained independence, it found that to win widespread loyalty and commitment to the nation was a far more complex process.

India in crisis. The violence which followed the departure of the British produced the greatest migration in the history of the world. More than 15 million people crossed the border between the new nations of India and Pakistan—Muslims fleeing north and Hindus south. Jobs and possessions were deserted; refugees flooded into both countries, homeless and often without food, money or promise of employment.

India's enormous population, then (1947) about 350 million, was desperately poor. It had too little fresh water, medicine, and sanitary facilities. These shortages jeopardized health on a massive scale. In the villages, where there was only one doctor for every 25,000 people and only one hospital for every 50,000, many people were suffering from cholera, smallpox, malaria, and malnutrition. The infant mortality rate was 146 per 1,000 people. An individual who survived infancy could expect to live only thirty-two years.

Nor was medical care all that was in short supply. India lacked food so acutely that she was compelled to sacrifice urgently needed capital to buy it abroad. Her two principal industries, those manufacturing cotton and jute products, lost much of their supply of raw materials by the formation of Pakistan, where these crops were chiefly grown. There was too little housing and clothing. There was widespread unemployment. The partition left India with 82 percent of the total population of the subcontinent, but only 69 percent of the total irrigated land. Fewer than half of the larger towns had electric power. Although the country had an extensive railroad system, it had almost no good highways or other forms of public transportation.

Underlying this partial list of woes was the population problem. When the century began, India's population was growing at a very low rate; famine and disease made the death-rate almost as high as the birth-rate. During the 1920's, however, government measures succeeded in lowering the death-rate. In the thirty years following 1920, India added more than 110 million people to her population. Even this staggering growth then was accelerated. By the 1950's she was adding more than five million people a year, by the 1960's, eight, and by the 1970's, thirteen. Life expectancy reached the age of 52 in

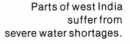

Parts of west India
suffer from
severe water shortages.

1969; the population soared over 570 million in 1971. Demographers were predicting that it would reach 775 million by 1986.

These masses of people were being squeezed into an area about two-thirds that of the United States. Whatever the nation produced was being rapidly consumed, leaving nothing for export. Factors which seemed to control population in other countries, such as the growth of cities, did not substantially affect the birth rate in India. More Indians continued to produce more children. The crisis of population was heightened by the fact that 40 percent of all Indians live in the Ganges River Basin, concentrating in the states of West Bengal, Uttar Pradesh, Bihar, Haryana, and Punjab. In the southwestern coastal state of Kerala there were 1,400 persons per square mile by the 1970's. There were 1,300 per square mile in West Bengal and 800 per square mile in Uttar Pradesh. Because it is a much larger region than Kerala, Uttar Pradesh has a population 4½ times greater—90 million. By contrast, the population of New York State (about seventeen million) has a density of less than 340 per square mile.

The New India

"*Unity in diversity.*" Prime Minister Nehru and other leaders of the Congress Party were quick to see that no amount of special pleading or lawmaking would persuade the millions of Indians to shift their loyalties abruptly from local to national authorities. Their guiding principle of government was to accept differences, and at times even to foster them, while seeking unity. Their premise was not unlike the one adopted by the founders of the United States. They forged a way to develop two levels of government within the framework of one.

The Union of India, as the nation was officially called, provides for a confederation of the former provinces and Princely States. During the British colonial period almost 600 of the latter were autonomous in their internal affairs but were under direct British administration, by agreement with their rulers, in external affairs. After independence, the whole of India was integrated into seventeen states, each with its own parliament. The division by states recognized linguistic and cultural differences but sought ultimate unity.

National policy is made by the Parliament of the Union of India. Like the British government, on which it was modeled, the government of India vests broad powers in a Prime Minister. This executive presides over a Council of Ministers, or cabinet, which is chosen by the majority party in Parliament. The Council is subordinate to the Parliament, which is made up of two parts, the Lok Sabha ("House of the People") and the Rajya Sabha ("Council of States"). This arrangement draws on the systems of both England and the United States, whose government was closely studied by the authors of the Indian Constitution.

A president is elected every five years. He is given the power to summon and to dissolve the Union Parliament. In practice, however, his powers are vague and limited to his own ability to influence the other members of government. The Prime Minister is India's recognized leader. He has the right to form the Council of Ministers and to appoint the nation's chief administrators: the ambassadors, governors, and commissioners. The Constitution of 1950 also guaranteed an independent judiciary headed by a Supreme Court, which has the power of ultimate judicial review.

The government of Nehru. The Congress Party had led the country throughout the struggle for independence. When independence was achieved, it gained and kept control of Parliament. Nehru was its most powerful figure. Writing in the 1930's under the pen name of "Chanakya," Nehru said of himself, "In normal times he would be an efficient and successful executive, but in this revolutionary epoch Caesarism is always at the door, and is it not possible that Jawaharlal might fancy himself as a Caesar?" For sixteen years, India's destiny was in Nehru's hands. With the death of Gandhi in 1948, the allegiance of the Indian masses was shifted to him. His authority was unparalleled in India. He became the living symbol of the independent nation. All major decisions affecting the well-being of the country were made by him. But Nehru, himself, always shunned temptations to Caesarism.

In his political outlook Nehru was a democrat. He sought to encourage freedom within constitutional limits, to recognize and even to encourage diversity. As we will see, he attempted to reconcile this viewpoint with the principle of a thoroughly planned economy. Although he believed in "socialism" and many of the ideas of Karl Marx, he rejected the applications of Marx's ideas in the Soviet Union, which he considered authoritarian. He insisted that socialism "conform to Indian conditions and have its roots in India's soil; it cannot be a mere imitation of socialism in any other country." It was a position similar in some ways to the one later vigorously asserted by Mao Tse-tung in China.

Under Nehru's leadership, the Congress Party groped for a formula that would permit freedom yet gain progress. In January, 1952, general elections were held and more than 60 percent of the people voted. Nehru led his party to a sweeping victory. Soon after taking office, Nehru discovered that the problems of running the government were vastly different than leading a movement for

Prime Minister Nehru showed
the strains of his high
office when addressing the
fifteenth session of the
United Nations.

independence. A glaring weakness of the Congress Party was its lack
of a coherent political program. Organized to promote the cause of
freedom from British rule, it was divided and uncertain how to
proceed after independence had been won. Not an experienced
administrator, Nehru found it difficult to control his subordinates.
Nehru's program for India was far more difficult to realize than
Gandhi's. He rejected Gandhi's social ideal of an India made up of a
decentralized collection of self-sufficient villages. The basis for
Gandhi's plan lay in the existing economy and social structure. But
Nehru's vision of an industrialized society called for enormous and
disruptive changes. Yet he perceived that industrialization was made
necessary by India's growing population and enlarging role in the
world. Under his leadership the Congress Party dominated the
Indian Parliament and took over many of the programs of the Praja
Socialist Party (P.S.P.). Yet the Congress Party found that, because of
the country's complexity and size, as well as the party's own administrative inefficiency, those ideas were not easily put into practice.

Political parties. Only a few of India's many political parties are
national; none offers effective competition to the Congress Party.
Four of them, however, have some influence: the Socialist and
Communist parties on the left, and the Jan Sangh ("People's Party")
and Swatantra ("Freedom") parties on the right. India's Socialist
Party has had little success because its policies often are
indistinguishable from those of the more popular Congress Party.

During World War II the Communist Party was considered unpatriotic by many Indians because it chose to work with the British rather than for independence. From 1947 to 1952, some Communists thought that India was ready for revolution and became guerrillas. The general population feared rather than followed them, however. Abandoning violence, in 1952 India's Communist Party sought popular approval through a national election. It won five percent of the vote and took several seats in the Lok Sabha. Its greatest gains were in south India where regional feeling ran high against the national government. There, Communists backed proposals for a multinational state (similar to the U.S.S.R.) in which each linguistic group would comprise a distinct nationality. Two years later they won a striking victory in an election in the southwestern state of Kerala. Although they lost the key administrative positions in that densely populated region in the next election, they regained them in 1967, both in Kerala and West Bengal.

Despite these isolated successes, it seems unlikely that Communism can become strong in India. Hindus view life as a circle and Communists view it as an ever-ascending spiral. The two philosophies—the one stable and tolerant, and the other dynamic and mistrustful of people who do not subscribe to it—are not likely to attract the same supporters. Moreover, Communists oppose caste structure, which has been at the heart of Indian life for centuries. These reasons, combined with the splintering of the Communists into factions favoring the Soviet Union, China, and historical Marxism, have prevented the spread of Communism in India.

The two right-wing parties in India also have failed to win popularity. The Jan Sangh seeks greater distribution of food and wealth but is based on Hindu principles. The many regions which prefer their own languages and cultures to Hindi have rejected the programs of the Jan Sangh. Nor does the Swatantra Party gain a significant part of the total vote. Its basic support comes from successful businessmen and large landowners. Thus it stands little chance of gaining wider appeal.

Nehru's successors. During the final years of his life, Nehru's immense popularity gave rise to the frequent question, "After Nehru, who?" It appeared that India would be lost without him. There were few administrators with his breadth of domestic and foreign-policy experience. When he died in 1964, the question was answered by the succession of Lal Bahadur Shastri, who had been an important official in Nehru's government.

Shastri did not have Nehru's charm or self-assurance. On taking office he seemed overwhelmed by the magnitude of his country's problems. His feelings of inadequacy were heightened by his inexperience in foreign affairs. Soon after he was elected Prime Minister, Shastri suffered a heart attack. Although he recovered sufficiently to govern, his mild temperament earned him little authority. Few Indians heeded his wishes and orders. The country regarded him with affection and amusement, rather than with the awe that had been reserved for Nehru. He won respect, however, for a firm policy against Pakistan, contending that India, not Pakistan, owned the former Princely State of Kashmir. This policy led to armed conflict in 1965. Shastri later concluded a peace treaty with the Pakistanis, but it was signed just a few hours before his death. He had held office for two years.

Immediately afterward, the Congress Party chose Nehru's daughter, Indira Gandhi, as its leader. Unlike Shastri, she was not chosen unanimously, but had to win an election among Congress Party members of Parliament. Madam Gandhi defeated her opponent by a margin of 186 votes out of a total of 526. She therefore became Prime Minister in January, 1966—a stunning victory for the progress of women not only in India, but throughout the world.

The fourth general election took place in 1967. The Congress Party won re-election, but by a smaller majority than before—only 54 percent of the seats in the Lok Sabha. This setback threw the party into confusion. Its fears were deepened by the hostility that many older party members felt for Madam Gandhi's policies. These older members, popularly known as the Syndicate, were headed by Morarji Desai, a Deputy Prime Minister who was also Minister of Finance.

Madam Gandhi proposed to follow the socialist program begun by her late father. One measure of this program, the nationalization of major private commercial banks, was particularly opposed by Desai. Overruling him, Madam Gandhi dismissed Desai as finance minister and brought India's fourteen largest private banks under government control. She next supported V. V. Giri for President against a candidate proposed by the Syndicate. After winning that election, the group led by Madam Gandhi swept into power in the other major offices of the party and the government.

The basis of political authority. To many students of Indian history, it was not surprising that India has been able to retain its democratic principles while conferring the bulk of national power on one party. The apparent contradiction is rooted in the complex nature of Indian society. India's major religion, Hinduism, expresses beliefs which almost all Indians share. Although the nation is divided linguistically and ethnically, it is thoroughly united in these beliefs. To many Indians the Congress Party resembles the nation. It encompasses many parts, some of which may conflict, but once its differences are resolved it moves forward in unity.

There are further reasons to explain the puzzling nature of the Indian democracy. Government has never been a primary force in Indian life. The caste system, the joint family, and the village have been far more powerful in affecting social thought. With a tradition that relies upon literature and abstractions rather than upon material things, millions of Indians believe in astrology more than in government. It is not unusual to see an Indian scientist casting a horoscope to learn when to begin an experiment involving nuclear chemistry or physics. Indian peasants traditionally chant hymns before using a new tool, hoping that the blessing will make it more valuable. Throughout India's cities, charts are sold in the streets to give people the exact position of the planets at any given moment. With this information they use the ancient practice of astrology to decide if and when to get married, change jobs, or make a trip.

In the fatalistic Indian view of life, government is incapable of changing an individual's higher destiny. Its role is to prevent violence and to encourage the fulfillment of dharma—the moral law; but it commands less of the individual's loyalty than his family, caste, community, and ethnic group. The *Mahabharata* suggested that Indians depose the ruler who repressed them with too much government. They should "slay the unjust king as if he were a mad dog," it said. In this view, "unjust" may be equated with "demanding." Traditionally, Indians have regarded government as a necessary evil.

While the individual is encouraged to pursue personal salvation as a more important goal than political activity, he does not deny the need for government. A belief in life, touchstone of every Indian faith, predisposes Indians to want an agency that will enable all living things to coexist. Government serves this purpose and thus supports religion. Unlike many Western countries, India has never been concerned that government would reduce the power of its religions or that its religions would cripple government. The two are parts of one another, with religion by far the more enduring and influential part.

Finally, the hierarchical nature of their society tends to cause Indians to accept their government's dynamic paternalism. In Indian families fathers are ideally benign and distant and the children are respectful and passive. Because they grow up in a society with many diverse parts and authorities, the children learn to tolerate the exercise of power if it does not hamper the practice of religion. India's socialist government has planned carefully, as a father would, for India's millions. However, it remains remote to them, an object for distant esteem; it draws its support from the groups to which they belong rather than from them as individuals.

The fate of linguistic reform. The essential conservatism of Indian philosophy has blocked many efforts at reform, particularly in the field of language. To gain local support for the struggle against the British, the Congress leaders had promised that after independence the country would be reorganized along linguistic lines. They failed to realize that such a policy would stimulate local loyalties and weaken Indian nationalism after the common anti-British bonds dissolved. Accordingly, they revised their program when writing the Constitution of 1950. A plan was announced to use existing languages for fifteen years. Meanwhile, the country was to work toward the use of Hindi nationally.

As the deadline of 1965 approached, many Indians rebelled at the prospect of giving up their languages for Hindi. As we have seen, Hindi is used in about one-third of the country and is chiefly confined to the Ganges River Basin. Elsewhere in the country riots broke out against any authority that might force its use. Parliament was compelled to retreat. In 1967, it enacted a measure that retained English as the national language until the indefinite time when the non-Hindi speaking states might accept Hindi. States which used Hindi were required to employ English when dealing with non-Hindi speaking states. The latter states were permitted to use English as well as their own languages. Thus, the whole issue of linguistic reforms was compromised.

Changing caste patterns. The caste system was officially abolished by the Indian Constitution of 1950. Today, in most large cities, educated workers and professionals of many castes intermingle. Caste taboos on eating and drinking with others tend to be ignored. Schools, public restaurants, apartment houses, and transportation facilities have been almost entirely desegregated. Caste lines in major cities are now so blurred that a Brahman who is sworn to priestly poverty may live in the style of a millionaire. Another Brahman may work as a cook. A person of the merchant caste may be an officer in the army, while a person of the military caste may be a prosperous business executive.

The condition of the Harijans or Untouchables has also improved. Discrimination against this large group, numbering about eighty million, was forbidden by an Act of Parliament in 1955. Harijans could no longer legally be prevented from drinking from public wells or from eating in public restaurants. In urban areas Harijans have been banded together to form street cleaners' unions—the average street cleaner's wage is higher than that of a school teacher. Some Harijans have risen to become college professors or lawyers. (The "Father" or author of the Indian Constitution was Dr. B. R. Ambedkar, a member of the Harijan caste.) Finally, in many of the

In the state of Kerala, these women celebrated a harvest in an ethnic dance that soon brought most of their village into the celebration.

cities intermarriages between castes have become common and have helped to break down old barriers and prejudices.

But although caste discrimination has been outlawed and weakened, it has not altogether succumbed. Discrimination against Harijans remains at levels which President Giri in 1973 called "a sin against humanity." He called it "the country's worst social evil" and proposed that offenders be executed rather than merely jailed.

Throughout Indian society the caste system has shown signs of reorganizing along different lines, of evolving into a more fluid class structure. While commercial practices are forcing Indians to discard the old castes, family life continues to employ them. In social relationships they are often tenacious. Many Kshatriyas would not consider visiting Sudras, let alone intermarrying with them. In place of the traditional distinctions between priest, warrior, merchant, and peasant, a new structure is developing, based upon wealth and education. As intermarriage has obscured the old *caste* difference, young Indians are becoming more acutely aware of their *class* status.

Compared to colonial India, the modern nation enjoys considerable mobility in its social life. In the village jati, leaders increasingly are selected on the basis of ability rather than birthright. Many jati are disappearing or blending with others, because the occupations upon which they are based are too specialized to persist in India's current economy. Promotions in business and success in professions no longer depend solely upon caste. But caste associations resembling American unions remain an important part of Indian life. As vigorous spokesmen for their members, they have not always withered with the blurring of caste lines. They have adapted to modern life and now represent their groups in parliamentary and cultural forums, as well as in the economy. With their increasing mergers they enable many of their members to gain more power and prestige than was formerly possible. The influence of these associations is increasing, not diminishing.

Thus India, slow to change but resilient and ever building on her past, is providing an answer to the many scholars who have raised the question, "Will the caste system prevent unity in India?" The answer seems to be that the caste system, by assigning different political and economic functions to many groups, has been a source of cohesiveness rather than of dissension. This system is being modified so that it can be made useful under modern conditions. The new caste structure is forming around common economic and political concerns rather than occupational and ritual interests. Ranking by castes is being limited to local communities in which it does not hamper the development of loyalty to the nation. At the same time, the unity of India is assured by common traditions, culture, and religion.

Position of women. The traditional ideal of Indian women is Sita, wife of Prince Rama. As described in the Hindu epic, the *Ramayana,* she was unfailingly loyal to her husband, even when separated from him. She was kidnapped, and after they were reunited she proved that she had been devoted to him by throwing herself into a fire. The fire rejected her. The practice of *sati* (or *suttee*)—in which a woman burns herself to death on the flaming burial pyre of her late husband—resembled Sita's act and was employed until recent years. It has been successfully outlawed. In many other ways, action by the government of India, coupled with changes in the economy, have slowly changed the relationship between husbands and wives.

Traditionally, the Hindu woman ranked far below the male in social status. A wife had few legal rights and could not publicly contradict or challenge her husband. She was not permitted to mention his name directly in public. This taboo proved particularly confusing when she was required to identify herself for legal purposes. In the Muslim and upper class Hindu communities of north India, and in some parts of south India, many wives practice purdah (from the Persian word *pardah,* or "veil"). This tradition encourages a wife to hide herself behind a *burka,* a flowing cloth including a veil, when she may be seen by any man except her husband. It is intended to protect her husband's rights over her.

Within the confines of her own home, the traditional Indian

woman enjoys considerable respect. Even there, however, she is obliged not to eat until her husband has eaten. Her life revolves around his. She performs rituals for his long life and success. Her chief source of social esteem is the degree to which he succeeds in his occupation. Quiet and retiring in his presence, she can rarely become his helpmate in the intellectual sense. Yet Indian husbands and wives develop strong affection for one another. The husband's respect for his wife is usually deep, especially after the birth of the children.

Gandhi was among the first to champion the cause of women's politcial and social rights in India. Since independence, the status of women, especially in the cities and large towns, has changed. To a surprising degree, this change has taken place without conflict. The improvement in the position of women has been largely the result of enlightened government action, designed to give the female a greater measure of equality and freedom of opportunity. Polygamy has been outlawed. Women have been granted the legal right to divorce their husbands. By law, a divorced woman becomes the guardian of her children; she has the right to administer her children's property until they reach adulthood. Even more important, women were granted the right to inherit property. Finally, they have been accorded the franchise and in the largest cities now enjoy equal job opportunities. Women have increasingly gained public offices, particularly since Indira Gandhi became Prime Minister in 1966.

While preparing dinner, this woman wears a garment that will enable her to practice purdah if men appear.

Despite the passage of many laws freeing women from their traditional bonds, in practice custom and ignorance have often thwarted these laws. The great mass of Indian women, especially in the smaller towns and villages, are still not confident enough to assert their legal rights. However, as the effects of urbanization and education become more widely felt, the woman's legal equality will undoubtedly become more of a reality.

Marriage and the family. As in most Oriental societies, marriages in India have always been arranged by the parents or other intermediaries. The love match is primarily a Western phenomenon, and indeed has gained wide acceptance in the West only recently. Indians have long considered marriage a financial and social arrangement, designed to strengthen the position of the whole family. Traditionally, one of the most important factors determining the choice of a bride has been the size of the dowry.

Because it is regarded as a union of families rather than of individuals, the marriage may take place when the husband and wife are only children. In 1955, it became illegal to arrange for the marriage of girls under fifteen and for boys under eighteen. In 1968, the minimum age for girls was increased to eighteen. But this law is not easily enforced. Almost twenty percent of all girls are married before they reach the age of eighteen. Only the educated elite, usually Indians who are able to live abroad, are able to make their own marriages on the basis of mutual attraction. Probably this is less than ten percent of the total number of marriages.

This dance is part of an ancient ceremony involving brass jars which these village women ordinarily bring to their well. It is supposed to bring rain.

To arrange a marriage, the men of a family travel through villages housing members of their jati. They identify potential mates for their eligible male relatives. A marriageable woman may be found at the village well, the man in the fields. Having seen the prospect, the marriage scouts visit someone who knows both potential parties to the marriage contract. Through this mutual friend or professional marriage broker, an agreement is reached and a dowry established. The dowry is intended to bind the woman to the contract. If she chooses to leave the marriage it remains her husband's possession. If he leaves, on the other hand, she receives some, but usually not all of his property. The larger the dowry, the more desirable the girl.

The woman is given little choice of mates. Yet probably neither she nor her prospective husband will reflect on the choice made for them, once the agreement is reached. A ritual is planned and the marriage, including an offering to a sacred fire, takes place before a rejoicing audience of other members of the family and jati.

Today, as more Indian women are becoming educated and finding employment, the importance of the dowry has diminished. The wishes of the marriage partners are given greater consideration when the marriages are being arranged. Other advances have been made, thanks to government initiative. Widows now are legally free to remarry, although custom often prevents them from doing so.

The family: basis of the value system. In rural India the institution of the joint family still persists. This family pattern is also still widely prevalent among the upper classes, where it offers certain economic advantages.

The Indian joint family system places the father or eldest brother at the head of the group. While the head of the family is the undisputed manager of the other males in the family, the woman looks after its females and its domestic concerns. There is undeniable authority in both the father and the mother, or in their substitutes; yet they are far from dictators. A democratic spirit prevails. Decisions of prime importance often are decided by a vote in which the heads of the family may be overruled.

The joint family often includes twenty-five persons. It may include over 200, but the average is six or seven. The parents, their sons, their sons' wives, and their unmarried children live together. Life is very difficult for the new bride who must live under the same roof and compete with her in-laws, especially her mother-in-law. Almost invariably she will join her husband and his brothers and sisters, however, in granting respect to the heads of the family. For the father, this respect is remote: he is benevolent but distant from his children. They tend to form a close bond with the mother rather than with him. The eldest son is destined to carry forward the family name and to perform the holy death rites which will insure peace for his father's soul. Therefore, he is closest to the male head of the family. Yet he, too, rises when his father comes near him, even when he is fully mature; and throughout his life he will greet his father with the *pranam*, the sign of deference in which one touches the feet of a highly respected figure. These relationships to their fathers and mothers no doubt have profound effects on Indian children for the rest of their lives. Indians tend to be respectful with authorities but more remote with male superiors than with female ones. They cherish courtesy. In their traditional greeting the head is bowed and the hands are clasped as if in prayer. The Sanskrit word "namaskaram" or the Hindu word "namaste" ("I bow to thee") is uttered softly.

It is the family, above all other institutions, which imparts social values in India. Its ancient traditions, still strictly practiced, imply the existence of an eternal law, one which causes young Indians to become conservative rather than rebellious. The defiance that is often a part of family life in the West is unlikely to be found in India. Nor is rebelliousness or defiance often found in social and political life. Gandhi's struggle against British rule was joined by groups rather than by individuals. The individuals are seen as parts of the group. The individuals will make sacrifices for the group, but it is the group which chooses to act, and it usually does so with the unanimous consent of its members. Confronted by the overwhelming tendency for group action and the traditional concept that the individual cannot escape his fate, most Indians quietly endure whatever happens in life. To the rest of the world their fatalism, accompanied by good humor and tolerance, is often a source of wonder and surprise. Yet it is broadly supported by the family, religious community, and social groups to which they invariably belong.

Beginning with the family, India's institutions have conditioned the millions of Indians to share a reverence for life. Not only humans and cows, but mountains, rivers, and plants are considered sacred within the Indian value system. The moral life is seen as a pursuit of selflessness, the achievement of true moderation through love and personal integrity. Morality exists in an acceptance of living things in all of their forms. Demands of the "self" are therefore said to be unworthy.

Urbanization, industrialization, and education are major forces working to affect the joint family and its value system. As more young couples move to the crowded cities, they will be obliged to live in apartments. Apartment living renders the joint family arrangement impractical. In schools and at work, more Indians are being taught to depend upon ability rather than caste for position. Increasingly

Indians have begun to doubt the need for the elaborate rituals of the past. Some of the values taught by the family, therefore, are fading. As the movement to the cities grows, more young people will escape the traditions that have tended to control them. They are visibly beginning to seek social experiences based on individual desires rather than on the requirements of a group. These changes in attitudes are supported by their government, which considers social change as essential to India's economic progress.

Education. Before the arrival of the British, Indian schools were associated with religions. Boys born to the highest castes were educated by Brahmanic teachers called *gurus.* Pupils were asked to memorize the Indian classics, and then to read and to write, for ten to twelve years. The Hindu educational system may have been operating when Alexander the Great invaded India in the fourth century B.C. Muslims developed a parallel school system, associated with mosques, in the eleventh century. Their schooling began at the age of four and also lasted for ten to twelve years.

In time these educational systems developed universities and continued to educate the upper classes for centuries. Under British rule, however, the administrators in India were urged to teach English and Christianity and to set up schools based on Western education. By 1837, English rather than Persian was the official language of India. British-style universities and secondary schools were established. Indians sought places in them, knowing that to be graduated from them was an important way to enter the civil service.

The rise of nationalism in India crippled to some extent the schools that the British had established. Unwilling to educate members of the nationalist movement, the British expelled them. In response, the Indian National Congress began to develop rival schools. Gandhi, meanwhile, had introduced his concept of a self-sufficient India, one whose people were willing to spin their own cloth. A system of "basic education" accompanied this concept. Through it students would be purified, in mind and body, by the study of the crafts. They would learn academic subjects during the course of studying crafts.

Gandhi's ideas affected educational thought in India after independence was achieved. Thousands of "basic schools" were established at the primary and junior high school levels, offering five-year programs; the Indian government had decided that it could satisfactorily replace British-style education in all elementary schools. During the next decade it concluded that all other schools in India could well follow the same basic school pattern.

The basic schools teach such subjects as pottery, leatherwork, weaving, and elementary engineering. Each school stresses the occupations prevalent in its region, involving its students with

Chandigarh, the union territory that serves as the capital of the states of Punjab and Haryana, is the site of this modern college of architecture.

materials they will probably see used outside of school. Students are encouraged to participate in their own educations, rather than to be guided by a fixed program.

The government has been unable to convert all elementary schools to the system of basic education. British schooling methods prevail in many regions. Practiced chiefly in rural communities, the basic system is increasingly regarded as a barrier to students' social progress. Many rural parents, aware of the more academic programs taught in city schools, have been urging their schools to modernize their educational methods.

The drop-out rate among Indian students is one of the chief indicators of discontent with the system. Only about half of Indian students complete their first five years of education. Neither the academic nor the basic schools succeed in keeping a majority of students throughout their programs. In 1950, the new constitution established as a national goal the education of all children to the age of fourteen by 1960. However, because of the growing population, illiteracy increased rather than decreased during that decade. Only about one-fourth of the Indian population can read and write. Before they can learn the language arts, students often leave school with the complaint that it involves too much memorization and too many lectures. In the basic schools, students often leave before they are graduated because they are needed to help support their families.

If judged by sheer numbers, India has made impressive educational strides since independence. Its school system, with more than eighty million students, is the second largest in the world. Although many students do not finish school, 80 percent of all who are eligible now attend elementary school, in contrast to 35 percent in 1947. India today has 74 universities and 3,000 colleges and research institutions. Enrollment in these institutions exceeds two million, in contrast to less than one-half million in 1950. About two-thirds of these students are in the humanities and one-third in the sciences.

However, the heartening increases in the quantity of education were not always accompanied by similar improvements in the quality of education. Indian students often are graduated from secondary schools without any skills that can be used in commerce or industry. Schools are largely controlled by local governments which cannot adequately guide students into areas where they are most needed. India needs many more teachers, particularly in mathematics, science, and English. Too many teachers still tend to stress the use of memory rather than of creative thought.

India's school system is attempting to reform as well as to expand. Plans are being made to limit enrollment in colleges, which annually produce hundreds of thousands of graduates who are unable to find jobs. There have been efforts to create a curriculum which varies according to the nation's requirements. More technical, vocational, and agricultural schools are being developed.

Currently, all secondary school students must learn mathematics and a language, usually English, in addition to their own language. They must take one year of social studies—history, civics, or geography—and to graduate they must study a second Indian language, a classical language, and general science. They may elect to take courses in specific sciences, the humanities, or agriculture. Students attend school in thirty-five minute periods, six days a week from 10 a.m. to 4 p.m. for at least two hundred days a year. In many schools there are double shifts, beginning at 7 a.m. and at 11:30 a.m., to accommodate the rising demands for education.

CHAPTER 9

A NATION UNDER PRESSURE

SUCCESSES AND FAILURES OF THE INDEPENDENT STATE

INDIA TODAY IS A MAJOR FORCE among nations. With its nuclear capacity and armed force of 1.2 million, it dominates the huge region of which it is a part. Its diverse economy appears to be awakening, with modern commerce and industry rising out of an ancient agricultural past. It has flung satellites into space and drilled for oil beneath the seas. Unlike most other developing countries today, India sells more than it buys from other nations and has been improving literacy and production.

But these signs of health can only be understood in a context of what is certainly the most complex nation on earth. No other country is as diverse in geography, climates, social system, arts, languages, religions, and technology. In India, any or all of these factors may vary within the space of a few miles. Some are unchanged from prehistoric times, while others are firmly contemporary.

India's 784 million people make up the second largest national population on earth. Increasing at rates between 2.5 and 3.5 per cent a year, they apparently will double their presently unmanageable number within 20 to 30 years. Before it was forty years old, the independent state of India added to its population 1.5 times more people than lived in the entire United States.

Even now the nation suffers from, and can trace many of its problems to, overpopulation. Local governments are unable to supply water, roads, and utilities for the millions who demand them. The country lacks housing, medical care, and often sanitation. Trains, filled to their roofs with passengers, slip off bridges. Overloaded bridges collapse into rivers. Floods kill thousands, wiping out whole villages clustered in slums near riverbanks. More die in droughts, victims of starvation. In one recent disaster, panic spread among crowds on a narrow staircase: forty-five people died in the stampede.

The most tormenting of recent disasters in India struck the slum-dwellers of Bhopal, a city of almost a million about 380 miles south of New Delhi. One night in 1984, Bhopal was the site of the worst

industrial accident in history. The agony began when winds from
the northwest plains carried toxic fumes from a Union Carbide
chemical plant into the nearby shacks of the sleeping poor. Children and elderly suffered the most. Thousands died. Others,
anguished with burning eyes, ran into the streets in panic, unable
to learn until much later whether their loved ones were alive or
dead. The accident was caused by the failure of controls designed
by the American company which made pesticides in the plant. The
tragedy was deepened, however, because tens of thousands of Indians had no other place to live but directly outside of the plant's
barbed-wire gates.

These are only the sporadic effects of overpopulation in India.
Even more persistent and dangerous are unemployment and poverty. Countless Indians labor up to fifteen hours a day to support
their large families. Many are forced to spend their lives scavenging
scraps of cloth or metal to sell, begging, sweeping streets, or pulling
rickshaws. With 40 per cent of the population under fourteen years
old, most Indian parents, traditionally dedicated to the support of
their children, must work almost constantly to feed, clothe, and
house them. Up to three-quarters of the students are undernour-

Almost any public event draws enormous crowds in the major cities of India. In this
Calcutta park, musicians or magicians regularly attract thousands.

ished and subject to disease.

Thus India's immediate problem may be stated simply: the number of people in the country far exceeds the resources. But the problem, like almost everything else in India, is not simple; it is made more complicated by India's historic inheritance. The increasing population is forced into a social framework which was created centuries ago. Even if its resources were greater, it appears, Indian society might still not allow equable distribution of them. Therefore the successes of this emerging nation—in science, mathematics, music, art, architecture, and industrial development—must be measured against a background of its social institutions and policies.

SOCIAL CONDITIONS

The cities. It is dawn. The first to arise in Calcutta are the thousands who have slept in doorways and alleys or near the banks of the Houghly River. Among them are men and women of all ages, including some mothers bearing infants. Many are emaciated or have missing limbs and teeth, pustulated skin and racking coughs. In the first light, most look for water. If they find some they splash it over their faces and drink a little more. Some practice ancient yoga exercises or pray; others limp off to find food or reach into their bag of possessions for what little they have saved. Thus begins their day of begging, picking over refuse, or selling bits of scavenged materials—firewood, metal, or cloth.

As a burning sun rises, construction workers pile into the rear of trucks to head for jobs. Bazaars come alive. Their merchants haul and arrange sacks of grains, vivid tropical fruits, fish, vegetables, and pungent spices. Soon the customers come to stroll over floors covered with fragrant straw, to inspect, compare, haggle, buy, or perhaps just to look.

By 9 a.m., the streets of all Indian cities are filled with a mixture of people who seem to represent the different ages of history. Throngs include individuals ranging from gnarled and primitive wanderers, dressed in rags, to alert and intelligent men and women, striding to air-conditioned offices. The cities begin to hum with fierce energy, resounding with the ring of builders' hammers and riveting machines, with cars, ear-splitting motorscooters, taxis, packed trams and buses, cows, pigs, dogs, chickens, bicycle rickshaws, the cry of vendors, and the pleas of beggars, of whom some cities have over 100,000.

In the heat of the midday sun, it is possible to feel new rhythms developing. Executives emerge from modern buildings for appointments in cool restaurants. They are prepared to spend more on lunch than many whom they pass will earn in a month. A barber may offer haircuts on the street. A fortune-teller nursing an infant may beg for customers to buy her wisdom. A boy, his feet bare and with sores on his legs, may urge people to pay for records showing how the movement of planets will shape their destinies. Men spend their days hoping someone will hire them to deliver a message, haul a burden, wash a car, or sweep the sidewalk.

By the end of the working day, as temperatures begin to decline, a few people head for comfortable homes on the edges of the cities. After dinner they may seek recreation in a club, at home with books or television, or at a movie. Young men, cradling soccer balls and swinging cleated shoes over their shoulders, start for the outlying fields to practice the game which, with cricket, is a national pastime. Others work until dusk, then after 12 to 15 hours of labor start for rooms in "development blocks," which resemble military dormitories. A single room in these buildings, often unvented, is usually about 12 by 5 feet. It may house as many as five people.

The shacks which make up the slums are even more crowded. As many as twenty people occupy small structures made of tin, bamboo, driftwood, and thatch in or near some of the major cities. Slum dwellings line a path about four feet wide. This thoroughfare is almost always laced with putrifying sewage or rotting garbage, issuing smells which mingle with those of the spices, liquors, and animals in the dwellings. A dinner for the people of these districts is often cooked on the top of a metal drum or over an open fire. In the absence of plates it may be served on a palm leaf and probably will consist of rice or flour mixed with curry, raisins, molasses, or an apple.

The pressure of population in Indian cities has abated only slightly in recent years. Despite all evidence that cities have little to offer, people continue to come to them for jobs or excitement. City governments struggle to provide services, but have not been able to cure the stench of open sewers, power blackouts, torn roads, filth, rodents, and failing communications systems. The water is often dangerous; there is disease, a shortage of jobs, housing, and recreational facilities. About 75 per cent of the people in Indian cities are said to lack adequate plumbing, water, or sewage.

Among India's major cities, Calcutta is often regarded as the one whose crisis is greatest. It is both India's pride and its shame, seemingly rightly named for the goddess Kali, who is in part gentle and in part fearsome. On the one hand it is a cultural center, for its leading ethnic group, the Bengalis, are among the country's leading writers, musicians, scholars, and film-makers. On the other hand,

At the cores of Indian cities, modern buildings rise among decaying ones.

the tides of people newly arrived in Calcutta, either from the countryside or by birth, have exhausted the city's ability to deliver services. Sewage runs down many streets. Garbage rots in the sun, which Mark Twain once found "hot enough to make a brass door-knob mushy." Calcutta appears to have come far from the time when William Bentinck, whom Britain sent to govern India in 1828, could remark that "The spectacle is altogether the most curious and magnificent I have ever met with." Today it more closely fits the more recent observation of George Trevelyan, an historian who wrote: "The place is so bad by nature that human efforts could do little to make it worse."

But the place has been made worse since India achieved independence. Calcutta's population, just 2.1 million in 1941, soared to 9.1 million within forty years. At least a third of them live in slums, while less than 1.5 million enjoy separate apartments or houses. Unemployment was deepened among them because, in the recent past, revolutionary terrorists drove businesses away. Less than 4 per cent of the city's people control more than 45 per cent of its wealth.

Corruption also threatens the power of city governments. The owners of many businesses keep two sets of books or deal chiefly in cash to avoid taxation. Police and judges often are said to accept bribes, and other public officials are said to be willing to overlook violations of law in exchange for money. In Lucknow, in 1971, police joined rioting students to attack the university in protests against high prices and a lack of opportunity. Thievery is common in such public places as postoffices and train stations. In Bombay, the smuggling of drugs and precious objects of Indian art is a major industry because narcotics are sought by visitors from nearby Middle Eastern countries.

Indians are quick to point out that no major city in the world, including those in the United States, Europe, and Japan, is without poverty and corruption. That people survive in urban India seems miracle enough to them. Some succeed in educating their children and increasing their incomes. Even a few members of the lower castes seem occasionally to gain better housing, plumbing, or electricity. Others die young. Life expectancy at birth in India is just fifty-two. In contrast, it is seventy-four in the United States and seventy-six in most of Scandinavia and Japan.

With its long tradition of charity and humanitarianism, India often produces or attracts people who hope to ameliorate these problems. Mohandas K. Gandhi (See page 90) was one example of the many Indians who have dedicated their lives to helping the poor and exploited in their country. In more recent times, a nun named Mother Theresa has offered another model of this behavior.

Born in Albania in 1910, at the age of fifteen the woman now known as Mother Theresa was drawn to work in India by accounts of the poverty there. She became a cloistered nun, but the anguish that she saw in the streets of Calcutta persuaded her to leave the cloisters. In 1950 she organized the Congregation of the Missionaries of Charity, whose twelve original members, all Catholic nuns, vowed to "help the poorest of the poor." This small group began to care for dying lepers, starving children, and the sick and homeless who wander, begging. The Congregation's efforts became world famous after 1957, when Pope Paul VI gave Mother Theresa his white ceremonial limousine. Without ever riding in it, she sold the car and raised enough money to build a haven for lepers in West Bengal. In 1979 the image of the five-foot, frail, weathered Mother Theresa became known throughout the world when she was awarded the Nobel Prize for Peace.

This one example shows how, in spite of their problems, Indian cities can be marvels of human drama and creativity, revealing substantial determination. Some, such as Bombay, have created acceptable public transportation, street sweeping, and garbage-collection services. Calcutta has greatly limited deaths from cholera, a disease caused by infected water. Calcutta, Madras, New Delhi, and other Indian cities struggle persistently against the force of population, trying to build at least as fast as decay sets in. Thus urban India limps towards the end of the twentieth century, hoping that the pride, energy, and intelligence of the Indian people can prevent the catastrophe that always seems to lurk in the future.

The countryside. There are almost 575,000 villages in India, and they contain approximately 80 per cent of the country's 740 million people. An Indian village may include between fifty and one hundred homes, the type and distribution of which tells much about India.

The largest home in the community is likely to be occupied by a Brahman (a word which some scholars who write in English also spell *Brahmin*) family. Not all Brahmans are wealthy, but the members of this highest caste predominate among landowners. The homes of major landowners are normally made of brick and mortar and have landscaping around a broad courtyard. These landowners may own between 50 and 200 acres of land, as well as part of a tractor shared with neighbors. To farm that large an area they need the help of members of the lower castes, whom they pay $4 to $8 (U.S.) a month and are said to beat if their work slackens.

The villagers of India must, of necessity, pursue self-sufficiency. While caring for animals, this woman produces cloth to sell and for her family.

Under Land Ceiling Acts passed since Independence, landlords are limited in the number of acres they may own. Socialist governments, beginning with the one headed by Jawaharlal Nehru, were determined to prevent the misuse of farm laborers by landlords. These laws have been largely ignored in recent years, however. Through bribery and fictitious records, the landlords can arrange to own almost triple the amount allowed.

The owners of larger parcels of land believe the government is unlikely to seize their surplus areas. If it did, there would not be enough to distribute to the millions of poor. Political and economic chaos would result. In the countryside most government efforts have been directed towards the development of public works such as roads and utilities. Such projects have increased efficiency and wealth on farms, but they done little to improve the distribution of land.

Therefore India's wealthier landlords go on drawing from the country's vast pool of labor. Some, unwilling to remain in the countryside, move to the cities and offer their farms to sharecroppers to work for them. The crop that they claim as rent is limited by law, but this law, like the Land Ceiling Acts, is often evaded. A sharecropper may be forced to give from half to two-thirds of his product to the landlord or face eviction.

The owners of smaller parcels, usually members of the lower castes, may try to support their families on as little as one-eighth of an acre of land. With this, they may own little more than a tiny home made of baked mud, whitewashed and with a small veranda. Even these limited possessions may be reduced when they must be split for inheritances or dowries. A man who has spent a lifetime earning a few acres knows that, if he has a daughter, he may have to share it with his future son-in-law. Daughters, therefore, are not always welcomed by Indian families.

At the bottom of this pyramid of humans are the Untouchables, whom Mohandas K. Gandhi called the Harijans ("Children of God") and whom Indian law now calls the Scheduled Classes. Wherever there are Harijans there are separate districts for them, usually consisting of huts made of bamboo, scraps of wood, mud, and dried leaves. A similarly poor, separate district in the village may be occupied by Muslims, descendants of Harijans who converted in the vain hope of escaping persecution during the six centuries of Muslim rule.

Together, the millions of Harijans and Muslim farm workers have supplied much of the brute labor which has enabled India to feed its people and, in recent years, even to export food. They have, in general, accepted this role, with its long hours, low pay, and back-

These Harijans live on the outskirts of a village in central India. A cow, their chief possession, finds little to eat on their impoverished land.

breaking struggle to wrest rice and wheat from the unwilling earth. Thus the full weight of India's caste system, which persists in great degree despite the efforts of the government to end it, falls on these most impoverished of Indians.

Since the Aryan conquests of India began about 2000 B.C., the Harijans have been treated contemptuously by members of the Brahman, Kshatriya, and Sudra castes. They have been denied the right to adequate food, housing, jobs, and even water. Forbidden to enter most shops and schools, they have been condemned to lives of endless poverty, prisoners in their separate districts.

But Gandhi and other moral leaders stirred India's conscience in the matter of the Harijans, and in 1955 the Indian Parliament passed the Untouchability Act. This legislation was intended to guarantee the members of the lowest caste access to temples, shops, and restaurants. Twelve years later, Parliament also guaranteed the Harijans the right to enter tea and barber shops and to use wells. The Harijans were assured that they would be granted extra places in schools and government.

The new laws have caused the Harijans, as well as many Muslims, to cry out for relief from their condition. Like civil rights laws in many other countries, including the United States, they are often ignored. For the first time, the Harijans have begun to protest these violations.

One example of the new sense of independence among Harijan farm workers involved a village in north-central India recently. There, Harijans of the lowest rank, who handle the carcasses of animals, can only reach the main road by passing the houses of Brahmans. The Brahmans often look and dress exactly like the Harijans, but they feel empowered, because of ancient Aryan ideas, to dominate the lower castes. When the Harijans pass their houses the Brahmans seize, threaten, and often beat them until they agree to work in Brahman fields. The Harijans are paid little for their labor and may be denied any payment at all. But lately they have been demanding an end to these practices. With new self-assertiveness, they have called upon the government to protect them. They petitioned for a new path to the main road, one which would enable them to avoid Brahman threats.

Efforts of this kind are based upon the influence Harijans may wield in the vast Indian democracy. Harijans number approximately 111 million people, or about half of the population of the United States, and can produce a substantial voting bloc. Throughout India, Harijan farm workers have begun calling for better pay and working conditions. Essentially they have been asking for nothing more than the enforcement of the law, but Indian police, responsive to property owners, often attack them. The sight of police shooting and beating impoverished laborers has infuriated Harijan leaders, who have called for further demonstrations. Their boldness has startled many upper-caste Hindus, creating a new awareness of centuries of prejudice.

Thus in the Indian countryside it is possible to see the forces of history and of modern democracy in conflict. The burdens of history may be painfully difficult to throw off, however. Within the complexity of Indian society, they often take new forms. For example, in place of the outlawed zamindars, the private tax collectors who became absentee landowners, there are new absentee landowners today. They are middle- and upper-caste Hindus who demand from half to three-quarters of a farmer's crop when he tills their land. They, like the zamindars of the past, often move to the cities, seeking pleasure with illegally high profits from their distant lands.

Much of India's economy, too, is based upon an ancient method of cooperation which has little to do with that modern part which depends upon high technology. This method is called the *jajmani* system, which creates an enduring link between a patron *(jajman)* and a tradesman or servant *(purjan)*. Normally this link persists for generations among families, even if the services offered, or the pay given in exchange, is inadequate. A man may be both a servant and a patron at the same time. For example, he may make all the sandals for one family, receiving a fixed price, while his wife receives all of her dresses, or *saris* from the head of another family at a fixed price. The price is usually paid in the form of food, labor, or the use of land. With the growth of cities, the jajmani system has been changing because tradesmen and servants have more competition for their places in the system. Yet it remains an essential part of the Indian economy.

Development of the arts and education. Under British rule, rebellious Indian leaders sensed that the arts and education might inspire the idea of nationalism among their people. They rightly believed that they could nourish pride in India by describing, through books, the stage, and the visual arts, a great past.

Today, long after the departure of the British, the independent government of India continues to stress the arts and education as a means of binding the country together. It finances a National Culture Trust whose three academies support the development of new literary, visual, and performing arts. It also publishes and distributes a substantial number of books with patriotic overtones.

A government may try to stimulate art, but cannot generate it, however. That remains the task of individuals such as Rabindranath Tagore, the poet and playwright who won the Nobel Prize for Literature in 1913. In India the problem is made far more difficult by the literacy rate, which less than half of the population. Widespread poverty and the country's many languages add to the difficulties. Newspapers and magazines regularly fail, and less than 10 per cent of the country receives them. Book publishers find it difficult to distribute their products nationally because of differences in regional cultures and the lack of sales outlets. The progress of Indian arts is largely centered in a few large cities, including Calcutta, Bombay, and Madras.

Film is the medium in which Indian artists are most successful. The work of Indian directors is seen and admired throughout the world. The finest Indian writers have also gained international attention, despite their difficulties in finding markets inside of the country. Many, such as Aubrey Menen, R.K. Narayan, and Santha Rama Rau, are masters of English and are widely read in the United States and Britain.

The obstacles in the path of Indian arts—poverty, overpopulation, and linguistic diversity—also plague education. Children are unable to concentrate or even to stay in school when they are sick or hungry. In Indian elementary schools the dropout rate has been as high as 65 per cent. Indians profoundly respect education and know that schooling is the key to economic survival and advancement. However, they are often discouraged when school graduates fail to find jobs. The Harijans especially suffer from the lack of opportunity. They may be unable, because of poverty, to send their children to schools. The teaching profession, with its low pay, lack of facilities, equipment shortages, and massive workloads, does not attract people of great skill. Teachers often need jobs so badly that they overlook cheating and poor scholarship in order to keep their students.

Despite these problems, the Indian government has struggled valiantly to draw increasing numbers of students into schools. National enrollment is reported to be between 80 and 87 million, though the reports must be viewed skeptically because schools and teachers are paid by the student. Now many times what it was during the British era, the enrollment, even at the low end of the scale, is a tribute to the new democracy. To increase enrollment the government has offered special incentives to Harijan students, including scholarships and lower entrance requirements. Tuition is often waived for females in the constant effort to break down prejudice against women. The government strives to improve school buildings, many of which have only one room and no drainage.

The Union government is not fully in control of education in India. It manages colleges and universities, but primary and secondary schools are mostly private, run by missionaries, organized religions, or businesses. Those which are public are run by local and provincial authorities who emphasize their own interests through education rather than national ones.

Indian students honor their country's ancient arts while studying contemporary subjects.

This division of authority has affected the curriculum in schools. Most Indian states require that students be taught three languages—the regional one, either Hindi or English, and one other which is widely used in the country. Burdened by this demand on their time, students are asked to develop their memories more than their creative or reasoning powers. Many, particularly in the universities, complain that India has a passion for teaching by rote. They say that the country can never progress unless education is reformed. The university students favor English as their language of instruction, knowing that it will open more opportunities for them later in government and business. In the lower schools, students have fewer choices. They have been concentrating on regional languages since the 1960's. At that time a number of southern states claimed that Hindi, which is spoken by 40 per cent of the population and so is the most widely used Indian language, was being forced upon them.

The Union government has tried to solve these massive problems in the most sensitive possible way. It withdrew its pressure for a national language, though certainly it hopes for one. It has focused its limited resources on expanding the education system to groups previously excluded from it. Meanwhile has increased the number of schools, sought to improve the quality of textbooks and teachers, and stressed the need for education in science and technology as a central way to raise national standards.

Science and technology. In parts of India, tribes slash and burn forests to fertilize land. Then, after planting and harvesting, they move on. They are applying the technology of prehistoric humans with rudimentary tools. By contrast, in many Indian cities brilliant scientists are developing new applications for atomic energy and telecommunications. Such dramatic differences are not unusual in India. They show a society divided by time as well as by space, and nowhere is this more evident than in the fields of science and its application.

Throughout its history, India has produced some of the world's finest mathematicians, physicists, engineers, and biologists. They have flourished despite an underdeveloped education system which tends to stress languages and philosophy over research. Indian scientists have won impressive honors, including many Nobel prizes, during this century. In addition to its successes in highly technical, fields India has won praise for its work in anthropology, archaeology, and political science.

The development of scientific learning is not enough to fuel a renaissance in India's economy, however. The country must also

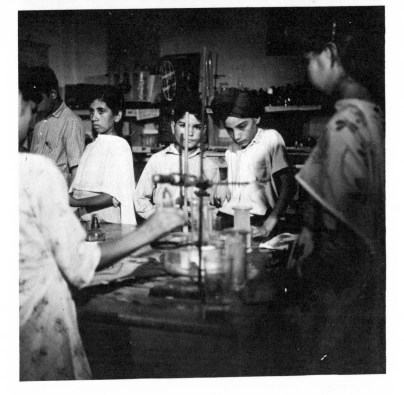

These young science students are in a Community Development Block, a rural program begun in 1952. This Block has 102 villages and 54,000 people.

keep and somehow use the fine skills that it has inspired. Indian industrialists tend to buy their more sophisticated equipment abroad and to hire foreign scientists to help them run it. As a result, Indian scientists are drawn overseas by jobs in superior facilities at higher pay than they could receive at home. Large numbers of them are educated in England, where many remain when beginning their careers.

Today, the Indian government is struggling to keep its scientific talent in the nation's service. It has financed more than thirty national laboratories and research institutes. The most celebrated of these are run by the Indian Atomic Energy Commission, the Council of Scientific and Industrial Research, and the Council of Agricultural Research. The effort has been fruitful. India has surprised the world with its progress in the field of atomic energy, and it has raised its own satellites. Progress in science, when combined with the new emphasis on technical training in schools, has therefore become one of the more promising aspects of the new India.

In 1971 India announced that it was able to separate uranium 233 from thorium, and three years later it exploded an atomic device underground. It would not develop an atomic bomb, its government said, but would use the new form of energy for earth-moving projects. Then, in 1980, it began to launch its own satellites by means of its own rockets, further demonstrating the substantial progress in its scientific efforts.

Religion and civil rights. The Hindu population of India, which represents more than 83 per cent of the country's 784 million people, is famed for its gentle tolerance of other faiths. Yet the intense pressures of population and poverty have, at times, brought frightening social angers to the surface. In those moments, the 11.6 per cent of the populations who are Muslim and the 2 per cent who are Sikhs may become involved in communal strife with their Hindu neighbors.

In recent years, riots between Hindus and Muslims have increased both in number and in violence. More than a thousand persons in the state of Assam died in them during a single month of 1983. But even this disaster seemed small when compared with the most startling example of communal strife since the attacks on Muslims with which modern India began. It involved the small Sikh community, which is concentrated in the state of Punjab.

India's 14 million Sikhs do not often complain of discrimination against them, as Muslims do. They are well represented in high places in government, the military, business, and agriculture. Their farms have helped to turn the Punjab, where they hold a small majority, into a granary for the entire country.

The Sikhs do, however, want more self-rule. Above many of their public squares in the Punjab, they fly the triangular yellow flag of

The Golden Temple, which India's Sikhs regard as their most sacred monument, became significant for the entire country when Indira Gandhi held office.

their sect. Hoping to control their own fate, they chaffed when Hindus won elections in their state in 1980. Soon afterward, they began to agitate for an independent Sikh community. Sikh radicals turned to violence, bombing and shooting Indian officials in the Punjab. They stoned buses and murdered more than 120 police officers. Within two years they assassinated more than six hundred Hindus. Meanwhile hundreds of Sikhs were arrested, and in 1982 at least sixty-two died in police custody. In protest, more than four thousand Sikhs stormed the national Parliament. At last, when the Sikhs began to place bombs in bus and train terminals, the Union government became determined to end terrorism in the Punjab.

To India's Prime Minister, who then was Indira Gandhi, Sikh terrorists appeared to be centered in the Golden Temple, holiest shrine of the Sikh faith. This sacred building, with its shining dome and quiet, flower-laden pools, became the scene of one of the fiercest religious battles in recent Indian history. In June 1984 the Indian government sent troops, armed with tanks and mortars, into the temple's courtyard. They were met with machine-gun and rocket fire. Before the struggle ended, hundreds were dead or wounded.

The raid on their shrine infuriated India's Sikhs. At least two thousand deserted the army. Then, in an act that stunned the world, two Sikh members of Indira Gandhi's personal bodyguard turned their guns on her, killing her instantly. Hindus responded with even more massive violence. Gangs began to pull Sikhs, identified by their beards, turbans, bandoleers and ceremonial daggers, out of cars, trains, and trucks. At least a thousand Sikhs were murdered, and often impoverished Hindus hauled away their property while police stood watching. The bloodshed lasted three days, driving more than twenty-five thousand Sikhs into refugee camps.

The violence abated only after Indira Gandhi's cremation. Yet Indians proved again, as during the Hindu-Muslim conflicts, that it was just below the surface, even in a nation known for its peaceful philosophies.

CHAPTER 10

GOVERNING THE NEW INDIA

INSTITUTIONS

INDIA'S DEMOCRACY, THE LARGEST in the world, has been tested severely during its brief lifetime. Western in concept, it was imposed upon an Eastern culture which had never before been fully unified under law. Indians adopted it eagerly at first, having been well prepared for it by their former British rulers. They saw in it an extension of their families, in which voting often takes place, and also in the *panchayats*, or councils which they have used to govern the countryside for centuries. But challenges to democracy must inevitably grow in a land so complex and difficult to rule. This chapter will examine these challenges, as well as the strengths, of the young Indian government.

Constitution. India's basic law closely resembles the ones of England's and, to a lesser extent, the United States:

> *All citizens shall have the right . . . to freedom of speech and expression; to assemble peaceably and without arms; to form associations or unions; to move freely throughout the territory of India; to reside and settle in any part of the territory of India; to acquire, hold and dispose of property; and to practice any profession, or to carry on any occupation, trade, or business.*

Like its Western counterparts, the Indian constitution also guarantees equal protection under the law and the right to a public hearing within twenty-four hours after arrest.

The Indian document goes beyond the law of Western democracies, however, to address the country's unique problems. Women and Harijans are specifically guaranteed the identical rights given all others, as well as the right to enter public places, drink from public wells, and gain consideration for any government job. All Indians are assured that the government will not force them to change their culture or language. It promises to defend them against the economic slavery which has long plagued the lowest castes.

Parliament. The Indian people's elected representatives are divided into an upper house, the Rajya Sabha (Council of States) and the Lok Sabha (House of the People). The upper house is not chosen by direct popular vote, but chiefly by twenty-one state legislatures. Its members hold six-year terms, with one-third of which expire every two years. Members of the lower house, chosen by direct popular vote, serve five-year terms.

In theory, the Indian Parliament forms an independent bulwark against any administration which might seek excessive power. In practice, it has been subject to strong prime ministers, yielding to them while proclaiming its support of democracy. Most of its members come from positions of money and power; they are likely to be conservative, despite their socialist rhetoric.

The executive. The administration of India is said to be headed by a president, but that office is chiefly ceremonial. Authority centers in the Prime Minister and his or her cabinet, which is selected from among the members of Parliament. The Prime Minister normally directs the president in his or her duties, which include making formal appointments of ministers and judges of the highest courts. The president is the neutral symbol of the whole of India, while the Prime Minister is the agent of the majority party.

To unify India when independence arrived, the central, or Union government was required to allow substantial powers to remain in the nation's twenty-one states. This federal system affords the Union government complete control over foreign affairs, defense, and communications, and partial control over such matters as economic planning, criminal law, and marriage and divorce. It offers services throughout the country, including the nine territories and more than five hundred princely states which also became part of the Union.

For more than twenty years, India's government has been seeking to limit the country's population growth by urging woman to use birth control methods.

Though its powers are constitutionally limited, India's executive branch has declared emergencies on twenty-two separate occasions. By doing so, it avoided most legal restrictions on its powers. In one case, the government claimed that a national emergency existed and so limited constitutionally guaranteed rights for the whole country.

The judiciary. India's courts were intended to check and balance both the Parliament and the executive. They have not always served that purpose, however. The fourteen members of the Supreme Court are appointed by, and may be dismissed by, the Prime Minister. Neither Parliament nor the people need be consulted when these appointments are made.

The courts have, nevertheless, at times shown their independence of the Union government. In recent years they resisted Parliament's nationalization of banks, the Prime Minister's move to cancel agreements with the princely states, and even the tenure of the Prime Minister. Eventually they proved unable to withstand the administration, which overwhelmed them with its power to replace them or to declare an emergency.

A MODERN INDIAN DYNASTY

Three members of a single family have dominated India's hundreds of millions of people since independence was gained. They are Jawaharlal Nehru, his daughter Indira, and his grandson Rajiv. They comprise a kind of dynasty which, after its founder won the blessing of Mohandas K. Gandhi, succeeded in shaping the destiny of the world's second most populous country.

It was Nehru who led India towards democracy and socialism. To many Indians, conscious of the complexity of their country, he was an indispensable leader with unparalleled insight into the minds and hearts of the Indian people. It seemed natural, therefore, that India would turn to other members of his family soon after his death. Their willingness to do so gave exceptional power to his only survivor, Indira. Their choice was all the more remarkable because she rose to the highest office of a country that has rarely honored women.

The life of Indira Gandhi. The first woman destined to govern India barely knew her famous father. An only child, she was largely in the care of her mother, who had never left India and taught her the ways of the Indian people. Her father, on the other hand, had been educated in England and had a dazzling array of international friends. He had inherited his political nature from his father, Motilal, a lawyer who became one of the foremost leaders of India's independence movement.

Nehru's sophisticated companions often treated his wife as a simple Hindu. That troubled Indira, who was lonely, too. Indira, with no friends, spent her childhood watching and following her father at receptions and rallies. She was often presented to famous political leaders who would smile and then tend to ignore her. At home, which was visited often by writers and journalists as well as politicians, life changed rapidly. The British soon began to arrest Indian leaders. They seized Nehru, and for years she knew him only through the letters he wrote in jail. He addressed them to the whole world rather than to her, collecting them in the form of an autobiography which dealt more with politics than with his own life.

Torn by the two ways of life followed by her parents, Indira combined them, she recalled later, by giving speeches to the servants on their rights as Indians. She kept this political instinct when her mother died and her father sent her to Oxford, England to be educated. There she became active among British socialists and met Feroze Gandhi (no relation to Mohandas K. Gandhi), who did accept his namesake's ideas. Returning to India together, they married and joined the independence movement.

Two sons, Sanjay and Rajiv, were born to Mrs. Gandhi. Her marriage did not last, however; she and her husband were widely separated culturally, for he was a Parsee, a descendant of immigrant Persian Zoastrians, and she was a Hindu. After her divorce, she became the hostess for her widowed father and, as millions began to recognize her when she stood beside him on podiums, entered politics herself. The Congress Party gave her a minor post in the cabinet of her father's successor, Lal Bahdur Shastri, and when Shastri died in 1966 it made her Prime Minister.

Mrs. Gandhi was not the easily managed woman whom party

After suppressing Sikh rebels, Indira Gandhi pleaded for unity.

leaders expected. She was guided more by the memory of her childhood than by her political associates. "There never has been any advice spoken to me that I needed much," she said. What influenced me more were the lives of the people I lived with—my mother and my father." Along with this influence came the loneliness she had experienced as a child. She disliked campaigns, speeches, dust, and noise, all staples of Indian politics. She was subject to illness and often locked herself in her office in the red sandstone Parliament building, aloof, withdrawn, and even rude to strangers.

Indira Gandhi's program was firm and demanding. She seized control of the state so vigorously that she bent the entire country to her wishes for almost twenty years. "Indira is India, and India is Indira," her followers said. Towards the end of her life she sought to perpetuate her control through her elder son, Sanjay, and when he was killed in a reckless airplane stunt over New Delhi she turned to the younger one, Rajiv. She tore Rajiv away from his job as a commercial airline pilot, which he enjoyed, so that he could carry on the political tradition of the Nehru family.

Then at last one of Indira Gandhi's sternest policies, a military assault on the Golden Temple of the Sikhs, brought an end to her life. It produced a reaction among the Sikhs and, as she walked in her garden, dressed in an orange sari and lost in thought, two Sikh members of her own bodyguard cut her down in a hail of bullets. Her only surviving son succeeded her, as she had planned.

THE USE OF INSTITUTIONS

Politics and change. The force of Indira Gandhi's personality dominated Indian politics for almost twenty years. Lacking a program or philosophy of her own, she continued to voice the legacy of her father, the late Prime Minister. Socialism and national unity were his central goals, and she pursued them by whatever political means were available. From the moment she assumed power she assailed private industry, moving to nationalize banks, coking coal mines, and oil, iron, and steel companies. Her most successful campaigns bore the slogan, "End poverty in India!" and her administrations did increase production, lower expenditures, and distribute a million acres of land to at least a half million families.

But Indira Gandhi's accomplishments must be measured against the effects that she caused within India's political system. Her forceful strategies devastated the opposition. None of her critics could stand for long against her popularity and desire to silence them. When she died, there was no effective opposition to her rule.

Thus for whatever economic progress she brought about, India paid a high political price. Upon her death India was neither more unified nor, because its population had increased by more than 250 million, were most people significantly better off than when she became Prime Minister.

Indira Gandhi came to office in 1966, a year of drought and famine. As she proceeded with nationalization, employing some nine million bureaucrats to run government-owned businesses and agencies, a dangerous inflation began. In some years, prices rose by as much as 20 to 30 per cent. These increases were caused in part by the rising price of oil sold by Arab countries. The cost of supporting some ten million Hindu refugees, flooding in because of persecution in what was then East Pakistan, added to inflationary pressures. Finally, the monsoons on which Indian agriculture depends were depositing moisture over the seas rather than over land, causing hardship among farmers.

Domestic crises were swept aside, however, because an international one had developed. In East Pakistan, the Hindu majority had begun open rebellion against its Muslim rulers. It was being repressed so vigorously that refugees were streaming into India for protection. The high cost of providing this protection, in addition to anger over Pakistan's occupation of what India regarded as its lands in Kashmir, soon led to war. India, bolstered by a newly signed treaty of friendship with the Soviet Union, quickly overwhelmed Pakistan on the battlefield. Its wartime triumphs led to Indira Gandhi's overwhelming victory in the 1971 elections.

The massive vote of approval for the Prime Minister encouraged her to take more forceful steps in domestic affairs, too. Her political opponents had been raising cries of corruption against her. They alleged that she had been using public money to win elections for herself and her supporters in the Congress Party. Her son, Sanjay, had received huge profits from government contracts because of her influence, they said. At last, when a judge agreed with some of these claims, ordering her removed from office, she struck back, aiming at the judiciary as well as the opposition.

Indira Gandhi refused to leave office. Instead, she ordered the President of India to proclaim "that a grave emergency exists whereby the security of India is threatened by internal disturbances." That night, police began to arrest her opponents in their homes. She imprisoned tens of thousands of her critics without formal charges or the right of bail. Indira Gandhi suppressed public discussion of these unparalleled events by threatening to close any newspaper, radio, or television station which attacked her or even dared to give the names and number of detainees.

Thus in one instant Indira Gandhi crushed freedom of speech, the independence of the judiciary, and dissidence in India. As the world learned of these moves, millions of people declared themselves astonished that the Indian democracy had collapsed without a protest. There were almost no demonstrations: the Congress Party which she headed gave Indira Gandhi its fullest support, the courts fell silent, and the people seemed to welcome the quieter political arena.

Equally surprising was the progress of the country under the national emergency. Inflation quickly fell to a quarter of its previous rate, which was 30 per cent. There were few strikes and more production. The spreading use of new high-yielding seeds gave rise, during this period, to the "Green Revolution" which increased India's food supply. Luckily the monsoons turned favorable, helping farmers to produce and adding to the amount of available hydropower.

Along with an emergency economic program, Indira Gandhi intensified one involving strict birth control measures. To limit the surging population she demanded that public employees restrict themselves to smaller families or be punished. Next, she pressed forward with a national policy under which millions of men and women had been sterilized.

Though they had accepted the loss of their democratic rights, Indians balked at the thought that they might lose their power to reproduce. They rejected Indira Gandhi and her Congress Party in the elections of 1977. In her place they elected Morarji R. Desai, who had helped to form a coalition of small political groups into the Janata (People's) Party. The new government quickly repealed Indira Gandhi's emergency measures.

Within two years, however, Indira Gandhi was back in office, returned by voters with an overwhelming majority in the Parliament. She had mounted a skillful campaign, regularly appearing after many of India's numerous disasters "to share the pain of my people." Opposition to her did not cease during this period; she was imprisoned for a week while her supporters and critics clashed outside the prison. But she emerged with full control of the government when internal quarreling brought about the collapse of the Janata Party. To win this victory she had formed her own organization, the Congress-I (for Indira) Party.

Indira Gandhi's new powers were greater than before. Yet in this moment of her triumph she was crushed by a personal blow, the death of her beloved son Sanjay in a reckless airplane flight over New Delhi. She had been grooming Sanjay as her successor. With him gone, she turned to her second son, Rajiv, determined that her

Rajiv Gandhi, though lacking experience in government, became the third member of his family to lead India. After his first speeches, calm returned.

family would retain control of India.

Rajiv, a commercial jet pilot, entered politics reluctantly, at his mother's request. He had been an engineering student at Cambridge, England, and knew little about government. Efficiency impressed him more than political ideas, and his British education and Italian-born wife gave him a world outlook. He won his first election to Parliament after a campaign against corruption.

It was during Rajiv Gandhi's rise in politics that Indira Gandhi confronted rebellious Sikhs and was assassinated. Within hours after her death leaders of the Congress Party chose him as their leader and, therefore, as Prime Minister.

Three months later, in 1985, the Indian electorate gave Rajiv Gandhi the largest vote in history. He made a strong start, removing many of his late mother's supporters in order to attack corruption in government. He spoke of streamlining public agencies and of increasing production on farms and in factories. He worked to find new accords with the angry and frightened Sikhs. His opponents were given greater freedom to speak out and to address the public on television. Rajiv Gandhi gained widespread support by promising to release industry from many of the government controls his mother had established.

NEHRU'S LEGACY

M.K. Gandhi had always wanted India to restore traditional ways of village life (improved to a degree with the use of machines in cottage industries). Nehru believed that industrialization was

essential if the poverty and pathetically low standard of living of the
Indian people were to be remedied. Nehru's government at first was
concerned with the possibility of a new type of imperialism—
financial imperialism created by vast foreign investments in India's
industrial development. To prevent this, the government introduced
legislation which prevented foreign firms from owning a majority of
the stock in any enterprise. Additional laws required that the
management of industries had to be in the hands of Indians. These
restrictions resulted in the failure of Westerners to make available the
capital needed by Nehru's government. However, several years after
independence, when the fear of foreign economic domination
subsided, the restrictive measures were removed, and foreign capital
began to flow into India. Nehru's government continued the policy
which placed all basic industries under the ownership or control of
the government. At the same time, it introduced an economic system
which allowed for private and public ownership. This "mixed
economy" resembles that of Sweden.

Nehru's treatment for India's economic ills was a series of "Five-
Year Plans." It should be noted that his program was democratically
implemented. The government recognized the limitations of India's
resources and was moderate in its goals. Unlike the Chinese Communists, Nehru wished to spare the people unnecessary hardships and
proposed modest goals. For example, the budget that he
recommended for the first year of the first Five-Year Plan was less
than New York City's budget for the same year.

Planning was undertaken through a series of laws which
empowered the Union government to control industrial production
and development. At the same time, the state governments were
permitted to retain their authority in agricultural matters. The Union
government was financed through tax revenues from individuals,
corporations, and foreign trade. The state governments got their
revenue from land taxes.

During the course of the first Five-Year Plan the Union government announced that the goal of industrialization was to reduce the
wide gap in income that separated the rich and the poor. It did not
foresee the need to nationalize all industry. Rather, it predicted that
government's role within industry would be increased because of its
gradually increasing capital investment. In time, government
controlled India's transportation, communication, irrigation,
nuclear, and hydroelectric industries. It played a major role in the
operation of the chemical, fertilizer, oil, coal mining, and steel
industries. The banking, insurance, and import-export industries
were jointly controlled by government and private industry.
Government claimed no ownership in most agriculture, construction, mining, manufacturing, and small business.

Many farms were organized as cooperatives. These cooperatives became miniature governments which planned and administrated farm production for a village or group of villages. The Union government expressed the hope that these agencies would spread throughout India, exerting influence in all phases of agriculture. The cooperatives were seen as the basis of a more democratic society, on both economic and political levels.

A planning commission, of which Nehru was the first chairman, was established in 1950 to implement the Five-Year Plans. To date it has prepared six plans and is in the process of developing a seventh.To draft a plan the Planning Commission consults the various ministries and leading state officials, economists, and businessmen. With the Administration's broad aims to guide it, the Commission reconciles the suggestions of the many agencies and individuals. Once the plan is developed, the Commission submits it to the National Development Council, which includes the chief ministers of the states, sitting with members of the Commission. Revisions are made by the Council and the Cabinet. Finally the plan is sent to Parliament for approval.

The First Five-Year Plan (1951-1956). The primary aims of the first plan were to rebuild what had been destroyed during the Hindu-Muslim conflict and to strengthen the social institutions that would help to unify India. Of the more than seven billion dollars spent to achieve these goals, ninety percent were provided by the Indian government and the remaining ten percent were obtained from foreign assistance programs.

Because food shortages were the most pressing problems, the First Five-Year Plan put great emphasis on increasing agricultural output. Approximately forty-six percent of India's public investment was reserved for expanding agricultural output, including irrigation and power projects. The results were unspectacular but noteworthy. Food-grain production increased 20 percent, industry 40 percent, national income 18 percent, and electrical output was boosted by more than 60 percent. Meanwhile the per capita income increased from $53 to $56 a year.

In the drive for rural development, about one-quarter of the villages in the nation were affected by government campaigns for rural self-help, road-building projects, school and hospital construction, and lessons in better methods of cultivation. By 1956, 123,000 villages had voluntarily participated in the government's efforts to assist rural areas.

Rural tax collection was one of the principal areas of reform. Historically, the Indian government claimed a percentage of the crop in any field. This annual tax (*zamindari*) was collected by the British with the help of the former Mogul administrators. After giving the

British ten-elevenths of the revenue, these collectors (*zamindars*) kept whatever remained. They naturally tried to collect as much as possible. They began to acquire land and to move to the cities, where they had little concern for the welfare of their tenants or the productivity of their land. Ultimately any intermediary who collected taxes became known as a zamindar. By the time India achieved independence, the zamindars were collecting taxes on 40 percent of all of the cultivated land in India. During the First Five-Year Plan, the despised zamindar system was abolished. By making direct contact with the farmers, the government eliminated many of the middlemen who had been keeping part of what they had collected for themselves.

Some progress also was made in the effort to reduce rents. In many areas, half of the crop was going to landlords as rent. During the First Five-Year Plan the state governments limited the amounts that could be paid to a sum ranging from one-sixth to one-quarter of the crop. Tenants were given the right to acquire land after they had tilled it for one year. The government limited the number of acres that could be held by any single owner. Small holdings were consolidated.

In order to redistribute land, the government had first to obtain tracts of it. It did this in large measure through reclamation projects. It also bought much of the land held by the zamindars. Millions of acres were purchased, improved, and distributed. In many cases land was given to rural cooperatives. The government retained only two large mechanized farms, which it proposed to use as models for other regions.

Indians fear unemployment and so do not welcome the use of machines on their farms. Many farmers have no reason to improve their crop yields because they are merely tenants working on land owned by an absentee landlord. Most farmers do not have the capital to buy good seeds, fertilizers, and equipment. Faced by long arid periods followed by unpredictable monsoons, they are often helpless before the elements.

The government confronted these problems through the Community Development Program. This program, launched during the First Five-Year Plan, was designed to link many of India's small farms into more efficient cooperatives. Not only were many of these farms small, but they were also fragmented. In the Punjab, a village of 12,800 acres was found to have 63,000 separate fields. Because of the pattern of inheritance in his family, a farmer might cultivate plots in many different parts of his village. He might also have acquired different plots to secure greater rainfall or better soil.

The Community Development Program treated entire villages as single units, managed by the village. Holdings of the cultivators were pooled, but the owners retained their rights in the land and were paid according to the size of their original contribution to the cooperative. For convenience the land was divided into blocks, with each block cultivated by a family or group of families. Payment was made on the basis of work accomplished by each family.

The Program offered a variety of services for each development block—about one hundred villages with a total population ranging from 60,000 to 70,000. Teams of specialists, led by block development officers, gave assistance on every level of rural life. In the villages advisers were selected from among the local population. Their job was to encourage people to help themselves to construct new projects and to educate each other. Ambitious as the program was, the administration of the Community Development Program did not produce the significant results that planners had expected. Instead of causing Indians to help themselves, it often produced greater reliance on the government. Officials began to emphasize outside advisers less and to turn, instead, to a more traditional means of local administration, the *panchayat* (literally, "Council of Five").

The Panchayat system had governed Indian villages for centuries before the arrival of the British. Under British civil servants its authority was diminished, but it was restored after independence was achieved. The weaknesses of the Community Development Program caused the Union government to ask each state to evolve a network of *Panchayati Raj* ("Rule by Council") to supplement the program. These following new levels of local government were organized:

The panchayat, perhaps the oldest form of government in India, is a council of village leaders who are elected to manage community problems.

1. The Panchayat. This is a group of people elected by the entire adult population of each village.
2. The Panchayat Samiti. The chairman of each Panchayat in the Community Development Block becomes a member of this group.
3. The Zila Parishad. This is the supreme council, composed of all of the chairmen of the samitis in the district.

Soon after the completion of the First Five-Year Plan, the system of Panchayati Raj spread throughout India, functioning as part of the Community Development Program.

The Program was introduced wherever two-thirds of landowners, who owned not less than one-half of the land in any village, were in favor of it. Many landowners resisted it. Where it was accepted, however, the Program, though limited, encouraged the spread of farm cooperatives. Traditionally, Indian farmers were exploited not only by absentee landlords, but also by moneylenders, whose interest rates ranged between 9 and 300 percent. The cooperatives were needed to help the farmers finance themselves without enslavement. Cooperatives began to offer low-interest loans and to provide help with processing and marketing, transportation, dairy farming, fisheries, industries, medical aid, and education. Nevertheless, surveys showed that much more help was needed. At the end of the First Five-Year Plan only about ten percent of farmers were receiving low-interest loans from the government or from cooperative societies. Because of the shortage of capital and the fact that farmers often could not prove themselves good risks, the other ninety percent continued to obtain loans in the old ways.

While the rural cooperatives proved useful, they also seemed hazardous to some Indians. Almost all of them were financed chiefly through government help, with the direct assistance of government officials. Many farmers appeared to be losing initiative and independence because outside advisers were helping to solve their problems. No cooperative was considered successful unless its members were enthusiastically managing it themselves. The government encouraged the development of cooperative associations that could become independent of outside financing and advice.

The Second Five-Year Plan (1956-1961). The modest but measurable success of the First Five-Year Plan encouraged the Union government to expand the aims in a Second Five-Year Plan. Broadly speaking, this plan called for: 1) a 25 percent increase in the national income; 2) rapid industrialization, especially in the basic industries; 3) expansion of employment; and 4) the removal of economic inequalities. The specific goals, among others, were an increase in the per capita income from $56 to $61 by 1961, a 21 percent rise in

An agricultural scientist came to Banskho Village, Rajasthan, to help a seed grower with his harvest. The government has a large advisory program.

consumer-goods production, schools for eight million more children, two million more houses, and three thousand rural health clinics. In heavy industry, the objective was to raise production by 64 percent.

This plan, although placing greater emphasis on the development of heavy industry, especially steel production and the fabrication of steel machine parts, did not ignore agriculture. Thanks to expanded irrigation projects, twenty-one million new acres of land were placed under cultivation, a greater total acreage than in all of India's previous history. Vast river valley projects were carried out with aid from the United States, Great Britain, and the Soviet Union. They are concentrated on the Indo-Gangetic Plain and the east coast. One effort undertaken with American help was the Bhakra-Nangal Project, the most productive concrete gravity dam in the world. It was designed to irrigate over 3.6 million acres in Rajasthan and the Punjab through a three-thousand-mile canal system.

Another impressive contribution by the United States was made to India through the Ford Foundation. The Foundation helped to open 6,000 new adult education schools in which farmers and artisans could be trained. At the request of the Indian government, the Foundation in 1959 sent a team of experts to India to determine how agricultural production could be increased. Their recommendations were developed into the Intensive Agricultural Areas Program. More than one-third of India's 325 agricultural districts received the benefits of improved credit, shipping and storage facilities, and planting and marketing advice as a result. At the same time, reports reached India about new varieties of rice and wheat, grown in Taiwan and Mexico, which yielded five to six thousand pounds of grain per acre. This was almost twice the amount of grain that could be produced in the average acre in India. The impact of such an increase in grain production would be especially welcomed in India, which has one of the lowest yields per acre in the world. Through its Intensive Agricultural Areas Program, the Indian government introduced the new seeds to its country.

The effects of this breakthrough were not to be felt until after the Second Five-Year Plan was concluded. Meanwhile, the nation struggled to meet its industrial goals—goals which, it turned out, were higher than could be achieved. The overall expenditure of the Second Five-Year Plan was in excess of $14.4 billion. Of this huge sum, all but $4.4 billion was provided by the national and state governments. The remaining money was drawn from private sources and was invested in industry and agriculture.

It was clear that India's emphasis would continue to be on public progress, with a lessening role for private enterprise. Despite the meager progress of the Second Five-Year Plan, the country drew

The Bhakra-Nangal Project
helps to irrigate
more than 3.6 million acres.

some hope from its results. By developing more heavy industries whose production could reduce the need for imports, the nation prepared the way for greater self-sufficiency during the course of the future five-year plans. During the Second Five-Year Plan, private industry, the people, and the government began to save money in larger quantities than ever before. Agriculture was much more promising. However, Nehru summarized India's position somewhat gloomily: "It would need many more five-year plans," he said, "to progress from the 'cow-dung stage' to the age of atomic energy."

The Third Five-Year Plan (1961-1966). India's population growth exceeded expectations by more than twenty-five percent during the Third Five-Year Plan. This fact, staggering in itself, was not the only unpredictable event of the period. India's conflicts with China and with Pakistan drained the economy. At the same time, two years of severe drought cut agricultural production. All of these factors crippled the Third Five-Year Plan.

The Plan had emphasized industrial growth at the expense of some agricultural goals. However, industry failed to grow as rapidly as had been hoped. While time and energies were being poured into the development of factories, consumers were deprived of the resources they needed to accommodate the growing population. Although Indian planners had carefully worked out a system of priorities, they came under heavy criticism for supporting industrial rather than agricultural expansion. Inflation, sweeping the entire world, eroded India's ability to buy goods abroad. This further hampered domestic efforts to strengthen the economy. Suddenly the nation was faced with the need to import more heavily, at higher prices. A food shortage developed. Savings, profits, and investments began to decline. In 1966, it was necessary to devalue the rupee, the unit of Indian exchange. Not even this move, however, prevented a recession in India.

The failure of the Third Five-Year Plan resulted in a delay in further long-range planning. Annual plans were instituted. Yet the failure of the Third Five-Year Plan left the national government stronger rather than weaker. Unable to supply investment capital alone, the states looked to the national government to do so. The central government supplied more than 90 percent of all of the funds required by governments to finance the Third Five-Year Plan.

There was another benefit from the Third Five-Year Plan. During the Second Five-Year Plan, India began to use the new high-yielding seeds that had been developed in Mexico and Taiwan. More extensive use of chemical fertilizers and irrigation was needed to make these seeds yield. Nevertheless, India was able to provide the fertilizers and the irrigation systems. The new high-yield agriculture was hailed as the "Green Revolution" throughout the world, but especially in India.

The Green Revolution was one of the most important achievements of the decade. Food production in India rose from 89 million tons in 1964–65 to 100 million tons in 1970. Production gains were spectacular in the wheat-growing areas, where the yield was increased from 12.3 million tons in 1964–65 to 20 million tons in 1970. Production would be doubled, it was hoped, in millions of acres.

But in spite of these strides, India's ancient social system prevented the country from experiencing the full measure of progress. The gains were unevenly distributed. The major beneficiaries were the owners of large farms. The small cultivators, landless laborers, and share-croppers received little. Increasing food production, therefore, widened the gap between India's rich and poor. Moreover, wheat-producing districts gained far more than those producing rice. This added to the maldistribution of income. Finally, the larger food supply was no answer to the problem of a swelling labor force. At the time of the Green Revolution, India's labor force was 220 million—larger than the entire population of the United States. Women comprised about one-third of this group; ten percent were children under the age of fifteen. With more than fourteen million unemployed, India could do little more than to ask countless millions to press cow dung for fuel, or to collect firewood. There was nothing else for them to do. The increasing food supply helped to feed these laborers. Yet at the same time the Green Revolution created more unemployment by enabling the owners of large farms to produce their larger yields with fewer hands.

The Third Five-Year Plan recognized the urgent need for birth control measures. A red triangle symbol is used to remind millions of Indians to limit families. "Stop at two!" signs say everywhere, referring to the number of children in families. The Indian government became one of the few in the world to support the use of contraceptives. Nevertheless, the birth rate soared to 41 per 1,000 in 1969. Farmers, eager for help in the fields, continued to hope for sons who would not only aid them with the harvests but also perform the funeral rites that would enable their souls to rest in the next life. While educated Indians accepted birth control, the masses of Indians did not. In Indian villages, a demographer observed, "The couple seen doing menial tasks in the absence of children is considered cursed—and consider themselves cursed as well. The whole concept of 'population control' is so foreign to the Indian way of life that barring major changes in other areas—such as female education—the likelihood of its being achieved through voluntary action is slim indeed—even with all the doctors, jeeps, and slogans the world could offer."

The Fourth Five-Year Plan (1969-1974). Wary of setting goals too high to be achieved, the government reduced its requirements for industrial expansion during the Fourth Five-Year Plan. Although it was six times the size of the first plan, the fourth was conservative. Planners concentrated on developing a larger food supply and on striking a more favorable balance of trade, foregoing short-term gains in industry. Small manufacturing plants were given greater assistance. On the social level, the government continued its efforts to redistribute the national income. While many businessmen received government support, the large monopolies were attacked. The government moved to nationalize the largest banks. Investment—in agriculture, industry, and transportation—was the largest factor in the plan. The government was to supply 59 percent of the capital needed for the planned investments, as well as funds for other aspects of the Plan. Private sources supplied the rest.

The national income increased by more than a third during the course of the Fourth Plan, despite inflation. India's increasing self-sufficiency reduced the need for foreign aid. Yet the country remained far from securing economic independence, and the majority of Indians continued to live on diets well below subsistence.

India is rich in iron ore and coal. Both are being used below by a Sikh. He is helping to double production in Asia's largest steelworks, the Tata.

The Fifth Five-Year Plan (1975-80). Throughout the 1970's it became apparent that some Indians, at least, were becoming wealthy. Modern office buildings had risen in the major cities, and each morning expensive cars delivered members of the upper classes to them. The country was showing the effects of its increasing economic independence. Its debt was relatively small compared with other countries, less than 25 percent of what Mexico, a much smaller land owed, for example. It had begun to increase its grain production dramatically and to develop its offshore oil resources.

Yet it still suffered from the problem of maldistribution of wealth. More than half of all Indians survived on less than $100 a year, and about one in ten suffered with incomes of less than $50 a year. In the cities millions of people had no personal water supply or plumbing. Four of every five schoolchildren were prone to disease and starvation. Almost half of India's total income found its way into the pockets of less than 4 percent of the people each year.

The Fifth Five-Year Plan was designed to attack some of these problems. It proposed more food, cotton cloth, coal, steel, and petroleum products so that the economic level of the entire country could be raised. Calling for annual growth of 5.5 percent, this Plan focused on improving conditions in communities where most Indians lived, the rural areas. Despite several severe droughts and floods it succeeded in bringing the economy to a new and higher level, but it did little to overcome the ancient prejudices which affected the lowest castes. The political turmoil surrounding Madam Gandhi, coupled with her growing desire to force an unwilling population to control its birth rate, brought confused results in the pursuit of this Plan.

The Sixth Five-Year Plan (1980-85). During Indira Gandhi's second term as Prime Minister Indian officials, after thirty years of planning, could claim that the trend was up. There had been failures, of course, but more often than not they were due to unpredictable events, such as droughts. Over the period per capita income had more than doubled, the public debt had declined, there had been much new construction, and exports had risen sharply. Encouraged, the government again called for 5 percent growth. Its national science program was accelerated, enabling it to contract for two major new power stations, one of them nuclear. India was drawing oil from the seas and preparing to launch its own satellite with American help. All of this suggested major advances in technology.

The central goals of this Plan were to improve farm areas and to increase the production of fuel, steel, cement, oil, and grains. Despite a major drought in 1983, this Plan was so successful that exports increased by 18 percent. Then, in 1983, the assassination of Madam Gandhi brought new perspectives to the management of the economy. Critics of her administration, suddenly free to speak, pointed out that Indians had paid a heavy price for the apparent progress. They noted that the widening gap between rich and poor, the growing misery of the lower castes, the erratic political climate, and a general sense of corruption in government were endangering the national morale.

The Present Economy

India's economy is 70 per cent agricultural. Only 13 per cent of it is committed to industry, mining, and construction. Services, including government workers, make up another 8 per cent of the work force, and 6 per cent is involved in commerce.

It took almost a decade for India to recover from the shock of economic disasters during the 1970's. Among the severest blows

In Bihar, the family of a steelworker waited for him to return from a Tata factory. The mother embroidered, the children read and played.

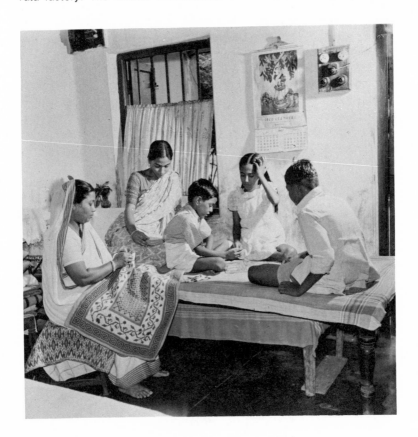

were poor monsoons, which in some years delivered only a quarter to a half of the normal rainfall. Then, too, there were floods which innundated whole cities, rising oil prices, and the costs of war with Pakistan. By the 1980's, however, grain production began to increase. Per capita income was $260 (U.S.) in 1982, in contrast to only $150 in 1976, and the rising trend continued.

Such figures do not clearly describe the distribution of increasing wealth. India is said to be adding at least 20,000 to its destitute population every day. People in this group may earn as little as $5 to $10 a month. At the same time, larger numbers of Indians are able to buy comfortable homes and expensive cars.

Many factors, taken together, have helped to bring about the recent improvements in India's economy. After Indira Gandhi declared a national emergency in 1976, the number of strikes and demands for higher wages declined, and factories began to produce more. At the same time the greater use of high-yielding seeds, combined with the return of normal rainfall, enhanced grain production. Finally, oil prices fell, enabling India to improve its trade balance and to enjoy lower inflation.

An increasing number of Indians have begun to question the nation's commitment to socialism, which began during the administrations of Jawaharlal Nehru and continued by his daughter. Under Indira Gandhi, government planners were often political appointees rather than experts in planning. Corruption became widespread, until even funds for disaster relief sometimes went into the pockets of officeholders. Millions of bureaucrats clogged the economy with paperwork as more and more industries were nationalized. Indira Gandhi herself, though a strong advocate of government economic controls, was forced to postpone the national regulation of wholesale rice markets because similar efforts in the wheat markets had failed badly.

Rajiv Gandhi became Prime Minister with the pledge that government would take an entirely new view of the economy. He had far more technical training than his mother and suggested that fewer socialist regulations would greatly encourage enterprise. Gandhi's first budget ended many of the controls over industries and investments. He moved to amend the Monopolies and Restrictive Practices Act, which had shackled hundreds of companies with regulations, and tried to stimulate the young electronics industry by lowering tariffs on the newest computers and computer equipment. Though he cut taxes he also managed to reduce the national debt.

Thus under the latest member of the "Nehru Dynasty" to take office India seemed to be entering a new era. It was a time when

Many parts of suburban India contain fine houses. The neighborhoods are not designed for motor traffic and often mingle businesses and residences.

private enterprise was being fostered in many countries, not only in Europe and the Americas, but in Asia too. Like its giant neighbor, China, India was undergoing profound economic change.

FOREIGN POLICY

India and the world. The end of World War II saw a new alignment of world powers. For the first time in centuries, instead of many divided nations seeking advantages by forming alliances with one another, there were two major camps—communist and non-communist.

India was a neighbor of the two largest communist powers, yet in many ways was committed to the non-communist democracies. It refused to join either of the two great camps and so became known as the leader of the "neutralist bloc," or "Third World." Nehru—in fact all of India— enjoyed this role in world politics. India claimed moral leadership for peace while most other nations seemed bent on destroying each other and perhaps all civilization. Nehru defined India's foreign policy in this way:

> *The pursuit of peace, not through alignment with any major power or group of powers, but through an independent approach to each controversial or disputed issue; the liberation of subject peoples; the maintenance of freedom, both national and individual; the elimination of racial discrimination; and the elimination of want, disease, and ignorance which afflict the greater part of the world's population.*

In the years after World War II, many factors complicated India's role as a peacemaker. The first of these was that India itself could not remain strictly peaceful because it had become embroiled in bitter disputes with Pakistan. The second, which did not develop with certainty until the late 1960's, was the split of the communist camp into two parts, one led by the Soviet Union and the other by the People's Republic of China. As we will see, events forced India to abandon the strict neutrality for which it hoped.

Pakistan. The wounds, physical and psychological, caused by the 1947 massacres have lingered in both India and Pakistan. The persecution of Muslims in India and of Hindus in Pakistan has continued, arousing deep suspicions. Efforts of either country to arm itself, even against remote threats, have aroused fears in the other.

Against this background, several major sources of friction arose. One concerned the distribution of water in the basin of the Indus River, whose tributaries flow through lands claimed by both countries. Which nation, India or Pakistan, should receive what part of this water? After a long dispute the World Bank mediated the question in 1954, proposing that Pakistan keep all of the water flowing into its lands except a small part which was drawn off for Jammu and Kashmir. (This name is given to one state, but the name Kashmir is more often used and so will be used here.) India was free to use rest and to prepare canals through which it could share the benefits of mutually owned water with its neighbor. As recently as the mid-1980's joint commissions were reviewing and often amending the decisions of those years following independence. The entire world encouraged these efforts to settle a dispute through conferences.

The problem of Kashmir was more emotional than the one involving water use. Both India and Pakistan claimed to own this region of more than 83,000 square miles. For years violence, verging on war, had flared among supporters of the two countries inside of the disputed land.

Kashmir was one of almost six hundred Princely States that were released by the British when the rest of the Indian subcontinent was offered independence. Kashmir, like the other states, was given the right to be autonomous or to join either India or Pakistan. Autonomy was difficult and perhaps economically impossible in the midst of the vast new countries that were being formed. Only three states, Hyderabad, Junagadh, and Kashmir, had delayed making their choice before India declared its independence on August 14, 1947. All the others had decided to join one or the other country.

There was a common reason for the indecision in the three remaining Princely States. In each case the ruler was at odds with the wishes of his people. Hyderabad, with a Hindu population, had a Muslim prince. Rather than turn his land over to India, in 1947 this monarch declared that his state would remain independent. A year later Indian troops stormed his palace, deposed him, and raised their flag over Hyderabad.

Junagadh also had a Muslim prince and a population that was overwhelmingly Hindu. This prince, too, wanted to avoid Indian domination, but when he announced that Junagadh would join Pakistan a rebellion broke out, and later there was an election in which the population chose to join India. However, Pakistan refused to acknowledge that Junagadh, a region some three hundred miles from its borders, had become part of India.

In Kashmir, this situation was reversed. There, a Hindu prince ruled a largely Muslim population. In 1947 Pathan tribesmen, carrying the Pakistani flag, drove him out of the country, and India sent troops to resist them. At the same time India agreed to an election, but it insisted that the Pathans inside of Kashmir withdraw to Pakistan. While consenting to this, Pakistan demanded that Indian troops should leave, too, lest their presence in Kashmir intimidate the voters.

When fighting broke out between the two armies in Kashmir the United Nations managed to gain a cease-fire at the end of 1948. Inconclusive meetings followed. Impatient, Nehru ordered an election held in the area occupied by Indian troops. Only one party ran in this election—the one led by Sheikh Abdullah, a fiery advocate of freedom for the people of Kashmir. The Sheikh's victory proved that Kashmir wanted to belong to India, Nehru said. But Abdullah denied this, claiming that he favored neither India nor Pakistan and preferred independence.

By offering Kashmir a special position inside of India, Nehru persuaded Sheikh Abdullah to join the Union. Nehru's domestic opposition objected to changing the constitution in order to acquire the area, but Nehru was adamant. His family had come from Kashmir, and he wanted it to be a part of the nation he had come to govern. In 1953, the Assembly of Kashmir voted to join India. Nevertheless, Sheikh Abdullah was dissatisfied with his agreement and again asked for independence. Furious, Nehru renewed his pledge to have another election held in the disputed territory. Then, in 1954, before the election was held, he also persuaded Kashmir's chief legislative body to declare the state a part of India.

Pakistan responded by offering to divide the region. India agreed; but the two sides could not settle upon where the new border should be. Then once again the diplomatic efforts broke down and were replaced by violence in 1955. Muslims reported that Hindus had broken into a mosque to steal a sacred hair of the Prophet Muhammad. Riots followed. They became severe when Prime Minister Shastri, who succeeded Nehru, declared that nothing could dislodge Kashmir from the Indian Union. In 1955, Indian and Pakistani troops opened fire on each other.

The conflict was halted and a border established in 1968. It was an uneasy truce, though. With neither side fully satisfied, the possibility of further conflict has remained, and even now Kashmir is one of the most menacing territorial issues in Asia.

In 1971, the continuing strife between India and Pakistan was transferred to another region—East Pakistan. As we have seen, the former Indian state of East Bengal was made part of Pakistan when the two countries declared their independence. Although it was separated from West Pakistan by one thousand miles of Indian territory, its population was predominately Muslim. East Bengal, renamed East Pakistan, contained more than half of the total Pakistani population.

The differences between East and West Pakistan proved greater than the similarities, however. Although they had a common religion, each had a distinctive language, culture, and way of thinking. We will see in the next chapter how a nationalist movement began and grew in East Pakistan. Ultimately it led to the establishment of the nation of Bangladesh. This independence movement caused West Pakistan to send troops into its eastern region. The civil war that resulted caused widespread havoc. Almost three million people died. At least ten million refugees fled over the border to India.

The flood of refugees greatly strained Indian resources. India announced equal concern for the millions who lived in its former state of East Bengal. Soon the Pakistanis and Indians were accusing each other of violating national boundaries. Sporadic shooting began over the border, and in December 1971 full-scale war broke out. Indian forces quickly invaded East Pakistan and with the help of local guerrillas whom they had helped to train, they defeated the West Pakistani army. East Pakistan became the independent nation of Bangladesh.

Throughout Indira Gandhi's tenure of office in India, the government of Pakistan proved less stable than that of its neighbor. One thread, however, persisted in the relations between the two countries: suspicion. Pakistan's fears were heightened when India developed its first atomic bomb, and it appeared to be seeking the ability to produce atomic bombs of its own. India, on the other hand, found reasons for concern when Pakistan began to rearm as a defense against the Soviet Union. The Soviets invaded Afghanistan, which lies directly to the west, late in 1979, prompting the Pakistanis to call for foreign aid from many sources. Although tanks and planes supplied by the United States and other countries to Pakistan are unlikely to be used against India, there remains a possibility, however remote, that they will be in the event of a conflict.

With the assassination of Indira Gandhi and the rise of her son Rajiv to power, the governments of Pakistan and India appeared to be searching for reconciliation. Pakistan's leader, General Zia, offered to cooperate and meet with Rajiv Gandhi to insure a peaceful relationship. India's new chief executive received this offer well, for he needed to focus his energies on domestic problems, as did Zia. Thus the two countries may be entering a new, less difficult period.

The United States. India has long admired the United States. Gandhi, Nehru, and other Indian leaders saw in the U.S.'s early struggle for freedom a model for their own efforts. The U.S. Constitution was admired and followed by the authors of India's Constitution.

Since gaining independence, India has been given many other reasons to regard the United States as a valued friend. Official American aid, as well as the substantial help from private institutions such the Ford Foundation (cited above), has provided clear evidence that the U.S. will do all that it can to preserve the world's largest democracy in India. From 1947 to 1970, India received more than $4 billion in American aid. It received nearly 60 million tons of

India is an atomic power with great influence in the international community, but retains many of the ancient practices which made its culture unique.

American grain under the Food for Peace Program, especially during the droughts of 1965-66. American advice and financial support helped India to achieve the remarkable results of the Green Revolution.

Further, in 1962 the U.S. sent both arms and financial aid after China invaded India. Competent American ambassadors, such as Chester Bowles, John Sherman Cooper, and John K. Galbraith, did much to promote the friendship. Visits to India by many American dignitaries, including President Eisenhower and Vice-President Johnson added to the relationship. The annual exchange of students, scientists, scholars, and businesspeople by the two countries continued to increase.

Yet there have been strains in the relations between these two essentially friendly nations. The United States wanted India's active support against communism in the years immediately following World War II. India was unable to give this support because of its policy of "nonalignment." Moreover, the experience of colonialism had left its mark. Whatever help the Americans gave was seen by many Indians as a continuation of Britain's old policy of keeping India an agricultural, rather than an industrial nation. India appreciated American sympathy and financial assistance but feared that the U.S., by then the wealthiest country in the world, had replaced European nations as Asia's colonizer.

As a developing nation, India regarded many American policies with apprehension. The United States had developed the atomic bomb and used it in warfare against an Asian country. Furthermore, the U.S. continued to build new atomic weapons. India did not share the American assessment of the threat from communism and feared the new weapons systems. India was in no danger of becoming communist, although many Indians admired Russia.

India did not share the American assessment of the threat from communism and feared the new weapons systems. It was in no danger of becoming communist, although many Indians admired the recent progress in the Soviet Union. When the U.S. clung to its recognition of Taiwan rather than Communist China, the Indians were angered. They said that this policy was based on a moral judgment rather than on the facts of world power. They did not see U.S. regional defense pacts, such as the Southeast Asia Treaty Alliance and the Central Treaty Organization, solely as efforts to contain communist countries. Rather, they said, these were efforts to perpetuate white colonialism in Asia.

The severest blow to the relationship between the United States and India was dealt by the military alliance of the U.S. with Pakistan. In 1954, the U.S. began to ship sophisticated arms to Pakistan as part of this alliance. These weapons were intended as a defense against the Soviet Union and China, but India saw them as threats to its own security. In 1965 and 1972, Pakistan used the weapons supplied by the Americans in its wars with India, confirming Indian fears. When India entered the war in East Pakistan, the U.S. declared that India had "the major responsibility for the hostilities. . . ." To restrict the war effort it cut off $87.6 million in development loans to India, although the loans were for non-military projects.

The Soviet invasion of Afghanistan in 1979 further complicated the situation. Soon after it took place, the Americans decided that they must support the resistance movement in Afghanistan by funneling arms through Pakistan and by sending advanced weapons to Pakistan itself. Shipments of advanced U.A. fighter jets to Pakistan alarmed Indira Gandhi. She sought both reassurance and aid from Washington to compensate her country for any lack of military balance that had been created. The U.S. complied, but the Indians still fretted.

Finally, India chafed when the U.S. insisted on attaching their own policies to the aid that they gave. For example, the Americans have consistently demanded that whatever funds they sent be used in the private rather than the public sector of Indian planning. To this insistence on capitalist rather than socialist programs, the Americans added a moral one during the administration of President Reagan. They declared that they would not allow any American money to be used for abortions, even in countries such as China and India, where population pressures were severe. Both the Indians and Chinese regarded this demand as interference in their national affairs.

To a large extent Rajiv Gandhi checked India's drift away from the United States. The U.S. had placated his mother by agreeing to send uranium to India if it were used for peaceful purposes, but she continued to side with the Soviet Union in many international incidents. Under Rajiv Gandhi, who favored less collectivism and more enterprise in the economy, Indian policies were more to U.S. liking. It appeared that the relationship had become stabilized and that India had returned to neutrality, at least.

The Soviet Union. India was cordial but aloof in its early relations with the Soviet Union. Its announced policy was to evaluate world issues on their merits rather than in terms of who supported them. The Soviet Union, when it was led by Joseph Stalin, regarded India's new government as capitalist because it was not "wholly socialist." This view changed when Stalin died in 1953. Two years later the Soviets helped India to build a steel mill. Nehru visited

Moscow, and the new Russian leaders, Nikolai Bulganin and Nikita Khrushchev, returned the visit. The Soviets began to endorse Indian policies and to support India's claims on Kashmir.

The military alliance formed by the United States and Pakistan in 1954 persuaded Nehru that he would need Soviet help in world forums. The USSR warmly reciprocated this wish after the first signs of its diplomatic break with China in 1959, although Nehru accepted Soviet military aid because of the threat of war with Pakistan and China. When the United States and Great Britain suspended arms shipments both to Pakistan and India during the 1965 clashes over Kashmir, the Soviets increased arms shipments to India. Then Premier Kosygin helped to resolve the Kashmir issue in 1966 by inviting the Indian and Pakistani leaders to the Soviet city of Tashkent. There, the two adversaries agreed to end hostilities and to respect a boundary. Both India and Pakistan were grateful for Soviet mediation.

Soviet advisers did not insist that their country's aid be used in any special way, as Americans often do. They left India relatively free to industrialize. The U.S., on the other hand, wanted its money to help feed India's starving millions rather than to industrialize. Moreover, as we have seen, it also required India to spend American funds in the private sector rather than in state-owned public industries. Later it opposed abortions anywhere in the world, and Indians were using this practice for birth control.

The Soviet Union cemented its relationship with India by taking advantage of cultural affinities between the two countries. The Soviets encouraged the study of Indian languages in Soviet schools and translated many important Indian literary works into Russian. India signed a long-range military pact with the Soviet Union when the quarrel with Pakistan spread to Bangladesh in 1971. This pact pledged mutual support and aid in the event of an attack on either country.

Many American diplomatic observers held the military pact to be the end of India's policy of nonalignment. Although the Indian government denied this, it was clear that India had moved much closer to the Soviet camp. The Soviets have since helped the Indians to build roads and dams, and in 1985 Indian cosmonauts flew into space on a Soviet craft. Pakistan's close ties with the U.S. and China have further driven India into its Soviet alliance. Rajiv Gandhi has tried to restore neutralism to a large degree, but how far he will go in this respect remains to be seen.

The People's Republic of China. "Indians and Chinese are brothers," was the most popular slogan in India during the 1950's. The Indian government, eager for international peace so that it could solve its domestic problems, sought to persuade its massive communist neighbor that it was friendly. India recognized the communist government three months after it took power. It supported China's efforts to join the United Nations and to gain other diplomatic recognition.

India was disturbed by China's invasion of Tibet in 1950 but did little more than protest. China had accused India of helping the United States to support an archaic Tibetan regime. Its leaders feared that Tibet was a back door through which an invasion of China might be launched. India responded by saying that China had been misinformed. Nehru said mildly that, in any event, the Chinese conquest of Tibet was an accomplished fact. When Nehru's opposition in India accused him of buckling under the communist giant, he replied that peace with China was essential to India's progress.

China, however, was not so easily placated. Almost immediately after signing a treaty recognizing China's rights in Tibet, India and China quarreled over their joint border. Chinese maps, circulated in China and abroad, depicted 50,000 square miles of Indian territory as Chinese. The Chinese argued that the land had been assigned to India by "illegal" treaties drawn by the British.

In 1957, the Indian government discovered that the Chinese had been building a road through Tibet, linking the Chinese province of Sinkiang with the disputed territory. India's protests were rejected by the Chinese, who in the next three years continued their work on the road and sent men and supplies over it.

In 1959, nationalist forces inside of Tibet rebelled, giving a new dimension to the quarrel. Tibet's leader, the Dalai Lama, fled and was given refuge in India, along with thousands of Buddhist refugees. Angered by the Indian sympathy for the Tibetans, the Chinese rebuked India for "wilfully upholding a colonial legacy." It was at this point that President Eisenhower visited India and ordered shipments of planes and arms to India so that China could be restrained. Thus, the stage was set for the conflict that began in 1962.

In that year, Nehru ordered his troops to "clear Indian territory of Chinese aggressors." Instead of retreating as he asked, the Chinese spilled over the Himalayas, driving the Indian army back to the plain of Assam. Fortunately, China did not press this advantage, but withdrew and called for negotiations. Since then the territory has remained in dispute, but there have been no major armed conflicts.

China's attack ended Nehru's conciliatory policy, and the two nations became angry with and suspicious of one another. This condition was worsened by China's support of Pakistan during the controversy over Bangladesh and, later, when the Soviets invaded Afghanistan in 1979. China's large Muslim minority and important contacts with Muslim states suggest that it is likely to continue to side with Pakistan in any dispute that it has with India. The tension between the two countries has forced India to strengthen its army and to deflect needed funds from peaceful to military development.

Other Asian countries. India has wanted Asia to unite economically, much as Europe has attempted to through the Common Market. Because its current relationship with China is unfriendly, India has turned to Japan to help it reach this objective. Japan buys up to one-third of India's exports and has sent India a large percentage of its manufactured goods.

Japan, however, has been creating closer economic ties with mainland China and is unlikely to sever them in order to respond to India. Conscious of this, India has also pursued other trading partners in Asia. Perhaps it is waiting for the time when its relationship with China will improve. In any case, it remains active among "nonaligned nations" and which in 1983 met in India.

Elsewhere in Asia, the effects of China's rising power have changed all of India's relationships. Indonesia, for example, shares Indian fears of China since 1965, when Chinese communists attempted to seize its government. It has been increasing its trade with India. Burma, India's neighbor to the east, also reacted negatively to China's effort to win support among its people. As a result, it has drawn closer to India.

Closer to home, a quarrel between India and Sri Lanka (Ceylon), caused by the presence of a substantial Indian minority in Sri Lanka, who migrated to that island during the past 125 years, has never been fully resolved. Native Sri Lankans resent economic competition from the Tamils, who are Indians or former Indians, among them. As recently as 1985 Sri Lanka accused India of fostering terrorism on the island. Finally, India enjoys good relations with its tiny border states of Nepal and Sikkim. India acts as protector of these countries, which are buffers against China.

The Middle East and Europe. Because of its large Muslim community, India has sought to forge lasting ties with the Muslim countries of the Middle East, which it calls "West Asia." India buys much of its oil from this region. For these reasons and because it does not want to confront a solid front of Muslim nations supporting Pakistan, it has generally sided with Egypt and Syria in their controversies with Israel.

In general its relations with Europe have been cordial. France has sold India nuclear materials which it was unable to buy elsewhere until the U.S. agreed to do so in 1985. West Germany, too, has supplied vital parts for nuclear and other machines. India's closest European friend is Great Britain. India is a member of the British Commonwealth and in 1984 was host to the heads of Commonwealth governments, with Queen Elizabeth II in attendance.

THE FUTURE OF THE INDIAN DEMOCRACY

The founders of modern India regarded capitalism as the chief source of their national problems. Western capitalists, they declared, had looted their country, forcing its people to labor in tasks which created profitable industries and products overseas while crushing Indian society. To preclude the rise of a capitalist class in India they proclaimed their vision of a socialist state which, unlike the one in the Soviety Union, was to be democratic as well as socialist. Jawaharlal Nehru established this aim, and Indira Gandhi pressed it further by nationalizing certain basic industries.

By the 1980's it was apparent that years of socialist planning had done little to alleviate the misery in India. A vast bureaucracy wallowed in its own inefficiency or corruption while more than half of the people continued to live at bare subsistence levels. The country suffered from high prices, widespread unemployment, and shortages. The relatively high birth rate promised even greater disasters in the future.

Under Rajiv Gandhi, the government began to change its course. Slashing regulations, trade barriers, and bureaucratic payrolls, it offered tax incentives to domestic and foreign investors. Moreover it withdrew government from the operation of some businesses and the control of others through licensing. Soon the economy responded. Agriculture, which in 1972 contributed almost half of the gross national product, yielded to less than a third by 1989. Meanwhile manufacturing, transportation, and trade surged. Industries began to modernize and turn out a stream of consumer goods such as television sets, computers, and motor scooters; exports jumped by 40 percent. The stock market boomed as industries poured money into the production of cement, steel, and fertilizers. In each of the five years ending in 1986 the rate of manufactured exports grew by an average of 5.1 percent a year, while in 1988 it exceeded 25 percent.

Most Indians welcomed the results of these new policies—the vastly increased amounts of goods and services and greater freedom of private businesses to operate. Yet there were many who pointed out that the new wealth was being absorbed by just 10-15 percent of the population. The rest of India still often bartered for its needs. Poor and unemployed classes, seeing a few people gathering possessions while they could not even find jobs, were becoming restless. In all of India there are only 25 million wage-earners, and the total of industries is only half of the total in Brazil.

As the decade drew to a close, it appeared that Rajiv Gandhi had reached an end in the first phase of his effort to revive the Indian economy. His program of deregulation was meeting with firmer resistance from bureaucrats and from businesses which enjoyed protection from their competitors. Almost 10 percent of all of the country's wage-earners were employed by the government, and they tended to reject any change in their status. Despite widespread incompetence, the 150,000 businesses in the public sector were not permitted to fail when they lost money. The Indian government hires 700,000 to work in its coal mines. This industry, however, produces no more than Australia's, whose coal industry hires just 30,000. Shortages of roads, vehicles, telephones, water, and especially electric power further curtail growth.

Despite these formidable limits, India appears more willing than ever to confront its problems. After four decades of independence it has more than doubled food production, increased national income at the rate of about 4 percent a year, and almost tripled literacy to more than 40 percent of the population. For the first time in history it has modern shipbuilding and auto industries, its own airline, and new supplies of energy, including offshore wells and atomic plants. It has reduced or eliminated many fatal diseases, including malaria, the plague, tuberculosis, cholera, and smallpox.

Powerful forces in India continue to threaten the country's fragile unity. Sikhs who resort to terror to gain independence, bureaucrats who want full control of enterprises, business owners who want unlimited profits, minorities which reject the national language in order to protect their own: these are only some of the groups which tear at the Indian nation. Facing their demands, India's leaders will need firm will and determination to preserve the world's largest democracy.

Chapter 11

CHALLENGES OF THE NEW ERA:
PAKISTAN AND BANGLADESH

Pakistan and Bangladesh are separate nations which until 1971 were united. They are situated on either coast of India, divided by one thousand miles of Indian territory. Each has one major seaport: Pakistan has Karachi, on the Arabian Sea; Bangladesh has Chittagong, on the Bay of Bengal. Joined by their Muslim faith, the two nations differ in most other ways—in language, culture, ethnic composition, land forms, and climate.

PAKISTAN

We have seen that Pakistan—or more formally, the Islamic Republic of Pakistan—originally included two parts or "wings." The western wing is the nation of Pakistan today. The eastern one, what was East Pakistan, became Bangladesh—"Land of the Bengalis"—after the civil war in which India became involved in 1971. The two wings were created when the British left the subcontinent in 1947. Predominantly Muslim, they incorporated Indian provinces, states, and territories in which there was a large Hindu minority. In the west the provinces included Punjab, Baluchistan, North-West Frontier, and Sind. The east unit included the province of East Bengal alone. When the new Islamic state was founded, most of its Hindu occupants fled to India while many of India's Muslims fled to Pakistan. This flight, said to be the largest short-term migration in history, created more than 15 million refugees.

The "father of Pakistan" was Muhammad Ali Jinnah, a brilliant leader of the Indian Muslim community. Jinnah predicted a need for the separate Muslim state long before the British left the subcontinent. He feared the voice of India's Muslims might not be heard in a nation so largely Hindu as India. Despite protests of the Indian National Congress and efforts of the British to prevent disunity, Jinnah and the Muslim League prevailed. When the British left, two nations, India and Pakistan, were established.

West Pakistan occupies an area of deserts and plains. To the north and west are the mighty Pamir and Hindu Kush mountains. The Indus River system flows south and westward across this region, providing some of the best natural irrigation known in agriculture. Farmers are thus compensated for a lack of rain. In summer, however, they suffer from floods caused by the melting of snow in the

173

high mountains. At times the same year that brings floods will bring droughts. In some regions, like Hyderabad, searing winds sweep down the mountains and over the plains. They turn the surface of the land into a hard crust.

Despite these hardships in the countryside, about three-fourths of the population is engaged in agriculture, producing vast amounts of jute, cotton, sugar, and wheat. Rice and tea are also important crops. In addition, timber, fish, and hides are processed. But Pakistan has been unable to achieve self-sufficiency in food production. Many of its people are desperately undernourished. While the average American spends about 16 percent of his income for food, the average Pakistani spends more than 66 percent—and he receives much less for it. Pakistanis consume large amounts of rice and wheat but have few fresh vegetables and dairy products available to them. The lack of proper diet—especially the lack of protein—severely limits the ability of many Pakistanis to work. The standard of living is one of the lowest in the world.

Many other factors limit efficiency and jeopardize the population. They include inadequate sanitation, pollution, and disease. The government of Pakistan has allocated large sums to improve drainage and insure access to fresh water. Yet raw sewage continues to flow into many canals, rivers, and ponds which are also sources of drinking and cooking water. The disease rate is high; leprosy,

This Pakistani shepherd works in a region at the foot of high mountains, where the parched land is rocky and windswept and the nights are cold.

tuberculosis, cholera, malaria, and smallpox take a heavy toll. Infant mortality and the adult death rate are among the highest in the world.

Pakistan has more than 99 million people and is growing at the rate of more than 3 percent annually—a dangerously high figure. The population has generally settled along the Indus River and its tributaries—the Jhelum, Chenab, Ravi, and Sutlej. With more than 310,000 square miles, its population is not as densely concentrated as parts of India, China, or Japan. In some areas of Pakistan there are only 100 people per square mile, while in others there are 1,000. Yet much of the land is not usable because it is too arid or steep. While the elevation of Karachi, on the Arabian Sea, is at sea level, in the far north of Pakistan the land soars to 25,000 feet. Some of the plains are too dry for any vegetation. Some of the highlands are covered by compacted trees and tough grasses, and in the middle elevations there are a few stands of chestnuts, oaks, and other broadleafed trees. In the deserts, on the other hand, there are broad expanses with no vegetation at all. In the deserts, years may pass before rain falls; the daytime temperatures soar to 105 degrees. Throughout Pakistan the average rainfall is less than 20 inches annually.

Pakistan occupies a strategic area bounded by Communist China, India, Afghanistan, and Iran. Despite its sheltering mountains it has been a field of battle since the time of Alexander the Great. Persians and Sythians fought in Pakistan. Kushans invaded from China and Huns from the north. During the 19th century the British sought to extend their empire into Afghanistan, but were expelled.

This combative past, combined with the Pakistanis' own cultural patterns, has resulted in a population that values the arts of war. Until its defeat in Bangladesh. Pakistan gave its army great prestige. In recent years the army administered the government in a state of martial law and did not permit the first general election to take place until 1972, fully 25 years after the country achieved independence.

Effective communication among Pakistanis is severely hampered by differences in language. In each administrative region different ethnic groups predominate: the Baluchis and Brauhuis in Baluchistan, the Pathans in North-West Frontier Province, the Sindhis in Sind, and the Punjabis in Punjab. Punjabi, the most frequently spoken language, is understood in about two-thirds of Pakistan. Sindhi, Pushti and Urdu are spoken by smaller numbers. Urdu, which uses a Persian-Arabic script and is based on Hindustani, has become the official language of Pakistan, but English is the language used in education and government. Less than a quarter of the population can read and write any of 32 or more languages in

Pakistan. In Bangladesh there is chiefly one language, Bengali. This language is particularly difficult to write because its alphabet is composed of 50 letters.

Ethnic differences in Pakistan are accentuated by ancient rivalries. The Punjabis hold many positions of power in government and the army. The Pathans, however, have a long history of militarism and are disdainful of the Punjabis' ability to run the army and government. Other groups resent the control over their lives exerted by the government and tend to live without reference to it. Nevertheless, these people are bound together by a common Muslim faith. Although the divisions in Pakistani society are severe, this powerful religious faith has superseded the ethnic differences. Until its civil war, Pakistan was the largest Muslim nation in the world.

BANGLADESH

In contrast to Pakistan, Bangladesh has no high mountains and little dry land. It has no military tradition or strong tendency to require a uniform belief among its people. Bangladesh is mostly delta; its three main rivers, the Padma (Ganges), Jamuna, and Meghna, traverse a huge plain. Rainfall, varying from 50 to 100 inches annually, is significantly greater than Pakistan's. Floods, cyclones, and earthquakes trouble Bangladesh. Its area of 55,000 square miles is bounded by the Bay of Bengal, Burma, and India. The temperate, humid climate is suitable for growing rice and tea. Jute and sugar are among the other large crops.

The presence of water is felt everywhere in Bangladesh. It provides the principal means of transportation. Dinghies (a Bengali word) and larger boats carry more than 75 percent of the passengers and material shipments in Bangladesh. But the process is slow. It takes almost twenty hours to cover the 125 miles between Dacca and Rajshahi. More than 16 percent of the country is covered by lush forests—about eight times the percentage in Pakistan. Palms and bamboos, ferns and mosses, reptiles, elephants, tigers, and wild buffaloes are typical of the plant and animal life of the country. There is one large jungle, the Madhupur. It consists of about 1,600 square miles. Isolated from the plains around it, surrounded by six earthquake faults, it is north of the capital city, Dacca. Finally, many of the tragic effects of surplus water occur during the summer monsoons. These high, storm-bearing winds rush in from the Bay of Bengal, regularly flooding a huge area. As much as three-quarters of the annual rainfall may be delivered in this one season. In some years, such as 1970, the uncontrollable waters have caused havoc.

Bangladesh has more than 98 million people, and its population is increasing by up to 3 percent a year. It has almost as many people as Pakistan does, but they have much less land available to them. The poverty, lack of proper nutrition, disease, and maldistribution of wealth that characterize Pakistan is even more severe in Bangladesh. Yet the society is probably more cohesive. Almost all Bengalis speak one language, Bengali, and participate in a culture that resembles India's more than Pakistan's. The large Hindu minority is far more readily accepted by the community than the smaller Hindu minority in Pakistan. Although Bangladesh has diverse tribes in its Chittagong Hills, it is more ethnically united than Pakistan.

While both countries have suffered in their independent state, they have achieved a basic goal—freedom from the caste system with which they were familiar in India. The Islamic faith opposes the rigid social structure which is inherent in the caste system. The Muslim religion holds to a belief in one God by one people, while India accepts and even thrives on a multiplicity of gods and peoples, all co-existing. Pakistan and Bangladesh are deeply divided on economic, ethnic, social and political levels. But in terms of religion, they are one.

For almost a quarter of a century East and West Pakistan succeeded in remaining under one government, despite their differences. Then in 1971, smoldering hostility burst into violence. The civil war that erupted was only one of the issues which brought India into conflict with Pakistan. Since gaining independence, India and Pakistan have been involved in vigorous disputes and combat over water rights and the state of Jammu and Kashmir.

SOCIAL AND CULTURAL DEVELOPMENT

In 1930, Muhammad Iqbal, the president of the Muslim League of India, proposed that part of India be set aside for a state "based on unity of language, race, history, religion, and identity of common interests." This idea attracted a group of Indian Muslims who were studying in London. The group issued a proclamation, "Now or Never," three years later. Their pamphlet went beyond the idea of Muhammad Iqbal. They suggested a separate Muslim state and offered a name for it:

> *Pakistan is both a Persian and an Urdu word composed of letters taken from the names of our homelands: that is Punjab, Afghana (North-West Frontier Province), Kashmir, Iran, Sindh, Tukharistan, Afghanistan, and Baluchistan. It means Land of the Paks, the spiritually pure and clean.*

The "common interests" shared by the Muslims of the Indian sub-continent had been introduced by Arabs who began to invade North India as early as the eighth century A.D. By 1000 A.D. they achieved a

In a village parade
these tribesmen
demonstrate their
military tradition.

firm foothold. Muslims occupied many communities and became the
ruling class. Hindus, mostly of the lower castes, became converts to
the Muslim religion. The wealthy Muslims came chiefly from Arabic
countries, Turkey, Persia, and Afghanistan. These upper class
foreigners gained the title *sherif*, while the poorer converts, the
former Hindus, were identified by the word *ajlaf*. Although they
were technically Muslims, the ajlaf did not substantially change their
Hindu ways or occupations. As we will see, the Islamic faith required
them to separate themselves from their former communities in other
ways, however.

It was against this background that the Muslim League joined the
call for a separate nation in the 1930's. We have seen how
Muhammad Ali Jinnah succeeded in persuading the British and
Indians that it would be necessary to accept the existence of two
nations. In 1947, the year after Pakistan achieved independence,
Jinnah died. No one of comparable stature was left to lead Pakistan
toward stability. The prime minister, Liaquat Ali Khan began to
develop the government. However, in 1951, he was murdered by an
assassin. Only their faith remained to hold Pakistanis together.

The Muslim basis of government. Islam ("Submission to God") has as one of its primary statements the prayer, "There is no God but Allah; Muhammad is the Prophet of Allah." This profession of the faith (the *shahadah*) is uttered daily in mosques throughout the world. While there is only one God in the Muslim faith, there are many prophets, however. Adam, Noah, Abraham, Moses, and Jesus are among them. Muhammad is regarded as the most nearly perfect of all the prophets. The concept of Muhammad's perfection was due to his ability to project Islam as a faith for all nations—an improvement, in the Muslim view, on the code for personal behavior that was preached by Jesus. For this reason, Muslims recognize the Hegira ("flight") of Muhammad from Mecca to Medina (622 A.D.) as the first year of their calendar. The Hegira symbolizes the social and political triumph of Muhammad's ideas.

Traditionally, there are five "pillars" to the Muslim faith. They are: the shahadah, prayer, almsgiving, fasting during the month of Ramadan, and making one pilgrimage to Mecca. Prayer, directed toward Mecca, is humbly offered, usually in Arabic, five times a day.

Like their acceptance of prophets before Muhammad, Muslims accept holy records which predate the Quran, their sacred book. Among these are the Hebrew Torah (or Law of Moses), the Psalms of David, and the Christian Gospel. But the verses of the Quran, they believe, are the final word of Allah and have the power to cure and enrich the mind and body. The Quran states that man is, literally, powerless before Allah. Angels rule humanity and have as their counterparts devils. The angels include Israfel, whose task is to blow the trumpet summoning the world to its final judgment; Azrael, who has the power of death; Michael, who controls nature; and Gabriel, who communicated the will of Allah to Muhammad. There will be a day, according to Muslim belief, when all men and devils will be forced to stand and be judged. Those who have honored Allah and his word (for even devils, or *jinn*, are thought to be capable of believing in God) may be permitted to enter heaven. Those who have not may expect to be sent to hell.

Muslims developed no priesthood. The will of Allah is said to be written on a tablet; it is fixed, scarcely subject to interpretation. In the view of some Muslims, man has a choice of actions. Other more traditional Muslims believe that all action is fated. In both perspectives the true Muslim accepts his destiny (*kismet*) as it is written. Both suggest that man can save himself from the wrath of Allah only by dedicating himself to Islamic law. Hence all who accept Islam fear Allah. For them the sole, unquestionable path to salvation lies in the Quran and its associated commentary, the Sunnah, which describes historical behavior in the Muslim community. Islamic society is based on the Quran, which is religious law. Therefore, to assail the nation is an antireligious act. All human communities, from neighborhood to earth itself, are controlled by Allah alone. Therefore, to propose change is futile.

Life in the new Muslim state. As in India, the joint family forms the basis of society in Pakistan. It is ruled by the eldest male, usually the father or, in his absence, the eldest son. Because it includes all of the sons and their wives and children in one household, it is larger than the nuclear family that is the social unit in the West. First, in Pakistan it may include up to four wives. Second, not only all of the sons and daughters, but their wives and husbands and children, and often the nephews and nieces of the master of the family, live together.

Women are regarded as subservient to men. To limit their appeal outside the family, they are required by their husbands to practice the tradition of purdah, in which they veil their faces unless they are alone or with their relatives. Although submissive to her husband, the woman is warm and nurturing to her children. Her chief role is as mate and housekeeper. While the husband governs their sons, his wife cares for their daughters.

The treatment of the sons is often severe. The object of discipline is to make the son strong enough to defend the honor of the family and the cause of Islam. Fathers and sons often are, therefore, formal and distant with one another. The sons are expected to observe the ceremonies of respect, such as standing when their father enters the room.

In 1961, Pakistan modified some traditional relationships among its people through the Muslim Family Laws Ordinance. Marriage, divorce, and inheritance laws were made uniform in both West and East Pakistan. Some restrictions were placed on the traditional power of the head of the family to dominate his relatives completely. Under the Ordinance a man is not permitted to take a second wife unless a government-appointed council consented to his action. This same council must be notified if he wishes to divorce. The Ordinance also helped to curtail child marriages by raising the minimum age for girls to marry from 14 to 16.

However, polygamy continues in Pakistan. Wealthy merchants and farmers take second or third wives to demonstrate their success in business. When the marriage takes place early in the lives of the couple, it is usually arranged by the fathers of the husband and bride. The economic, social, and religious needs of the families are considered before the feelings of the couple. Even Pakistanis who have been educated in the West may take a second wife if they were married by arrangement in their youth. But women can take only one husband at a time. If they fail to please their husbands they may be cast out of the family. The husband needs only to say, "I divorce thee" three times before two witnesses to make the divorce legal. The woman then usually returns to her family. She may try to remarry, but prejudices against divorced women are likely to prevent that. The husband, on the other hand, probably will remarry soon after the divorce. Under some circumstances a woman may divorce her husband, but only with the consent of a judge. She does not keep her dowry in that event. When a husband dies, a woman will often be persuaded to marry one of his brothers so that the dowry will remain in the family.

The strong relationships in family life have created inward-looking societies in Pakistan and Bangladesh. High walls are constructed around homes to keep strangers from catching intimate glimpses of the family, especially the women. Distant relatives, rather than strangers, often are employed as servants. They are permitted to live in the home and to receive the family's love and protection, but they are unlikely to earn much pay. In these circumstances, most people learn to live chiefly with the people nearest to them. The loyalty of most individuals is committed to

This modern hotel in Karachi is a convention site. Extremes of wealth and poverty characterize Pakistan's capital, as well as its outlying areas.

people rather than to ideas, principles, or institutions. A kind of courtly formality is admired in individuals as an expression of the society's most closely held values. In businesses, schools, and bureaucracies these concepts cause people to form personal relationships resembling those first taught in the family.

Modern technology has begun to modify these traditional views and practices. With more machines and recreation, young people are less dependent on the family for all their needs and pleasures. Fewer girls observe purdah, and more are permitted to go to school. As a new briskness enters the economic pace, young people tend to think more of how their abilities will compare with those of others, rather than of their family relationships. Islamic scholars have begun to think of how the Quran can best be interpreted for modern times.

Education. Primary schools are free, and most parents send their children to them. However, only about 25 percent of the children who finish primary school enter secondary schools. Although this figure is low when compared to other countries it is more than twice the percentage of the early 1950's. About half of Pakistan's school-age children presently attend classes. The country had hoped to achieve free compulsory education through the age of 13 by the mid-1980's, but it could not achieve that objective.

The secondary schools, which include grades six through eight, introduced new, more practical curriculums in 1961. This reform was undertaken to aid the many children who planned to seek jobs rather than to continue their education. Under the British, the educational system was designed to produce recruits for the civil service. The bureaucratic skills were cultivated. In more recent years, Pakistan has recognized that the demands of an increasingly industrial society require a more technical curriculum.

Despite many efforts to reform its university system, Pakistan's efforts have met with little success. In the past, students have complained that universities have made learning secondary to examinations. Too much time was wasted in idle talk, they said. In 1969, violence broke out on many of Pakistan's 13 campuses, including the one in Dacca. For the most part, these outbursts were in protest to the ineffectiveness of the university system. Responding to this pressure, higher education in Pakistan appears to be slowly taking a course given it by Sir Syed Ahmed Khan (1817–98), one of its most imposing thinkers, during the British rule. In protest against foreign domination, India's Muslims had formed religious schools that enabled them to stand apart from the British-sponsored education system. Sir Syed pointed out that the world was growing increasingly scientific. This fact demanded that the community give students a broader education than the religious schools could provide, he said. He led Pakistan toward the Westernization of its university system. Although conservative Muslims have long resisted this course, students in Pakistan, today, seem increasingly ready to adopt it.

Conditions, values, and cultures. Both Pakistan and Bangladesh are still largely rural. The British left some industry, but most of it was concentrated in West Pakistan. In the ancient buildings of both nations, Mogul influence is plain. Domes, minarets, and true arches recall the prosperous pre-colonial rule. There is much evidence of a brilliant talent for terra cotta sculpture in Bangladesh.

Mud bricks, baked in the sun, are used in many Pakistani houses. Wood is scarce. Most houses have two or three rooms. In cities the houses of the poor, made of any material from paper and sticks to stones, provide a haunting contrast to the magnificent brick homes of the rich. Whatever the quality, a Pakistani house will almost always demonstrate the Muslim desire for seclusion. In Bangladesh, this is also apparent, but to a lesser degree than in Pakistan. In Bangladesh, the houses often are made of bamboo and straw. Because of the heavy rains they are raised above the earth on small mounds that are usually surrounded by fences.

The villagers live quiet, generally unchanging lives. Their social relationships are chiefly local ones. Behind high, clay walls the women run their households, dealing chiefly with the members of their families and occasionally with other members of the village. Each day the head of the family goes to the fields outside the village to work. In this environment, in which the need for manual labor is widespread, the people respect anyone wealthy enough to avoid it. The highest esteem is given to the businessman or professional who has servants to do his manual labor for him. Displays of wealth, such as opulent surroundings or ceremonies, are granted social esteem.

These attitudes are changing in the newly industrialized areas of Pakistan. When Pakistani workers take jobs in factories, they are likely to change some of their older attitudes. They recognize a need to value ability rather than rank. But the middle class remains small in Pakistan. For the most part, they live in these cities: Islamabad, the new capital, a thoroughly planned and beautiful city a few miles south of Jammu and Kashmir; Karachi, the seaport, on an arid plain; Lahore, an historic former Mogul center on the Ravi River, near India; and Rawalpindi, a few miles southwest of Islamabad. The principal city of Bangladesh is Dacca, the capital and center of the country's intellectual activity.

Although increasingly Western clothing is seen in both Pakistan and Bangladesh, the more common dress is the *shalwar-qamiz,* which are cotton pants resembling pajamas. Punjabis often wear the *lungya*, a band of cotton wound around the waist. Woman wear the flowing clothing called the *burqa*, a cotton outer dress which enables them to practice purdah. In cities and villages the women of both Pakistan and Bangladesh wear jewelry made of silver and embedded with stones or etched with designs.

Pakistanis are a conservative people. They disapprove of dancing, songs that emphasize sexual love, and clothing that is alluring. Their chief recreation is conversation. Music is a major part of their lives, though. Plucking stringed instruments and sounding drums with their fingers, the Pakistanis produce sounds that resemble chants. They excel in visual arts, both traditional and modern. The Bengalis, more emotional and oriented toward Indian culture than the Pakistanis, enjoy dramatic representations of the *Mahabharata* and *Ramayana*, performed by touring actors.

Throughout Northern India and Pakistan clothing may reflect the traditions of the area as well as some of the fashions in Western countries.

The enduring epics of India, the *Mahabharata* and the *Ramayana,* provide a rich supply of material for touring actors. This gesture is symbolic of royal power.

POLITICAL DEVELOPMENT

Early struggles: Pakistan. The death of its first two national leaders left Pakistan a heritage of instability. Islamic tradition was the chief bond of nationhood. East Pakistan, however, began immediately to strain for greater independence. In a general election in 1954, it chose an 18-year-old student over the Muslim League's chief minister for its region. A "constituent assembly," made up of the leaders of the various national groups, had been preparing for a parliamentary government. Faced with the embarrassing results of the election, it dissolved itself.

By 1962, a newly constituted assembly had adopted a new constitution. It asserted that Pakistan would dedicate its life and laws to the Quran. Only a Muslim could become president. To help it pass legislation, the government was to form an Advisory Council of Islamic Ideology and an Islamic Research Institute. But although the members of this assembly were almost all members of the Muslim League, they were unable to agree on a structure for government. The various ethnic groups all were demanding a voice in what was to become the new Parliament. East Pakistan continued to express fears that it would not be adequately represented in a government 1,000 miles away. Its people resented West Pakistan's pressure to make Urdu, a language few of them knew, the national language. While refugees poured into the country from India, homeless and expecting help from the government, no effective government was operating.

As disputes continued, Pakistanis began to question whether the parliamentary form of government was appropriate for them. The four major ethnic regions of West Pakistan—which before independence had been the Indian provinces of Baluchistan, Sind, Punjab, and North-West Frontier—were combined into a single administrative province called One Unit. This was accomplished through Punjabi influence in government, over the protests of the Baluchis, Sindhis, and Pathans. As these groups formed a political coalition with the Bengalis to resist the submerging of their ethnic identities, the political confusion was abruptly resolved by a proclamation of martial law.

Under pressure from the army the president, Iskaner Mirza, dissolved Pakistan's legislatures and declared its two-year-old constitution invalid. The army then forced him to appoint General Muhammad Ayub Khan to head a new government. Within a month after seizing control, Ayub Khan forced Mirza out of office and into exile. Pakistan was in the total control of the military.

There were two phases to Ayub Khan's government. The first, lasting through 1958, revised administrative procedures and removed nearly 3,000 civil servants as inefficient or corrupt. In fact, many were merely opposed to the new administration. Ayub Khan later moved to prevent these and other opponents from returning to government. Under his decree anyone challenging his administration could be prevented from entering politics for six years. Charges against the opposition were often vaguely worded, including "misconduct," "contributed to the instability of the state," or "guilty of subversive activity."

In 1959, Ayub Khan launched a program that he called "Basic Democracy." He declared that the American and European versions of democracy could not work in a country divided as Pakistan. Under Basic Democracy, local governing councils were established. The basic units were the union councils, or panchayats, with one representative for every 1,000 to 1,500 people. These groups, scattered throughout the country, supervised local public works, health, and sanitation programs. Above them in the government hierarchy were: regional administrators, district councils, divisional councils, provisional advisory councils, and, finally, the president. In all there were 80,000 "Basic Democrats" serving on the various administrative councils. Although supposedly elected by secret ballot

Ethnic concerns,
rather than national ones,
often absorb Pakistanis.

by the population at large, they were chiefly sponsored by the army. When called upon to vote for a president in 1960, they elected Ayub Khan to a five year term.

In 1962, Pakistan's constitution was changed in order to provide for a more centralized federal government. Stronger powers were vested in the president, henceforth to be elected by the people rather than indirectly. Under the new constitution the Basic Democrats were permitted to send representatives to the newly elected National Assembly. Thus although martial law was lifted and a parliamentary form of government was restored, it remained under Ayub Khan's firm control. His plan proposed that democracy be achieved in stages. Rival political groups were permitted to function, but in a limited way. The nation, Ayub Khan said, should be "partyless," however. Soon, a coalition that was unable to accept these limits was formed to defeat him. Nevertheless, he won re-election in 1965 by an overwhelming majority.

In many ways the 1962 constitution was a liberal document. It guaranteed freedom of speech, assembly, association, movement, and guaranteed the right of due process of law. It did not provide for a check on presidential powers, however. Ayub Khan was able to postpone exercise of the constitutional guarantees by stating that the country was not ready for them. In 1967, the number of Basic Democrats needed to elect the president was increased from 80,000 to 120,000. These electors were to have been chosen by the people in 1969. But instability remained the hallmark of Pakistani politics. The elections scheduled for 1969 were never held.

The restoration of martial law. One source of strife centered about One Unit, the single administrative area created by merging West Pakistan's four provinces. The Pathans, who have a fierce pride in their region, the former North-West Frontier Province, demanded more independence. Joining them, Ayub Khan's political adversaries began to clamor for more ethnic independence. Ayub Khan responded by clamping down on political campaigning for two months.

At the same time, however, another issue emerged. Pakistan's students were demanding reform of the education process. It was too rigid, they said, and required much useless learning. When they rioted, many of them were arrested. More than 125 opposition legislators were detained, too, on grounds that they had encouraged the students. The leaders of the opposition declared that under these circumstances it would be impossible to have a free election in 1969. They announced that they would not participate in the campaigning. Ayub ordered the army to put down student riots more harshly. In East Pakistan, meanwhile, general strikes were called to protest what was said to be police brutality.

But the riots continued. Desperately President Ayub Khan announced that he would withdraw from office as soon as national free elections could be arranged. He arrested two of his major opponents, Zulfikar Ali Bhutto, one of the legislators who supported students; and Sheikh Mujib-ur Rahman, leader of the opposition in East Pakistan. To conciliate the rioters, he released both men. It was too late. His offer to resign produced only greater anger. In East Pakistan farmers sought to destroy any sign of Ayub Khan's power. Government officials were hunted down; some public buildings were burned; rent collectors and Basic Democrats were beaten and a few were lynched.

The pressure was more than Ayub Khan could bear. ". . . conditions are now beyond the power of the government," he announced. ". . . every problem of the country is now being solved in the streets . . . . There is no legal and effective organ remaining, other than the defense forces." On March 25, 1969, more than a decade after he himself had taken power and declared martial law, another general replaced him to do the same. His successor, Agha Muhammad Yahya Khan, commander-in-chief of the army, became the third military man to head Pakistan's government.

President Yahya Khan said that he would permit his country's first general elections to be held in 1970. In order to achieve national stability, he said, Pakistan must undertake "the difficult challenge (of) . . . abolishing poverty and ignorance from the country." Responsive to the demands of the ethnic groups, he dissolved One Unit and permitted local government to be restored. In October, instead of election through the Basic Democrats, there were direct elections in the provinces. Power was decentralized, to the relief of many social groups who had been protesting their loss of independence. Yahya Khan encouraged the nation to resume its striving toward the goal of true parliamentary democracy with guaranteed rights.

While seeking to meet many of the popular objections to the former administration, President Yahya strengthened the army's control over Pakistan. The 1962 constitution and the national and regional assemblies were dissolved. Military courts were established. No court, legislature, or assemblage of groups was left with the power to challenge the president's authority.

Like his predecessor, President Yahya said that his government was a bridge leading toward full democracy. Through consultation with the leaders of student, labor, and consumer and tenant groups he instituted a series of reforms. He acknowledged that the wide division between rich and poor was one of the central problems of Pakistan's government. Although political parties opposed to him were not permitted to level open criticism of his administration, they were allowed to organize. He promised that a national election would be held by 1972.

These promises did not quiet the opposition, however. In East Pakistan there were ceaseless demands for local autonomy based on the differences between Pakistan's two wings. At length, in December, 1970, Yahya Khan was prompted to issue a stern declaration, Martial Law Regulation Number 60, "Political Activities Regulation." In it he said, in a statement reminiscent of the ones leading to the decline of President Ayub, that "No political party shall propagate any opinion or act in a manner prejudicial to the ideology or the integrity or the security of Pakistan." This document withdrew any right to free speech. No public meeting could be held without the consent of the government. No one who had been jailed could run for public office for five years after the end of his sentence. Yahya thus became Pakistan's absolute ruler. His generals were given control of the newly autonomous provinces. Military men became judges who were responsible to Yahya, their commander-in-chief.

The elections that Yahya Khan promised were held. They led, however, not to the reconciliation of Pakistan's diverse groups, but to disaster. In East Pakistan the most energetic political party was the Awami ("People's") League. Organized in 1949, it was led by Sheikh Mujib-ur Rahman, whose goal was independence for East Pakistan. With more than 56 percent of the country's population, East Pakistan argued that it could not be governed from West Pakistan. The people of East Pakistan were angered by what they regarded as exploitation by the West Pakistanis who comprised more than 85 percent of the major government administrators. When the British left the sub-continent the average income in West Pakistan exceeded the average in East Pakistan by 10 percent. By 1970, the difference was more than 60 percent.

Sheikh Mujib's domestic program was basically socialist, calling for the nationalization of land and basic industries. He thus gained the bitter opposition of wealthy members of the government of West Pakistan. They could not forget that he not only opposed their religious program, but their political and economic status as well.

Tibetan features are evident in this Bengali tea picker.

Although he was a Muslim, the Sheikh resisted any interpretation of Islam that supported economic monopolies—a tendency in the government of West Pakistan.

The election campaign of 1970 pitted two major coalitions against one another. The Awami League and other groups which sought either autonomy or independence for East Pakistan were on one side. On the other side were the military men and incumbent officials who supported President Yahya Khan. To open the campaign, the president announced that the National Assembly would be chosen through a general election and that it would be asked to write a new constitution. Martial law would be ended when a new government was prepared to take over. That would mean greater participation in government by all citizens; more free elections would insure more democracy.

In the 1970 election the Awami League won 167 of the 313 seats in the National Assembly. This solid bloc of power startled West Pakistan's incumbent officials. They feared that East Pakistan, resentful of its distance from the central government, would attempt to control the assembly or even to divide the country. Z. A. Bhutto had won the second largest majority. At his request the central government announced that the National Assembly would not convene on March 3 as promised. This move was met by violent protests in East Pakistan. On March 23, 1970, East Pakistan declared itself independent. The stage thus was set for a tragedy of enormous proportions.

On the night of March 25, the government in West Pakistan ordered the army to crush the rebels. Equipped with tanks, machine guns, and bomb-laden planes, the army moved swiftly through East Pakistan. The soldiers were treated as invading enemies. East Pakistan became the scene of massive destruction and murder. With the arrest of Sheikh Mujib for treason, the badly equipped rebels began to fight West Pakistan, using sticks and obsolete guns against modern weapons. The result, according to later estimates, was the death of more than three million people, including many women and children. More than ten million refugees began to stream across the border into India.

As we have seen, this movement of refugees and the struggle inside of East Pakistan drew India into the civil war. Hostilities between India and Pakistan broke out in December, 1971. Each side accused the other of violating its territories, and a full-scale war began. On December 16, Indian forces captured Dacca with the help of the East Pakistani guerrillas. Pakistan quickly surrendered; East Pakistan declared itself to be the new nation of Bangladesh.

Reduced to less than half of its former size, Pakistan underwent dramatic change. President Yahya Khan resigned and was replaced by his antagonist, Bhutto, who had won 80 of the 130 National Assembly seats in the election. In what had been East Pakistan, meanwhile, Bangladesh, bleeding and impoverished, began its history as an independent nation under the leadership of Sheikh Mujib.

THE POSTWAR NATIONS

Pakistan: internal politics. The rise of Z. A. Bhutto to the presidency marked the end of the army's long domination of politics in Pakistan. The military was blamed for the division of the country and for the widespread misery that had been caused by the civil war. As head of the Pakistan People's Party (PPP) that had won most of West Pakistan's National Assembly seats, Bhutto stood in opposition to the army. Immediately upon taking office he therefore proposed to change Pakistan's basic political orientation. Bhutto declared himself to be a socialist whose goal was to create a more general distribution of wealth in Pakistan. To understand why this was a popular cause, it is necessary to examine the history of great wealth in Pakistan.

In an agricultural economy, land is the most valuable resource. Mogul leaders had claimed ownership of most of the best land soon after their invasion of the region that was to become Pakistan. Under the British, descendents of these Moguls were chosen to be tax collectors. However, the tax collectors were not paid by the British. Rather, they were permitted to keep whatever funds they could collect above the amounts required by the government. Small land-owners fell increasingly into debt to the tax collectors. In 1793, the British passed the Permanent Settlement Act, under which the tax collectors were permitted to convert debts owed to them to direct ownership. The Act also allowed the revenue collectors to will the land that they gained to their heirs, thus establishing a permanent class of wealthy landowners (*zamindars*). In exchange for these privileges the landowners agreed to turn over approximately ten-elevenths of their revenues to the British. By the time Pakistan achieved independence in 1947, this fixed percentage was much different from the amounts originally anticipated. The increasing population and rising prices and land values meant that the landlords could collect much more for themselves than in previous years. Many of them invested these gains in land and other properties. Thus the zamindars acquired substantial power which often enabled them to exert a far greater influence on government than the propertyless classes.

With their profits assured, the landlords often sublet their land and moved to the cities to live sumptuously. Their tenants usually had the right to sublet and often did. This process of subletting might continue forty or fifty times, leaving farmers in debt to a long chain of unknown creditors. While many farmers were able to preserve their right to own a half acre of land, many more were forced to work on the enormous holdings of the zamindars. In recent years, the government of Pakistan has tried to reduce these holdings. Landowners were permitted to retain a maximum of 500 acres of irrigated land or 1,000 acres of non-irrigated land. But by this time a few families had accumulated vast amounts of wealth. According to one estimate, twenty families control 80 percent of the banking, 97 percent of the insurance, and 66 percent of the capital invested in industry. When independence was achieved agricultural production accounted for 60 percent of Pakistan's gross national product. Today, because of increased industrialization, agriculture produced about 45 percent of the gross national product. But this new emphasis has not shifted control of the economy from the families who gained it in previous years.

Thus, Bhutto was applauded for announcing that he would attempt to redistribute wealth. Beginning with his inauguration, Bhutto addressed himself directly to the people rather than to its members of the propertied classes or the military. Soon after he took office the various political groups were permitted to become active again. They sought and gained an end to the martial law that had repressed freedoms in the country for years.

Bhutto next introduced an interim constitution, one borrowing from the Government of India Act of 1935 and the Indian Independence Act of 1947. Meanwhile, the new government commenced work on the draft of a new permanent constitution. Throughout its pronouncements the Bhutto government seemed to favor a strong president, but at the same time it conceded the need for local autonomy. The people were to choose their provincial presidents in direct elections. They would also choose the members of a National Assembly that was to be made up of two houses.

The degree of autonomy granted to the provinces proved to be one of the major problems in the drafting of the new constitution. As they had throughout Pakistan's history, the minorities in the provinces feared that they would be controlled by the Punjabi majority. Behind their hope for more autonomy lay the fact that East Pakistan, when dominated by a power which it could not accept, rebelled. It was possible that the fiery, militaristic Pathans, who occupy the mountainous area below the Khyber Pass, might seek a similar course if the government failed to recognize their differences with the Punjabis.

Bhutto's search for a new form of government, when combined with his socialist principles, earned him many enemies. In 1977 a group of military officers stormed his offices and arrested him, ending his seven years as president. In his place they installed Mohammad Zia-ul-Haq, who promptly placed the country under martial law and declared that Bhutto would be tried for the murder of an adversary. Zia formed an agency known as the Higher Command Council, consisting of the president, prime minister, defense minister, and the chiefs of the army, navy, and air force. He said this group would have a permanent place in government.

Zia's martial control of Pakistan might soon have weakened, as others had before him, if not for the Soviet Union's invasion of Afghanistan in 1979. Zia seized upon the war in a neighboring country to tighten his grip on his own land. He censored the press and forbade all political activity. Soldiers placed his leading critics under arrest; and Bhutto, whose party was still a threat, was exe-

This Pathan tribesman is rarely separated from his rifle.

cuted. According to Amnesty International, there were more than six thousand political prisoners in Pakistan in 1982, and almost two hundred of them had been severely tortured.

Confident of his authority, Zia declared that "The president as the chief martial law administrator shall have and shall be deemed always to have had the power to amend the constitution." This order nullified any action by the courts to restore the constitution of 1973. But it reached deeper into Pakistani society as the war in Afghanistan began to create problems for the whole region. More than twenty-eight million refugees streamed over the border, victims of Soviet bombs. Drugs became widespread, imported both from Afghanistan and from the Arab countries of the Middle East. The number of drug addicts in Pakistan rose from one hundred to more than three hundred thousand during 1982-84 alone. American guns poured into the country. They were meant to help Afghans resist their attackers but often were turned to criminal use.

All of these problems were a major factor in what has become known as "islamization" in the Middle East. From the time that Israel was founded in 1948, Arab countries have tended to become more religious. They expressed a measure of Islamic unity during the 1970's by forming the nucleus of the Organization of Petroleum Exporting Countries (OPEC). This group quickly raised the price of oil to record levels. Hoping to find solace for military defeats and grievances against colonialism, they were further propelled towards religion when the people of Iran overthrew their Western-minded ruler, the Shah, in 1979. A worldwide movement for "islamization"—a stricter adherence to the laws of Islam—followed. It was largely financed by OPEC's leading and richest member, Saudi Arabia. In 1984 President Zia placed this measure on a national ballot in Pakistan:

> *Do you support Pakistan President Zia's program which he has started to bring Pakistan laws in line with the Islamic principles, in accordance with the injunction of the Holy Quran and the Holy Prophet—peace be upon him—and to safeguard Pakistan's ideology; and do you support the continuance, the further strengthening of this program and the transfer of power to the elected representatives of the people in an organized and peaceful manner?*

Pakistan's Islamic clergy quickly rallied behind the measure and, as a result, behind Zia. Since people could only vote either yes or no and heard of no opposition, they voted overwhelmingly to support what they believed to be their religious faith. But at the same time they were supporting Zia, who claimed a nationwide mandate reaching 98 percent. He felt strong enough by 1986 to revive the constitution, while at the same time he kept the repressive laws governing treason, subversion, freedom of speech and movement. He continued to control the Supreme Court.

Before he would agree to limit his martial law order, Zia demanded certain protections for himself and other officials who had been accused of torture and murder. He required that the legislature pass a law which indemnified the administration for all of its past actions. "For all practical purposes," his opposition declared, "martial law is being perpetuated in civilian form." But Zia responded that he had clearly moved the country towards greater freedoms, and he uttered this ambiguous threat: "Anyone trying to derail the train of democracy will have to face terrible consequences."

Zia was apparently addressing himself to the large and probably growing group of Pakistanis who resented his execution of his predecessor, General Bhutto. Zia had punished the whole Bhutto family, but had allowed the late President's daughter, Benazir, to join her mother in London. As Zia began to lift martial law this young woman returned to Pakistan to the triumphant cheers of thousands of people. She became the focus of the opposition, openly threatening to overturn the administration, but was allowed to speak.

Some foods, such as the fruits and vegetables shown here, are plentiful in Pakistan. Others, including much needed proteins, are in short supply.

Zia's embrace of islamization, however, seemed to have gained him the support of Muslim leaders who held almost unshakeable power. His religious orthodoxy affected all Pakistanis. Women complained that they had fewer freedoms than ever. In 1982, women field hockey teams were forbidden to play in front of men, for example, and women who did not veil themselves in public were frowned upon. Religious courts ordered the public flogging of adulterers or young people found to have become sexual before marriage. The hands of pickpockets were removed. The campaigns against alcohol and tobacco became more vigorous. Though Pakistan has one of the highest birth rates in the world, birth control was forbidden. By 1986, the country's population soared over 95 million.

The war in Afghanistan had economic consequences as well as social ones. The growth of the economy declined as more and more money was poured into arms. A rate of 7 percent growth in 1978 had slumped to less than 5 percent by the mid-1980's. Inflation was running almost 10 percent a year, and the balance of payments deficit was at record levels. Luckily, by 1986 oil, which accounted for more than a quarter of all imports, was declining sharply in price, offering greater hope for recovery.

Foreign relations. Much of Pakistan's foreign policy has been based on its relations with India. Because of its conflicts with India in 1948, 1965, and 1971, and because of its continuing dispute with India over Jammu and Kashmir, Pakistan has sought military alliances. Muslim countries throughout the world have agreed to these alliances, further arousing India's fears. The Indians believe that Pakistan has been using its growing atomic industry to manufacture atomic bombs. They have also resented Pakistan's efforts to submit the Kashmir dispute to international judges, despite an agreement in 1972 that the issue would be settled by the two countries alone. Pakistan's growing military budget has been a major concern. Relations have improved since Rajiv Gandhi's rise to power in India, however, and communications between the leaders of the two countries are warmer.

Of all of Pakistan's friends, the United States has proved the most generous. American aid has increased in direct proportion to the Soviet threat at the borders. The Americans have sent F-16 jet fighters as well as other military and economic aid. Despite this help from the U.S., however, Pakistan's government continues to insist that it is "nonaligned" between the two great powers.

The Soviet Union's invasion of Afghanistan has also enabled Pakistan to gain more economic, scientific, and economic aid from the People's P ~ublic of China. Communist China had first begun to support Pakistan during the 1971 war with India, no doubt to preserve its relationship with the long line of Muslim countries extending into the Middle East. At that time the Soviets were courting India, seeming to resent Pakistan's U.S. ties, and this attitude continues. In addition to China, Pakistan has developed good relationships with other Asian countries, especially Japan, which has sent substantial loans, trade, and technical advice.

THE FUTURE OF PAKISTAN

Historically, it has been difficult for the diverse political movements to develop in countries as deeply committed to a single religion as Pakistan. The party which gains the unified support of the clergy generally emerges triumphant. This has been so in Pakistan, and it has greatly benefited conservative military groups. Together with the Islamic faith, the military has been one of the most unified and influential social forces.

The external threats to Pakistan, combined with its lack of resources, make it likely that the military will continue to hold power. With less than 25 percent literacy, Pakistanis are poorly informed. The combined circulation of all of the country's newspapers is only about 700,000, though there are more than 95 million Pakistanis. Language differences and the lack of education compound the social problems merely compound the difficulty in a country where the annual per capita income is just $280.

Thus it seems unrealistic to expect democracy in Pakistan. Religious fervor and military control there suggest that, at best, the world can hope that Pakistan will remain stable and self-contained and seeks neither war nor civil unrest as solutions to its problems.

BANGLADESH

Problems and policies. The civil war which brought independence to Bangladesh began less than four months after a cyclone and tidal wave ravaged some of the region's most populated areas. The high winds and waters killed tens of thousands of people, either directly or by rendering them homeless and without food. Disease swept the land. Almost in the wake of this disaster, the Pakistani army confronted the starving, poorly armed guerillas who were seeking to form the new nation. A battle ensued for nine months; the Pakistani army, through superior numbers and machines, came close to crushing the dissidents. Again the destruction was widespread and severe.

When the war was over, the problems which resulted from these events were multiplied many times by the return of refugees from

Bangladesh contains a large Hindu minority.

India. More than ten million of them had settled in camps just over the Indian border. They came back when the war was over to find their homes destroyed and their possessions gone. Another ten million people who had not fled were made homeless by the war. There were few jobs. The war had destroyed many industries, farms, and farm implements.

Bleak as the economic picture was, it was not nearly as grim as the problem of health and welfare in Bangladesh. The country normally imported about one million tons of grain. Following the war, this quantity quadrupled. There were no funds to import food, nor any effective way to ship it to the people.

The starving millions in Bangladesh had committed themselves to the leadership of Sheikh Mujib. Yet it was evident that if his socialist program for the country did not remedy some of the hardships, more radical ideas might become appealing to them. Influenced by Communist China, there were many political activists who were calling for the "Chinese solution" to the problems of

Bangladesh. While opposing this group, Sheikh Mujib had also to restrain others which wanted to punish collaborators with Pakistan during the civil war. Many of these collaborators lived in the region of Bihar in the north, where violence later broke out against the 1.5 million inhabitants.

At last discontent led to Sheikh Mujib's assassination in 1974, and the bewildered population was plunged into a series of economic and political disasters. As floods, declining markets, and military coups plagued the country, workers began to strike for higher wages. The resulting chaos made some political leaders more determined than ever to install a dictator in the government.

For a time it appeared that Ziaur Rahman, founder of the Nationalist Party in 1978, might gain and keep a place as the country's strongest leader. Elected President, he outlawed most of his critics, focusing on the communists who had led the strikes. Then he, too, was assassinated. The winner of absolute power, it turned out after a period of confusion was the Army Chief of Staff, Lt. General H.M. Ershad.

In 1982 Ershad seized control of government, running it either directly or through a puppet. He executed many of his critics and silenced most others by threatening to arrest them for "crimes against the state." Students found themselves facing the guns of Ershad's army when they protested their loss of freedoms and declining educational standards. Public officials were hanged for what Ershad called "corruption."

Ershad declared that the country needed a strong leader to prevent its collapse. Severe floods took 1,000 lives, destroyed 60,000 homes, and ruined 5 million acres of rice crops in 1982. They affected more than 30 million people. In response, Ershad declared full martial law and forbade activity by all political parties. He closed universities and ordered a curfew in Dhaka, the capital. By these actions Ershad cancelled the elections which he had been promising for years. It was apparent that the people supported him overwhelmingly, he said, from the results of local elections which all three hundred of his supporters won.

Not everyone in Bangladesh quailed before Ershad's threats. Small opposition parties united into the Movement for the Restoration of Democracy (MRD). This group demanded that Ershad at least allow them to organize votes. But though it won some local support, the MRD failed to ignite much enthusiasm among the wider population. Overriding its complaints, Ershad extended his own term and continued to rule under martial law.

The turmoil in Bangladesh sprang chiefly from the widespread poverty, which in turn resulted from complex problems involving land, climate, and culture. Probably the central problem was the size and growth of the population. With an area slightly less than the state of Georgia, it now contains more than 100 million people. Its population is increasing at the rate of at least 2.8 percent annually and so may soon total more than half of the number of Americans. More than 8,000 infants are born in Bangladesh every day.

To revitalize the economy, Ershad has sold off almost all of the industries which had previously been nationalized. He shut down any state-owned companies which were losing money and opened the country's leading industries to foreign investors. As some funds arrived for the potentially profitable jute, fertilizer, sugar, and mineral industries, production improved. Bangladesh moved closer to the ability to feed itself but still was far from that goal. In most years it had to import two to three times the amount that it sold overseas.

The struggling country has received considerable help from abroad. Loans have poured in from China, Europe, the United States, including nations which have formed the Bangladesh Aid Consortium. Within six months after the disastrous civil war the U.S. sent more than $275 million, almost half of the amount requested by the United Nations to aid Bangladesh in 1972. India gave $80 million in money and equipment and sent technical advisers to help in reconstruction. India continues to work for a stronger Bangladesh, though it has become alarmed by the growing use of Ganges River waters and the tide of refugees that has been coming from the north. Finally, the World Bank has been generous with its help.

Detachment from Pakistan has opened new trading opportunities for Bangladesh, particularly from India. China, Japan, and the United States have done everything possible to buy the country's products. But hopes in Bangladesh are often crushed by natural disasters, rising population, and political turmoil. The per capita income was just $105 a year in the 1980s, and the life expectancy at birth was just 46 years. Only a quarter of the people were literate. Thus Bangladesh, wobbling to its feet in the first years of its history, faces a longer period of desperation before it can expect stability.

APPENDIX A

STATISTICAL PROFILE OF ASIAN NATIONS

All figures were assembled in 1986, reflecting data obtained earlier. They are given for relative purposes only and should not be considered currently precise.

1. Population in millions.
2. Area of country in 000's sq.mi.
3. Population density per sq. mi.
4. Percentage population increases.*

5. Years for population to double.
6. Average life expectancy at birth.
7. Per capita income in dollars.∤
8. GNP in billions of dollars.

	1.	2.	3.	4.	5.	6.	7.	8.
Bangladesh	98.7	55	1,775	2.7	27	48	130	105
Burma	37.6	261	144	2.5	28	55	180	5.6
China	1,043	3,696	282	1.2	60	67	296	301
India	768	1,183	605	2.2	32	52	260	190
Indonesia	167	741	226	1.7	42	52	560	87
Japan	121	147	827	0.6	120	76	10,100	1,204
Kampuchea	7.2	69	104	2.5	27	45	159	1.1
Laos	4.1	91	45	1.7	42	50	152	.6
Malaysia	15	127	122	2.4	30	70	1,870	27
Pakistan	100	307	326	2.7	27	50	370	35
Philippines	54	116	472	2.5	28	64	760	39
Singapore	2.5	239	10,704	1.1	65	73	7,100	16
Taiwan	19.1	14	1,376	1.4	51	72	3,040	46
Thailand	51	198	258	1.8	40	63	812	40
Vietnam	60	128	462	2.5	27	52	170	1

*World average, 1.8; U.S, .7
∤U.S., $16,270

APPENDIX B

GUIDE TO THE PRONOUNCIATION OF INDIAN WORDS

When they appear in standard transliterations of Indian words, the letters given below indicate original sounds closely resembling the English shown in parentheses after them:

a (as i in it), o (oh), u (uh), a (ah), i (ee), u (oo), e (ay), ai (i), au (ow), c (ch), s (occasionally as sh). Stress is usually given to the next to the last or to the third from the last syllable of the word.

APPENDIX C

GLOSSARY

Agni (AH-gnee)—Aryan god of fire, worshipped as the protector of man and his home.
Agra (AH-grah)—City in north India, site of the Taj Mahal.
ahimsa (Ah-HIM-sah)—The Jain doctrine of nonviolence.

arhat (AHR-hat)—A Buddhist worthy of Nirvana.

Arjuna (ahr-JUNE-ah)—The warrior in the *Mahabharata* to whom the god Krishna related the *Bhagavad-Gita*.

Artha (ARCH-ah)—The Second End of Man in Hinduism: the pursuit of material wealth.

Arthasastra (arth-ah-SHAS-trah)—"Economic Science": a political treatise by Kautilya.

Asoka (ah-SHOK-ah)—The "philosopher-king" of the Maurya period, a Buddhist who renounced warfare. (Also Ashoka.)

asuras (as-SHUR-ahs)—Demons and enemies of the Hindu gods.

atman (AHT-mon)—The divine essence in man that seeks to become one with Brahman.

bania (bah-NEE-ah)—An Indian moneylender.

Bhagavad-Gita (BAH-gas-vad GEE-tah)—The part of the *Mahabharata* called "The Lord's Song," which the god Krishna related to the warrior Arjuna.

bhoodan (BHOO-dahn)—Program introduced by the Indian, Vinoba Bhave, calling for gifts of land to the poor.

Bodhisattva (bod-HIS-aht-vah)—A saintly Buddhist of the Mahayana school who postpones going to Nirvana in order to help others in the world.

Brahman (BRAH-mahn)—The Supreme Reality, with whom all Hindus seek union. (May be Brahma.)

brahman (BRAH-mahn)—Hinduism's highest class: teachers and priests. (Also brahmin.)

Buddha (BOO-dah)—"The Enlightened One" of India, Prince Gautama or his images.

candala (chan-DAHL-ah)—The lowest group of Indian Untouchables; menials in India.

chettyara (CHET-yar-ah)—Indian merchant group residing in Burma.

dasyus (DAHS-yous)—Dark-skinned Indians who were enslaved by Aryan invaders.

dharma (DHAR-ma)—Hinduism's First End of Man: the laws and duties which dominated the lives of all hindus.

dhyana (dh-YAN-ah)—The Indian word "meditation," which was adopted by Japanese Zen Buddhists.

Durga (DUR-gah)—An eighteen-armed form of Siva's consort, Parvati.

Gautama Siddhartha (GAU-tamah SID-harth-ah)—The prince later called Buddha, founder of the great philosophical religion, Buddhism.

ghats (gahts)—"Hills," or "mountains" in India.

ghazi (GHAH-zee)—A Muslim "slayer of infidels."

gupta (GUPT-ah)—The classical period of Indian civilization.

harijan (HAH-ree-jahn)—The word meaning "Children of God," given by Gandhi to the Untouchables.

hartal (har-'tahl)—A day of worship used as a form of economic strike by followers of Gandhi.

Hegira (HEE-ji-rah)—The "Flight of Muhammed" from Mecca to Medina in 622 A.D., the first year in the Islamic calendar.

Hinayana Buddhism—See "Theravada Buddhism."

Indra (IN-drah)—The chief Aryan god of war.

Jain (jine)—An ancient Indian sect that preaches nonviolence and self-denial.

jati (JAH-tee)—An Indian word meaning subcaste.

jiva (JEE-vah)—"Conqueror": the Jain concept of a liberated soul that escapes rebirth.

Kali (KAH-lee)—The Hindu goddess of destruction; consort of Siva.

kama (KAH-mah)—Hinduism's Third End of Man: the pursuit of pleasure.

karma (KAHR-mah)—The matter around the soul, formed as a moral consequence of one's actions, which determines the station of rebirth.

khaddar (KHAD-dahr)—"One's own cotton"; the rough, home-made cloth that became symbolic of India's struggle for freedom.

Krishna (KRISH-nah)—A benevolent Hindu god, one of the incarnations of Vishnu.

kshatriya (CHAT-ree-yuh)—The second-highest, or warrior class in Hindu society.

Ladakh (lahd-AKH)—A region between Tibet and India that has often been claimed by China.

Laksmi (LAHX-me)—The gentle consort of the Hindu god, Vishnu.

Mahabharata (mah-HAB HARAH-tha)—The philosophical epic poem of India which means literally, "Great India."

Mahatma (mah-HAT-mah)—"Great Soul"—a Hindu title given M. K. Gandhi by his followers.

Mahayana Buddhism (MAH-ha YARN-ah BOOD-ism)—"The Great Vehicle": a major school of Indian Buddhism which altered the religion, permitting new saints (bodhisattvas) in order to increase its appeal.

Maurya (MOR-ya)—The earliest historical dynasty established in northern India.

maya (MY-yah)—The Indian concept of illusion for which man pays with rebirth.

Mogul (MOHG-ul)—A dynasty established by Islamic Turks in India. (Also Mughul.)

Mohenjo-Daro (moe-HEN-joe-dah-ROE)—The earliest culture known in Asia, formed in the Indus Valley ca. 4000 B.C.

moksha (MOK-sha)—Hinduism's Fourth End of Man: deliverance from rebirth.

Monsoon (mon-SOON)—"Season" in Arabic: the intense, recurring rainstorms in sub-tropical Asia.

mudra (MOO-drah)—Hand positions, each having meaning, in Buddhist icons.

Muslim. (MUSH-lim)—A believer in Islam; a follower of Muhammad. (Also Moslem.)

nataka (na-TAH-kah)—Indian drama of the Gupta period.

Panchatantra (PAHN-cha-TAHN-tra)—Collection of children's tales about animals in ancient India; resembles Aesop's *Fables.*

Parvati (PAR-vah-tee)—The benevolent counterpart of Kali; the Hindu goddess of feminity and the wife of Siva.

Puranas (pur-AHN-ash)—A collection of post-Vedic Hindu legends and religious instructions.

purdah (PUR-dah)—The practice of seclusion of women in Muslim societies, character-ized by the wearing of veils in public.

rajputs (RAJ-puts)—A sub-caste of the kshatriya class in Indian society.

Rama (RAHM-ah)—The hero of the epic, *Ramayana;* symbol of light and goodness.

reincarnation (re-incarn-A-shun)—The belief that man is reborn when he fails to live according to the moral codes of his society.

Rig-Veda (RIG VAY-dah)—The first Vedic text; the basis of Brahmanism.

sati (SAH-tee)—Female devotion in India. The condition which Hindu widows achieve in full measure when they throw themselves upon the burning pyres of their husbands. (Also suttee.)

satori (sah-tor-e)—"Sudden Enlightenment" in Zen Buddhism.

satyagraha (SUT-yah-gruh-ha)—"Truth Force": Gandhi's nonviolent demonstrations.

Sikh (sick)—A member of a benevolent brotherhood in the Punjab which became aggres-sive after it was persecuted by Aurangzeb.

Sita (SHEET-ah)—The consort of Rama in Hinduism; the symbol of female loyalty.

Sitting Dharna (DHAR-nah)—A nonviolent tactic: sitting until an injustice or social ill is remedied; sometimes the fasting unto death.

Siva (SHE-vah)—"The Destroyer," the Hindu god of reproduction. (Also Shiva.)

stupa (stoo-pah)—Burial mounts, or domed temples, supposed to contain some remains of Gautama Buddha.

sudra (SOOD-RAH)—The fourth, or menial class in Hindu society.

sutra (SOO-trah)—"Thread," or Buddhist parable in India.

swadeshi (swah-DESH-she)—The Indian practice, introduced by Gandhi, of boycotting English goods.

swaraj (SWAH-rahj)—The Indian demand for self-rule during the British occupation; the word itself means "freedom."

Theravada Buddhism (THERA-vahda BOOD-ism)—"The Lesser Vehicle": a major branch of Buddhism, which stresses that the individual can become enlightened and achieve Nirvana only through his own efforts. (See "Mahayana Buddhism.")

thuggee (THUG-ee)—Hindu secret society which offered human sacrifices to Kali.

transmigration (trans-mi-GRAY-shun)—Hindu and Buddhist concept that the soul is reborn unless Nirvana is achieved.

Tripitika (trih-PIH-tih-kah)—"Three Baskets": the major collection of Buddhist doctrines, comprising the "Bible" of Buddhism.

Untouchables—Outcastes, considered below the four major classes of Hindu society.

Upanishads (uh-pahn-EE-shads)—Philosophical treatises which are a basic source of Hinduism.

Vaisyas (VAIHS-yahs)—The third, or commercial class of Hindu society.

varna (VARH-nah)—A ritual class color, or class, in India.

Varuna (vah-RUHN-nah)—The chief Vedic god, who possesses all knowledge.

Vedas (VEH-dahs)—Ancient Aryan religious texts from which the religion of Brahmanism was developed in India.

Vishnu (VISH-noo)—The benevolent god of the Hindu Triad (Vishnu, Siva, Brahma); he is the protector of mankind.

Yakshis (YAK-shes)—Minor Hindu gods, considered "good" and usually identified with the cult of fertility.

yoga (YO-gah)—The practice of "involvement without attachment" inherent in various Hindu religious activities.

zamindari (zah-MIN-dah-ree)—Indian tax-collectors whom the British permitted to take title to the land in payment of debts.

APPENDIX D

BIBLIOGRAPHY

The mark (*) indicates a book especially useful for young readers, as well as for adults.

Journals & Periodicals (to 1986)

Encyclopedia Brittanica Yearbook, Asian Survey (Berkeley: University of California Press); American-Asian Review (New York: St. John's University); Asian Pacific Community (Tokyo: Asian Club).

Books: General

AGARWALA, P.N. *The History of Indian Business.* New York: Advent, 1985.
   A text which traces the ancient origins and modern role of India's commerce.

AKBAR, M.J. *India: The Siege Within.* Baltimore: Penguin, 1985.
   A clear, wide-ranging study of Indian politics.

BALASUBRAMANYAM, V.N. *The Economy of India.* Boulder: Westview, 1985.
   A careful study of how caste, class, and modern technology are mixed.

BASHAM, ARTHUR L. *The Wonder that Was India.* New York: Macmillan, 1954; Grove, 1959; ✓ Sidgwick & Jackson, 1983.
   The best available survey of India's pre-Muslim culture, illustrated.

_____ (ed.). *A Cultural History of India.* Oxford: Oxford University Press, 1975.
   India's enormous contributions to the arts and sciences are assembled here.

BETEILLE, ANDRE (ed.). *Equality and Inequality: Theory and Practice.* Oxford: Oxford University Press, 1985.
   Analyzes the astounding complexities in Indian society.

*BOWLES, CHESTER. *Promises to Keep.* New York: Harper & Row, 1972.
   A compassionate, informative view by the former ambassador.

*BOWLES, CYNTHIA. *At Home in India.* New York: Pyramid Books, 1962. (Paperback).
   The daughter of an American ambassador in India tells her colorful story.

BROWN, JUDITH M. *Modern India: The Origins of an Asian Democracy.* Oxford: Oxford University Press, 1984.
   "Short Oxford History of the Modern World Series."

CAMBRIDGE UNIVERSITY. *Cambridge History of India.* 6 vols. Mystic, Conn.: Verry, 1955-70.
   The most complete and scholarly work of its kind.

CARMICHAEL, JOEL. *The Shaping of the Arabs.* New York: The Macmillan Co., 1967.
   A thorough and valuable study of a primary influence in Indian history.

CHANDRA, BIPAN. *Communalism in Modern India.* New York: Advent, 1984.
   Analyzes the chauvinism which all too often has ended in violence.

*DEBARY, W.T. (ed.) *Sources of Indian Tradition.* New York: Columbia University Press, 1958.
   The best available compilation of original works about India.

DUTT, ASHOK K. & GEIB, MARGARET. *An Atlas of south Asia.* Boulder: Westview, 1985.
Social, cultural, economic, historical, and geographic factors, with emphasis on India, in graphic and textual form.

✓*FORESTER, E.M. *A Passage to India.* New York: Harcourt Brace, 1971.
A great novel describing the relationship between East and West.

*GARRETT, G.T. (ed.). *The Legacy of India.* Oxford: The Clarendon Press, 1951.
Superb essays on India society, showing its religion, caste, music, science, and literature.

KANGAS, G.L. *Population and Survival in India.* London: Heinmann India, 1984.
Focuses on what may be the nation's most pressing problem.

✓ *LAMB, B.P. *India: A World in Transition.* New York: F.A. Praeger, 1963.
A brilliant and humane study of India's people and institutions.

✓ MABBETT, IAN W. *A Short History of India.* new York: Praeger, 1970.
An outline history, giving the main thrust of India's past.

*MARKANDAYA, KAMALA. *Nectar in a Sieve.* New York: Signet, 1963. (Paperback).
The vivid story of a South Indian family.

MEHTA, VED. *A Family Affair: India Under Three Prime Ministers.* Oxford: Oxford University Press, 1982.
How the Nehru family came to lead the world's largest democracy.

METCALF, T.R. *Modern Indian: An Interpretative Anthology.* New York: Macmillan, 1971.
A comprehensive view of Indian life.

NAIPAUL, V.S. *A Wounded Civilization.* New York: Random House, 1978.
One of the finest of modern Indian writers analyzes the burdens of history in the present.

NAKAMURA, HAJIME. *Ways of Thinking of Eastern Peoples.* Honolulu: East-West Center Press, 1964.
One of the most insightful books of its kind, covering India, China, Tibet, and Japan.

*NEHRU, JAWAHARLAL. *The Discovery of India.* New York: John Day, 1946.
Reflections on India by one of her greatest statesmen.

SHINN, RINN-SUP, *et al. Area Handbook for India.* Washington, D.C.: U.S. Government Printing Office, 1969.
A guidebook including statistics and maps, to all aspects of India.

SMITH, VINCENT. *The Oxford History of India.* Oxford: Oxford University Press, 1981.
Offers a wide if often pedantic view.

*SEAR, PERCIVAL. *The Oxford History of Modern India: 1740-1975.* Oxford: Oxford University Press, 1978.
A companion to *The Oxford History of India.* (*See* Smith, Vincent, above.).

Politics, Economics, and Government

AGARWALA, P.N. *The History of Indian Business.* New York: Advent, 1985.
A text which traces the ancient origins and modern role of India's commerce.

BANDYOPADHYAYA. J. *The Making of India's Foreign Policy.* New York: Paragon, 1970.
Traces India's course from nonalignment to publication.

BARNDS, WILLIAM J. *India, Pakistan, and the Great Powers.* New York: Praeger, 1972.
Explains the alliances in the ongoing conflict.

BROWN, D.M. *The White Umbrella: Indian Political Thought from Manu to Gandhi.* Berkeley: University of California Press, 1982.
A wide-ranging compilation of works by India's most influential thinkers.

_____. *The Nationalist Movement: Indian Political Thought from Ranadeto Bhave.* Berkeley: University of California Press, 1962.
A later companion to *The White Umbrella.*

FISCHER, LOUIS. *The Essential Gandhi.* New York: Random House, 1962.
A collection of important statements by Gandhi, organized in the form of a narrative that is richly annotated by a knowledgeable author.

FRANKEL, FRANCINE R. *India's Green Revolution: Political Costs of Economic Growth.* Princeton: Princeton University Press, 1971.
One of the few works about the consequences of agricultural change in India.

*GANDHI, M.K. *The Story of My Experiments with Truth.* Washington D.C.: Public Affairs Press, 1948.
The great teacher's own discussion of his methods and ideals.

MORAES, FRANK. *Jawaharlal nehru*. New York: The Macmillan Co., 1956.
Early but thorough to its date, by a distinguished journalist who knew Nehru well.

NANDA, B. *Mahatma Gandhi: A Political Biography*. London: Allen and Unwin, 1958.
A competent study of Gandhi's life, thought, and teachings.

PALMER, NORMAN. *The Indian Political System*. Boston: Houghton Mifflin, 1961.
An analysis of Indian politics and foreign relations.

ROBINSON, E.A. AND ROBINSON, MICHAEL (eds.). *Economic Development in South Asia*. New York: St. Martin's Press, 1970.
A regional view of economic strengths and weaknesses.

SALETORE, B.A. *Ancient Indian Political Thought and Institutions*. New York: Asia Publishing House, 1971.
Traces the roots of enduring ideas.

SWAMY, SUBRAMANIAN. *Indian Economic Planning: An Alternative Approach*. New York: Barnes & Noble, 1972.
Stresses the uniqueness and values of Indian planning.

*VAID, K.B. *Steps in the Darkness*. New York: Orion Press, 1962.
A realistic novel of modern India, showing the conflict of old and new ideas.

VENKATASUBBIAH, H. *Anatomy of Indian Planning*. Mystic, Conn.: Verry, 1969.
A useful description of methods and goals.

Religion and Philosophy

*CAMPBELL, JOSEPH. *The Masks of God: Oriental Mythology*. New York: Viking, 1962.
Brilliant discussions of Asian mythology, with contrasts to the West.

_____. *The Hero with a Thousand Faces*. New York: Pantheon Books, 1961.
A unique work suggesting that one image is the basis for many gods.

DEBARY, WILLIAM THEODORE. *The Buddhist Tradition in India, China and Japan*. New York: Random House, 1972. (Paperback).
The best available short collection of original material and commentary.

ELIOT, C.N. *Hinduism and Buddhism*. 3 vols. New York: Barnes and Noble, 1957.
An excellent standard work on India's greatest religions.

MAJUNDAR, R.C. (ed.). *The Vedic Age*. London: Allen and Unwin, 1951. ✓
Essays by Indian scholars on India's formative culture.

SEN, K.M. *Hinduism*. Baltimore: Penguin Books, 1961.
A basic description of the origins and nature of the religion.

WEBER, MAX. *The Religions of India*. Glencoe: Free Press, 1958.
The pioneering sociologist traces the roots of Indian faith.

ZIMMER, H. *Philosophies of India*. New York: Pantheon Books, 1951.
An outstanding work, based on Sanskrit and other primary sources.

Sociology and Customs

DAS GUPTA, JYOTIRINDRA. *Language Conflict and National Development*. Berkeley: University of California Press, 1970.
An exposition of one of India's most critical problems.

DUBOIS J.A. *Hindu Manner, Customs, and Ceremonies*. Oxford: The Clarendon Press, 1959.
Deals with a cultural subject which scholarly works often ignore.

ISSACS, HAROLD. *India's Ex-Untouchables*. New York: Harper & Row, 1972. (Paperback).
A noted scholar explains essentials of the caste system.

MACKAY, E.J. *Early Indus Civilizations*. London: Luzac, 1948.
A good survey, with emphasis on the Harappa culture.

*NAIR, KUSUM. *Blossoms in the Dust*. New York: F.A. Praeger, 1962.
A study of Indian social life in villages, showing evolving changes.

Literature and Art

*ANDERSON, G.L. *Masterpieces of the Orient*. New York: Norton, 1961.
Includes many Indian works.

*ASHTON, L. (ed.). *The Art of India and Pakistan*. New York: Coward-McCann, 1950.
A series of essays by Indian scholars on sculpture, bronzes, textiles, and paintings.

BROWN, PERCY. *Indian Architecture.* 2 vols. New York: Asia Publishing House, 1942.
An excellent study of Hindu, Buddhist, and Islamic influences on Indian architecture.

DASGUPTA, S. (ed.). *A History of Classical Sanskrit Literature.* New York: Asia Publishing House, 1947.
A comprehensive study, including generous selections.

*DUTT, R.C. (trans.). *Ramayana and Mahabharata.* New York: Dutton, 1961.
A fine translation of India's two most famous epic tales.

*GARGI, BALWANT. *Theatre in India.* New York: Theatre Arts Books, 1962.
A good introduction to India's traditional and modern theater.

*GOETZ, HERMAN. *India: 5000 Years of Indian Art.* London: Methuen, 1959.
An excellent review of Indian sculpture, architecture, and painting.

*MASCARD, JUAN (trans.). *The Bhaqavad Gita.* Baltimore: Penguin Books, 1962.
A readable translation of one of India's most influential works.

NYROP, RICHARD F. *et al. Bangladesh: A Country Study.* Washington, D.C.: U.S. Government, 1975.
One volume of what may be the most comprehensive survey of foreign lands.

_____. *Pakistan: A Country Study.* Washington, D.C.: U.S. Government, 1983.
See above.

*ROWLAND, BENJAMIN. *The Art and Architecture of India.* Baltimore: Penguin Books, 1956.
A good introduction to the history and techniques of India's artists.

*RYDER, A.W. (trans.). *The Panchatantra.* Chicago: University of Chicago Press, 1958.
An excellent translation of the ancient "beast fables" of India.

*_____ (trans.). *Shakuntala and Other Writings.* New York: Dutton, 1959.
An outstanding translation of the works of the great dramatist, Kalidasa.

SEEGER, ELIZABETH. *The Five Brothers: The Story of Mahabharata.* New York: John Day, 1948.
A readable exposition of the classic poem.

UPPAL, J.S. *Indian Economic Planning.* New York: Macmillan India, 1985.
A symposium of scholars warn of a coming crisis due to factionalism.

WOOD, JOHN R. (ed.). *State Politics in Contemporary India.* Boulder: Westview, 1985.
A symposium of scholars warn of a coming crisis due to factionalism.

ZIMMER, H. *Myths and Symbols in Indian Art and Civilization.* New York: Pantheon Books, 1946.
A penetrating analysis of key motifs in India's legends, myths, and folklore.

_____. *The Art of Indian Asia.* (2 vols.) New York: Pantheon Books, 1960.
An excellent study of Indian art, with fine illustrations.

APPENDIX E

A CHRONOLOGY OF ASIAN HISTORY

China*		India		Japan		Southeast Asia		The West	
B.C.		B.C.		B.C.		B.C.		B.C.	
ca. 2205	Hsia Dynasty	ca. 4000	Indus cultures					ca. 3500	Egypt united
1766	Shang Dynasty	ca. 2500	Harappa falls					ca. 2750	Sargon I in Sumeria
ca. 1500	Eight Trigrams	ca. 2000	Aryan invasions					ca. 2750	Cuneiform used
ca. 1300	Supreme Being	ca. 1600	Rig-Veda					ca. 2169	Babylon founded
	concept spreads		Classes develop					ca. 2000	Stonehenge
1122	Chou Dynasty	ca. 1500	Aryan-Dravidian					ca. 2000	Cretan culture
1119	King Wu's empire		Synthesis					1800	Hammurabi's Code
ca. 1119	Central government	ca. 1200	Vedas, Brahmanas					ca. 1450	Mycenean Age
	Feudal landholding	ca. 800	Upanishads	ca. 1000	Jomon Culture			ca. 1200	Phonecian alphabet
	Civil service begins	ca. 567	Birth of Buddha	ca. 660	Legendary origin			ca. 1000	Assyria rules
		ca. 500	Post-Vedic Period	ca. 500	Yayoi Culture			ca. 1000	Aryans move south
		ca. 500	Jain Sect founded					950	Reign of Solomon
		ca. 500	Buddhism					ca. 800	Carthage built
604	Lao-tzu born	327	Alexander in India			ca. 400	Indians arrive	776	First Olympiad
551	Confucius born	322	Chandragupta's			ca. 300	Bronze-Iron Age	753	Founding of Rome
ca. 400	"100 Schools"		victory			ca. 300	Buddhist	722	Iron in Assyria
371	Mencius born		The Arthasastra				missionaries	590	Roman Republic
329	Chuang Tzu born	273	Reign of Asoka					539	Persian Empire
220	Highways built	270	Code of Manu	260	Great Shrine of Ise			521	Darius I in Persia
206	Han Dynasty	ca. 232	Asoka dies					490	Periclean Age
	Liu Pang's reign	185	Fall of Mauryas					ca. 469	Socrates born
	Huns invade							431	Peloponnesian War
188	Liu's widow reigns							323	Alexander dies
180	Wen Ti emperor							323	Hellenistic Epoch
156	Ching Ti reigns							ca. 264	First Punic War
140	Reign of Wu Ti							146	Carthage destroyed
								44	Caesar murdered
								27	Augustus:
									Pax Romana

*The traditional and Wade-Giles transliterations are used until the 1970's, when the Chinese government mandated the use of Hanyu Pinyin.

	China	India	Japan	Southeast Asia	The West

China — A.D. 1–499

- 9 Wang Mang's reign
-    Land distributed
-    State monopolies
-    Prices, taxes fixed
- 22 "Red Eyebrows"
- 58 Han Ming Ti
-    Buddhism
-    Empire expanded
- 62 Pan Ch'ao's cavalry
-    Silk Road defended
-    Court conspiracies
-    "Yellow Turbans"
-    Gentry class
-    Sundials, clocks
- ca. 100 Paper invented
- ca. 175 Engravings
- 265 West Chin Dynasty
-    Barbarian invasions
- 317 East Chin Dynasty
- 386 North Wei Dynasty
- ca. 400 Sporadic warfare

China — 500–999 A.D.

- 575 Buddhism spreads
- 589 Sui Dynasty
-    Yang Ti's reign
-    Grand Canal
-    Great Wall repaired
- 612 Korea defeats China
- 618 Yang Ti murdered
- 618 T'ang Dynasty
- 626 Li Shih-min
-    Turkish invasions
- 640 Defeat of Turks
-    Land distributed
-    Ch'an Buddhism spreads

India — A.D.

- ca. 50 Scythians invade
- ca. 150 Kushans invade
-    Kanishka reigns
-    Gandhara art
-    Buddhist schism
- ca. 250 Literature develops
-    Lawbooks
-    *Mahabharata, Ramayana*
- 320 Gupta Era begins
- 380 Chandragupta II reigns
-    Art, science flourish
-    *Panchatantra*
-    Mathematics develops
-    Hinduism emerges
- 540 Gupta Empire falls
-    *Bhagavad-Puranas*
-    "Four Ends of Man"
- 606 Harsha victorious

Japan — A.D.

- ca. 400 Imperial Clan forms
- 552 Buddhists arrive
-    Soga clan is Buddhist
-    Civil wars
-    Shintoism vs. Buddhism
- 593 Buddhism made state religion
- 593 Buddhism is official
- 593 Envoys go to China
- 645 Soga clan in power
- 645 Taika Reforms
- 701 Taiho Codes

Southeast Asia — A.D.

- ca. 50 Chinese in Tonkin
- ca. 100 Mon in lower Burma
-    Cult of Siva
-    Funan begins
- ca. 190 Champa founded
- ca. 400 Kaundinya rules Funan
- ca. 500 Cult of Vishnu
- ca. 539 Khmers in Funan
- ca. 600 Burmans arrive
- ca. 640 Sailendras on Java
- ca. 650 Thai migrations
- ca. 650 Sri Vijaya on Sumatra
- ca. 670 Sri Vijayan envoys in China
- ca. 700 China trade increases
- ca. 750 Burmans take Prome

The West — A.D.

- 29 Death of Christ
- 180 Marcus Aurelius dies
-    Decline of Rome
- 325 Council of Nicaea
-    Constantine aids Christianity
- 247 Goths cross Danube
- 277 Mani crucified
- 378 Battle of Adrianople
- 410 Alaric sacks Rome
- 527 Justinian
- 622 Hejira of Mohammed
- 717 Battle of

China	India	Japan	Southeast Asia	
713 Hsuan-tsung reigns	712 Arab invasions	710 Capital at Nara		
755 An Lu-shan rebels		Writing develops		
763 T'ang power high		Confucianism, Buddhism		
845 Buddhists killed		Arts flourish	ca. 785 Sailendra expands	
874 Hsi-tsung rules			ca. 802 Jayavarman II: Angkor	
874 Huang Ch'ao rebels		794 Heian is capital		
889 Chu Wen		ca. 800 Land ownership spreads	ca. 850 Sailendra, Sri Vijaya unite	
890 Empire dissolves		814 Minamoto clan begins		
Commerce develops			ca. 898 Mataram established	
Currency spreads				
Books distributed				
960 Sung Dynasty		889 Taira clan begins	ca. 980 Khmers invade Champa	732 Battle of Tours
Reign of T'ai Tsu		995 Height of Fujiwara power	ca. 985 Mataram conquers Bali	800 Charlemagne
Confucianism aided				962 Otto crowned
Central government				987 Hugh rules France
Hsi-hsia, Liao attack				

A.D. 1000-1499

China	India	Japan	Southeast Asia	
1069 Wang An-shih	ca. 1000 Mahmud's raids		1006 Sri Vijaya takes Mataram	1016 Canute in England
Economic reforms			1025 Cholas raid Sri Vijaya	1054 Roman-Greek Orthodox schism
1100 Hiu-tsung reigns				
Arts flourish			1044 Burma expands	1066 Normans invade England
1127 Jurchen wars			1050 Mataram ends: Kadiri formed	
1130 Chu Hsi born		1160 Taira clan in control	1050 Khmers conquer Mon	1071 Seljuk Turks revive Islam
Neo-Confucian Synthesis		1183 Minamoto clan victorious	1056 Anauratha is Buddhist	1095 Crusades begin
1215 Mongols in Peking	ca. 1175 Ghori's invasions	ca. 1186 Kamakura is capital	1057 Anauratha takes Thaton	
1226 Jenghis Khan dies	1211 Delhi Sultanate	1192 Yoritomo is shogun	1177 Chams sack Angkor	
ca. 1260 Marco Polo in Asia		Buddhism, arts flourish	1100 Sri Vijaya declines	
1276 Kublai takes Hangchow		1205 Hojo Tokimasa regency	1180 Jayavarman VII	
1279 Mongols seize South China			1190 Angkor rebuilt	
1294 Kublai dies		1274 Mongols repulsed	1190 Khmers rule Champa	
1356 Chu Yuan-chang succeeds		1281 Mongols defeated	ca. 1190 Thais in north Burma	
1368 Chu destroys Karakorum	1398 Timur sacks Delhi	1333 Go-Daigo attacks regency		
Ming Dynasty	1498 Da Gama in Malabar	1338 Ashikaga Takauji Two Courts		
1403 Reign of Yung-lo				

China	India	Japan	Southeast Asia	The West
			1200 Conversions to Islam	1215 Magna Carta
			1222 Singhasari subdues Kadiri	1274 St. Thomas dies
			1257 Mongols overrun Annam	Middle Ages end
			1268 Kertanagara rules Java	1293 Roger Bacon dies
			1286 Kertanagara in Sumatra	
			1287 Mongols attack Pagan	
			1291 Kertanagara murdered	
			1293 Vijaya founds Majapahit	
		1368 Shogunate of Yoshimitsu	1300 Moslem conversions	1300 Renaissance
		Height of Ashikaga	1350 Majapahit Wars	1348 The Black Death
		1392 Imperial courts joined	1350 Thais expand	1378 Christian schism
		1400 Feudalism elaborated	1365 Majapahit rules islands	1400 Chaucer dies
1405 Cheng Ho			1395 Malacca founded	1452 Leonardo da Vinci born
ca. 1405 Early novels			1400 Gujerati trade increases	1453 France wins 100 Years War
Imperial City built			1419 Siam attacks Malacca	Turks capture Byzantium
Trade with Europe			1431 Annam independent	1477 Polo's *Travels*
ca. 1421 Nomadic invasions			1431 Thais seize Angkor	1492 Moslems lose Spain
1432 Mings close China		ca. 1467 Ashikaga shogunate decays	1489 Malacca defeats Siam	Columbus's voyage
				1486 Voyage of Diaz

A.D. 1500–1599

China	India	Japan	Southeast Asia	The West
ca. 1516 First Portuguese traders	ca. 1500 Delhi Sultanate collapses	1500 Sengoku Period Feudal warfare	1509 D'Alburquerque is Viceroy	1517 Reformation
	1505 Portuguese in Goa	1542 Portuguese in Japan	Portugal attacks Malacca	1519 Magellan's voyage
	1524 Babur in India	1549 Francis Xavier	1521 Magellan dies	
	1526 Mogul Dynasty			
	1556 Reign of Akbar			

China	*India*	*Japan*	*Southeast Asia*	
1557 Portuguese take Macao	High culture	1582 Oda Nobunaga dies 1582 Hideyoshi takes power 1587 Christians persecuted 1590 Korean expeditions 1590 Spaniards arrive 1592 Conflict in Korea 1598 Hideyoshi dies	1556 Burmans invade Siam 1564 Spanish in Philippines 1577 Franciscans in Philippines 1577 Drake in Moluccas 1597 Dutch attack Malacca	1530 Pizarro in Peru 1543 Copernicus 1558 Death of Charles V 1564 Birth of Shakespeare 1589 Henry IV: strife wanes

A.D. 1600–1699

China	*India*	*Japan*	*Southeast Asia*	
1601 Ricci in Peking 1622 Dutch attack Macao 1644 Last Ming ruler 1645 Manchus in Nanking 1662 K'ang-hsi regency Dual government created Campaigns: Tibet, Mongolia	1605 Reign of Jahangir 1609 English arrive 1627 Shah Jahan's reign Hindus persecuted Taj Mahal built 1659 Aurangzeb's reign New persecutions Rajput art ca. 1675 France wins trade	1603 Tokugawa shogunate (Edo) 1605 Reign of Ieyasu 1615 Hideyoshi-Tokugawa War 1616 Christians persecuted 1622 Iemitsu in control 1636 Spanish, English excluded 1637 Shimabara Rebellion 1639 Portuguese banished 1640 Japan closed to West 1641 Dutch confined	1620 French in Annam 1623 Dutch in Amboyna 1640 Dutch take Malacca ca. 1680 French trade in Siam 1687 Siamese massacre French	1608 Jamestown 1613 First Romanov Czar 1648 End of Thirty Years War 1649 English revolution 1661 Louis XIV 1688 England's Parliament supreme

A.D. 1700–1799

China	*India*	*Japan*	*Southeast Asia*	
1723 Missionaries banished 1736 Ch'ien-lung rules	ca. 1700 British open bases 1707 Downfall of Moguls 1739 Persians invade 1740 Mahrattas attack 1756 British-French War 1757 Battle of Plassy 1760 Sikhs seize Punjab 1761 Mahrattas retreat	ca. 1700 Bushido Code ca. 1780 Ukiyo-e, Kabuki	1740 Java rebels 1763 Spain regains Philippines 1790 British in Penang	1709 Russia takes power 1727 Death of Newton 1740 War of Austrian Succession 1765 End of Seven Years War 1776 Declaration of Independence

China	India	Southeast Asia	Japan	The West
	1763 British triumphant			1789 French Revolution
	1780 Mahrattas attack British			1799 Bonaparte is First Consul

A.D. 1800–1899

China

- ca. 1815 First British envoys
- 1829 Manchus ban opium
- 1839 Opium seized
- 1840 Britain declares war
- 1842 Treaty of Nanking
- 1842 British gain Hong Kong
- 1843 British gain ports
- 1850 T'ai-p'ing Rebellion starts
- 1856 British-French campaigns
- 1860 Allies enter Peking
- 1864 T'ai-p'ings defeated
- 1874 Japan in Ryukus, Formosa
- 1882 Japan attacks Korea
- 1894 Sino-Japanese War
- 1896 New concessions
- 1898 100 Days of Reform

India

- 1804 Mahrattas defeated
- 1818 Gurkhas defeated
- 1844 Sikhs lose
- ca. 1850 India conquered
- 1857 Sepoy Rebellion
- 1858 British India Act; Company replaced
- 1869 Birth of Gandhi
- 1877 Victoria becomes Empress
- 1885 National Congress

Southeast Asia

- 1804 British in Dutch colonies
- 1819 Raffles buys Singapore
- ca. 1846 British in North Borneo
- ca. 1850 Siam "Westernizes"
- 1851 Burmans invade Malaya
- 1852 British take south Burma
- 1862 France seizes Cochin-China
- 1885 Britain annexes Burma
- 1887 France founds Indochina: Annam, Tonkin, Cambodia
- 1893 Laos added to Indochina
- 1898 Admiral Dewey at Manila Bay

Japan

- ca. 1800 Shinto Renaissance; Provincial rebellions
- ca. 1850 Samurai titles sold
- 1853 Commodore Perry arrives
- 1854 Japanese-U.S. treaty
- 1856 U.S. consul arrives
- 1858 Civil war in Japan
- 1863 British shell Kagoshima
- 1867 Tokugawa shogun resigns
- 1868 Meiji Restoration
- 1869 Emperor regains power
- 1873 Reforms enacted; Imperial Army created
- 1873 Christianity legalized
- 1877 Samurais rebel
- 1880 Zaibatsu gain power
- 1880 Liberal Party founded
- 1882 Kaishinto founded
- 1883 Ito visits Prussia
- 1889 New Constitution
- 1889 Ito made premier
- 1890 First general elections
- 1894 Japan joined Korea

The West

- 1815 Battle of Waterloo
- 1823 Monroe Doctrine
- 1825 First Railway
- 1830 Revolutions
- 1837 Victoria is queen
- 1848 The Communist Manifesto
- 1852 Napoleon III
- 1854 Crimean War
- 1858 Origin of the Species
- 1861 Civil War in U.S.
- 1861 Russian serfs freed
- 1866 Bismarck unifies Germany
- 1870 Franco-Prussian War
- 1898 Spanish-American War

China	India	Japan	Southeast Asia / Philippines	World
1900 Boxer Rebellion	1905 Bengal partitioned: riots	1902 Treaty with Britain	1902 U.S. annexes Philippines	1904 British-French alliance
1911 Chinese Revolution	1906 Reform Act	1905 Treaty of Portsmouth	1908 Indonesian nationalism	1914 World War I
1912 Chinese Republic	1906 Moslem League founded	1910 Japan seizes Korea	1918 Volksraad in Indonesia	1917 Bolsheviks win
1912 Sun Yat-sen elected	1909 Morley-Minto Reforms	1914 War on Germany	1921 Burmese constitution	1920 Peace of Versailles
1913 Yuan Shih-kai supreme	1910 Terrorism	1917 German colonies annexed	1934 Tydings-McDuffie Act	1920 League of Nations
1915 21 Demands	1915 Gandhi returns to India	1918 Rice riots	1935 Philippine Constitution	1922 Mussolini
1915 Nationalists at Nanking	1916 Tilak's leadership	1920 More riots, strikes	1935 Quezon elected	1928 Stalin's Five-Year Plan
1917 China joins Allies	1920 Satyagraha	1922 Parliament dissolves	1935 British Burma Act	1929 World Depression
1919 Allies reject China	1921 Gandhi rallies India	1922 Communist Party founded	1937 Ba Maw, U Saw take power	1933 F. D. Roosevelt
1921 Communist Party formed	1935 Limited self-rule	1922 Washington Peace Conference	1940 Japan, Siam sign treaty	1933 Hitler in Germany
1924 Mongolian Republic	1941 Nehru in power	1923 Great earthquake	1940 Siam invades Laos, Cambodia	1936 Spanish Civil War
1924 "Three Principles"	1942 Civil disobedience	1925 Peace Preservation Law	1940 Japan takes Indochina	1938 Munich Conference
1925 Sun Yat-sen dies	1942 "Quit India"	1927 Tanaka becomes premier	1941 Japan in Siam, Malaya, Burma, Dutch East Indies, Philippines	1939 World War II
1928 Chiang attacks Communists	1943 Famine in Bengal	1928 Troops sent to Shantung	1942 Singapore falls	1940 Defeat of France
1931 "The Manchurian Incident"	1944 Gandhi freed	1930 London Naval Conference	1942 Guerrillas in Vietnam	1945 Defeat of Germany
1934 The Long March	1946 Hindu-Moslem strife	1933 Japan seizes Manchuria	1942 Hukbalahaps (Philippines)	1945 Atomic energy
1936 The Sian Incident	1947 India, Pakistan formed	1933 Japan quits League of Nations	1945 Japanese withdraw	1945 U.N. founded
1937 Japan in China	1948 Gandhi assassinated	1936 Military coup	1946 Burma demands freedom	
1937 United Front	1951 First Five-Year Plan	1937 Invasion of China		
1942 Allies aid China	1951 Ali Khan murdered	1940 Axis Pact		
1943 Cairo Conference	1952 Nehru is Prime Minister	1940 Japan attacks Burma		
1944 Communists advance	1954 India's treaty with China	1941 South Indochina seized		
1945 Russia gains Outer Mongolia	1955 Bandung Conference	1941 Pearl Harbor		
1945 Nationalists in U.N.	1956 Pakistan's Constitution			
1946 General Marshall's mission	1956 Second Five-Year Plan			
1946 Civil war resumes				
1948 Communists rout Chiang				

China	India	Japan	Southeast Asia	The West
1949 Chiang seizes Formosa		1942 Philippines conquered	1946 France regains Vietnam	
1950 Landlords dispossessed		1942 Japanese sea losses	1947 Elections in Burma	
1951 China takes Tibet		1943 Guadalcanal	1947 Cambodian constitution	
1951 "Volunteers" in Korea		1944 Southeast Asia defeats	1948 Collaborators executed	1948 "Cold War" begins
1953 First Five-Year Plan		1944 Premier Tojo resigns	1948 Vietnam divided	
1953 Korean armistice		1945 Atomic bombs dropped	1949 French leave Laos	
1954 Constitution		1945 Emperor seeks peace	1949 Karens revolt (Burma)	1950 Korean War begins
1956 Free speech invited	1956 V. Bhave	1945 Surrender of Japan	1950 Indochina War	1952 Stalin dies
1956 Strict controls resumed		1946 National elections	1951 Guerrilla warfare	
1957 Second Five-Year Plan		1946 Emperor disavows divinity	1954 French surrender	
1958 Communes begin		1947 New Constitution	1954 Cambodia is independent	
1959 Plagues widespread		1948 Land, education reforms	1954 SEATO	1957 Man-made satellites
1960 China aids nationalism		1950 Purge of Communists	1955 Jungle warfare	
1962 China invades India	1961 India seizes Goa	1951 U.S.-Japanese Treaty	1959 Thailand coup	1960 European Common Market
1963 Sino-Russian strains	1962 China invades India	1952 End of occupation	1961 Truce in Laos	
1964 Diplomats tour Africa	1962 India mobilizes	1955 New parties formed	1963 Viet Cong gains	1963 President Kennedy dies
1964 France recognizes China	1963 Border disputes	1958 Production soars	1963 Malaysia formed	1964 Russia denounces China
	1964 Nehru stricken	1960 Riots against U.S.	1964 Indonesia warns Malaysia	
		1962 Socialists gain	1964 Philippines progress	
		1963 Ikeda's re-election		
		1964 Striking economic gains		
		1964 Increasing China trade		

China	India	Japan	Southeast Asia	The West
1964 1st nuclear warhead exploded	1965 Clash with Pakistan	1971 Defense budget doubled	1966 Sukarno overthrown	1964 U.S. launches Gemini spacecraft
1965 Army ranks abolished	1967 Indira Gandhi Prime Minister	1972 Tanaka visits China	1966 U.S. bombs Hanoi	1964 Racial violence in U.S.
1965 Lin Piao foresees world revolution	1967 Clash with China	1973 Tanaka visits United States	1966 U.S. defoliates Vietnam jungles	1964 Johnson elected
1966 Cultural Revolution	1968 Alliance with Russia	1974 Critical inflation	1970 Sihanouk overthrown	1965 1st "walks" in space
1966 Red Guards riot	1969 Banks nationalized		1970 U.S. troops in Cambodia	1965 Peace demonstrations
1967 Cultural Revolution abates	1969 Communist victory in Bengal elections		1971 U.S. troops in Laos	1965 Watts riots
1969 Lin Piao named Mao's successor	1971 Army supports Bangladesh		1972 Martial law, Philippines	1966 U.S. student riots
1969 Border clash with Russians	1972 Bhutto leads Pakistan		1972 U.S. mines Haiphong harbor	1967 Israel wins "6-Day War"
1971 Lin Piao dies	1974 1st nuclear bomb		1973 U.S. bombs Hanoi	1967 "Black Power" movement
1971 Admitted to UN			1973 Armistice in Vietnam	1967 Anti-pollution movement
1972 Nixon's visit			1973 Armistice violations, Vietnam	1968 Martin Luther King dies
1972 Britain recognizes China			1974 War Spreads in Cambodia	1968 Russia invades Czechoslovakia
1973 Increasing world trade				1968 Nixon elected
				1969 My Lai charges
				1970 West German-Russian treaty
				1971 U.S. devalues dollar
				1972 Nixon visits China, Russia
				1972 Army limitation talks (SALT)
				1972 Britain joins Common Market
				1972 Peace negotiations
				1972 Nixon re-elected
				1973 Watergate investigation
				1973 Jupiter probe
				1973 4th Arab—Israeli war
				1973 Arab oil embargo
				1974 New energy sources explored

China	India	Japan	Southeast Asia	The West
1974 Jiang Jieshi dies	1974 Atomic power gained	1972 U.S. returns Okinawa	1975 Communism in Laos	1974 Ford succeeds Nixon
1976 Zhou Enlai dies	1974 Sikkim annexed	1972 Disputes with USSR	1975 Khmer Rouge triumphs	1976 Viking II on Mars
1976 Mao Zedong dies	1975 "National Emergency"	1980 Exports soar	1975 Lon Nol flees	1976 South African riots
1976 Rise of Hua Guofeng	1977 M.R. Desai elected	1981 U.S. warns of tariffs	1975 Vast Thai inflation	1977 Carter defeats Ford
1976 Massive earthquakes	1977 Army seizes Pakistan	1982 Nakasone elected	1976 Kampuchean migrations	1977 First space shuttle
1977 Deng Xiaoping returns	1978 Mrs. Gandhi imprisoned	1983 Tanaka convicted	1976 Vietnam controls Laos	1978 Inflation rages
1978 China raids Vietnam	1980 Mrs. Gandhi reelected	1985 Soaring prosperity	1976 Vietnam united	1979 Thatcher elected
1979 U.S. recognizes China	1980 Muslim-Hindi riots	1986 Increasing trade	1977 Cambodian border war	1979 U.S. hostages in Iran
1981 "Gang of 4" convicted	1982 Bangladeshi martial law		1978 Suharto reelected	1979 3-Mile Island
1981 Incentive programs	1984 Golden Temple stormed		1978 Kampuchean holocaust	1979 Afghanistan invaded
1982 New laws end Maoism	1984 Massacres of Punjabis		1978 "Boat People"	1980 Riots sweep Poland
1985 Huge economic gains	1984 Mrs. Gandhi dies		1978 Soviet-Viet alliance	1980 Rising technology
1986 Growing world trade	1984 Rajiv Gandhi elected		1978 Viets in Kampuchea	1980 Reagan elected
	1984 Bhopal incident		1979 Pol Pot overthrown	1980 Interferon created
	1985 Sikh terrorists		1980 Singapore prospers	1980 Iran-Iraq War
	1985 Zia ends martial law		1983 Suharto's 4th term	1981 Mitterand elected
			1983 B. Aquino murdered	1981 Polish martial law
			1984 Sino-Viet conflict	1982 OPEC weakens
			1985 Khmer Rouge crippled	1982 British-Argentine War
			1986 Marcos deposed	1983 Reagan reelected
			1986 Malaysia prospers	1985 Terrorists in Europe
			1986 Viets raid Thailand	1985 Inflation abates
				1985 Advances in genetics
				1985 Gorbachev heads USSR
				1985 "3rd World" debt soars
				1986 Oil prices plunge
				1986 Economies improve
				1986 South African unrest
				1986 Central American wars
				1986 Space shuttle explodes

CONSTITUTION OF INDIA

SUMMARY OF THE CONSTITUTION

INDIA is a sovereign, democratic republic. The Constitution provides for a federal form of government, and there is a division of power between the Union and the States. The distribution of power provides for three legislative lists. List I enumerates the legislative powers of the Union, List II those of the States, and List III describes the concurrent powers. The Union has exclusive power over the residual matters. The executive power of the Union and the State is co-extensive with the legislative power. Both in the matter of legislation and exercise of executive power, the competence of the Union and the States is subject to the fundamental rights in Part III of the Constitution.

PART III

FUNDAMENTAL RIGHTS

GENERAL

12. In this Part, unless the context otherwise requires, "the State" includes the Government and Parliament of India and the Government and the Legislature of each of the States and all local or other authorities within the territory of India or under the control of the Government of India.

¹13. (1) All laws in force in the territory of India immediately before the commencement of this Constitution, in so far as they are inconsistent with the provisions of this Part, shall to the extent of such inconsistency, be void.

(2) The State shall not make any law which takes away or abridges the rights conferred by this Part and any law made in contravention of this clause shall, to the extent of the contravention, be void.

(3) In this article, unless the context otherwise requires,—

(a) "law" includes any Ordinance, order, by-law, rule, regulation, notification, custom or usage having in the territory of India the force of law;

---

¹ In its application to the State of Jammu and Kashmir, in art. 13, references to the commencement of the Constitution shall be construed as references to the commencement of the Constitution (Application to Jammu and Kashmir) Order, 1954, *i.e.*, the 14th day of May, 1954.

(b) "laws in force" includes laws passed or made by a Legislature or other competent authority in the territory of India before the commencement of this Constitution and not previously repealed, notwithstanding that any such law or any part thereof may not be then in operation either at all or in particular areas.

RIGHT TO EQUALITY

14. The State shall not deny to any person equality before the law or the equal protection of the laws within the territory of India.

15. (1) The State shall not discriminate against any citizen on grounds only of religion, race, caste, sex, place of birth or any of them.

(2) No citizen shall, on grounds only of religion, race, caste, sex, place of birth or any of them, be subject to any disability, liability, restriction or condition with regard to—

(a) access to shops, public restaurants, hotels and places of public entertainment; or

(b) the use of wells, tanks, bathing ghats, roads and places of public resort maintained wholly or partly out of State funds or dedicated to the use of the general public.

(3) Nothing in this article shall prevent the State from making any special provision for women and children.

[1](4) Nothing in this article or in clause (2) of article 29 shall prevent the State from making any special provision for the advancement of any socially and educationally backward classes of citizens or for the Scheduled Castes and the Scheduled Tribes. [2]

16. (1) There shall be equality of opportunity for all citizens in matters relating to employment or appointment to any office under the State.

(2) No citizen shall, on grounds only of religion, race, caste, sex, descent, place of birth, residence or any of them, be ineligible for, or discriminated against in respect of, any employment or office under the State.

[3](3) Nothing in this article shall prevent Parliament from making any law prescribing, in regard to a class or classes of employment or appointment to an office [4][under the Government of, or any local or other authority within, a State or Union territory, any requirement as to residence within that State of Union territory] prior to such employment or appointment.

---

[1] Added by the Constitution (First Amendment) Act, 1951, s. 2.

[2] In its application to the State of Jammu and Kashmir, reference to Scheduled Tribes in cl. (4) of art. 15 shall be omitted.

[3] In cl. (3) of art. 16, the reference to the State shall be construed as not including a reference to the State of Jammu and Kashmir.

[4] Subs. by the Constitution (Seventh Amendment) Act, 1956, s. 29 and Sch., for "under any State specified in the First Schedule or any local or other authority within its territory, any requirement as to residence within that State."

(4) Nothing in this article shall prevent the State from making any provision for the reservation of appointments or posts in favor of any backward class of citizens which, in the opinion of the State, is not adequately represented in the services under the State.

(5) Nothing in this article shall affect the operation of any law which provides that the incumbent of an office in connection with the affairs of any religion or denominational institution or any member of the governing body thereof shall be a person professing a particular religion or belonging to a particular denomination.

17. "Untouchability" is abolished and its practice in any form is forbidden. The enforcement of any disability arising out of "Untouchability" shall be an offense punishable in accordance with law.

18. (1) No title, not being a military or academic distinction, shall be conferred by the State.

(2) No citizen of India shall accept any title from any foreign State.

(3) No person who is not a citizen of India shall, while he holds any office of profit or trust under the State, accept without the consent of the President any title from any foreign State.

(4) No person holding any office of profit or trust under the State shall, without the consent of the President, accept any present, emolument, or office of any kind from or under any foreign State.

RIGHT TO FREEDOM

[1]19. (1) All citizens shall have the right—

(a) to freedom of speech and expression;

(b) to assemble peaceably and without arms;

(c) to form associations or unions;

(d) to move freely throughout the territory of India;

(e) to reside and settle in any part of the territory of India;

(f) to acquire, hold and dispose of property; and

(g) to practice any profession, or to carry on any occupation, trade or business.

---

[1] In its application to the State of Jammu and Kashmir, for a period of fifteen years from the 14th May, 1954, art. 19 shall be subject to the following modifications:—

(i) in clauses (3) and (4), after the words "in the interests of," the words "the security of the State of" shall be inserted;

(ii) in clause (5), for the words "or for the protection of the interests of any Scheduled Tribe," the words "or in the interests of the security of the State" shall be substituted; and

(iii) the following new clause shall be added, namely:—

(7) The words "reasonable restrictions" (occurring in clauses (2), (3), (4) and (5) shall be construed as meaning such restrictions as the appropriate Legislature deems reasonable.

[1](2) Nothing in sub-clause (a) of clause (1) shall affect the operation of any existing law, or prevent the State from making any law, in so far as such law imposes reasonable restrictions on the exercise of the right conferred by the said sub-clause in the interests of ¶[the sovereignty and integrity of India,] the security of the State, friendly relations with foreign States, public order, decency or morality, or in relation to contempt of court, defamation or incitement to an offense.

(3) Nothing in sub-clause (b) of the said clause shall affect the operation of any existing law in so far as it imposes, or prevents the State from making any law imposing, in the interests of [2][the sovereignty and integrity of India or] public order, reasonable restrictions on the exercise of the right conferred by the said sub-clause.

(4) Nothing in sub-clause (c) of the said clause shall affect the operation of any existing law in so far as it imposes, or prevents the State from making any law imposing, in the interests of [2][the sovereignty and integrity of India or] public order or morality, reasonable restrictions on the exercise of the right conferred by the said sub-clause.

(5) Nothing in sub-clauses (d), (e) and (f) of the said clause shall affect the operation of any existing law in so far as it imposes, or prevents the State from making any law imposing, reasonable restrictions on the exercise of any of the rights conferred by the said sub-clauses either in the interests of the general public or for the protection of the interests of any Scheduled Tribe.

(6) Nothing in sub-clause (g) of the said clause shall affect the operation of any existing law in so far as it imposes, or prevents the State from making any law imposing, in the interests of the general public, reasonable restrictions on the exercise of the right conferred by the said sub-clause, and, in particular, [3][nothing in the said sub-clause shall affect the operation of any existing law in so far as it relates to, or prevents the State from making any law relating to,—

    (i) the professional or technical qualifications necessary for practicing any profession or carrying on any occupation, trade or business, or

    (ii) the carrying on by the State, or by a corporation owned or controlled by the State, or any trade, business, industry or service, whether to the exclusion, complete or partial, of citizens or otherwise.].

---

[1] Subs. by the Constitution (First Amendment) Act, 1951, s. 3, for the original cl. (2) (with retrospective effect).

[2] Ins. by the Constitution (Sixteenth Amendment) Act, 1963, s. 2.

[3] Subs by the Constitution (First Amendment) Act. 1951, s. 3. for certain original words.

20. (1) No person shall be convicted of any offense except for violation of a law in force at the time of the commission of the act charged as an offense, nor be subjected to a penalty greater than that which might have been inflicted under the law in force at the time of the commission of the offense.

(2) No person shall be prosecuted and punished for the same offense more than once.

(3) No person accused of any offense shall be compelled to be a witness against himself.

21. No person shall be deprived of his life or personal liberty except according to procedure established by law.

22. (1) No person who is arrested shall be detained in custody without being informed, as soon as may be, of the grounds for such arrest nor shall he be denied the right to consult, and to be defended by, a legal practitioner of his choice.

(2) Every person who is arrested and detained in custody shall be produced before the nearest magistrate within a period of twenty-four hours of such arrest excluding the time necessary for the journey from the place of arrest to the court of the magistrate and no such person shall be detained in custody beyond the said period without the authority of a magistrate.

(3) Nothing in clauses (1) and (2) shall apply—

(a) to any person who for the time being is an enemy alien; or

(b) to any person who is arrested or detained under any law providing for prevention detention.

[1](4) No law providing for preventive detention shall authorize the detention of a person for a longer period than three months unless—

(a) an Advisory Board consisting of persons who are, or have been, or are qualified to be appointed as, Judges of a High Court has reported before the expiration of the said period of three months that there is in its opinion sufficient cause for such detention:

Provided that nothing in this sub-clause shall authorize the detention of any person beyond the maximum period prescribed by any law made by Parliament under sub-clause (b) of clause (7); or

(b) such person is detained in accordance with the provisions of any law made by Parliament under sub-clauses (a) and (b) of clause (7).

(5) When any person is detained in pursuance of an order made under any law providing for preventive detention, the authority making the order shall, as soon as may be, communicate to

---

[1] In its application to the State of Jammu and Kashmir, in cl. (4) of art. 22, for the word "Parliament," the words "the Legislature of the State" shall be substituted.

such person the grounds on which the order has been made and shall afford him the earliest opportunity of making a representation against the order.

(6) Nothing in clause (5) shall require the authority making any such order as is referred to in that clause to disclose the facts which such authority considers to be against the public interest to disclose.

¹(7) Parliament may by law prescribe—

(a) the circumstances under which, and the class or classes of cases in which, a person may be detained for a period longer than three months under any law providing for preventive detention without obtaining the opinion of an Advisory Board in accordance with the provisions of sub-clause (d) of clause (4);

(b) the maximum period for which any person may in any class or classes of cases be detained under any law providing for preventive detention; and

(c) the procedure to be followed by an Advisory Board in an inquiry under sub-clause (a) of clause (4).

RIGHT AGAINST EXPLOITATION

23. (1) Traffic in human beings and *begar* and other similar forms of forced labor are prohibited and any contravention of this provision shall be an offense punishable in accordance with law.

(2) Nothing in this article shall prevent the State from imposing compulsory service for public purposes, and in imposing such service the State shall not make any discrimination on grounds only of religion, race, caste or class or any of them.

24. No child below the age of fourteen years shall be employed to work in any factory or mine or engaged in any other hazardous employment.

RIGHT TO FREEDOM OF RELIGION

25. (1) Subject to public order, morality and health and to the other provisions of this Part, all persons are equally entitled to freedom of conscience and the right freely to profess, practice and propagate religion.

(2) Nothing in this article shall affect the operation of any existing law or prevent the State from making any law—

(a) regulating or restricting any economic, financial, political

---

¹ In its application to the State of Jammu and Kashmir, in cl. (7) of art. 22, for the word "Parliament," the words "the Legislature of the State" shall be substituted.

or other secular activity which may be associated with religious practice;

(b) providing for social welfare and reform or the throwing open of Hindu religious institutions of a public character to all classes and sections of Hindus.

Explanation I,—The wearing and carrying of *kirpans* shall be deemed to be included in the profession of the Sikh religion.

Explanation II.—In sub-clause (b) of clause (2), the reference to Hindus shall be construed as including a reference to persons professing the Sikh, Jaina or Buddhist religion, and the reference to Hindu religious institutions shall be construed accordingly.

26. Subject to public order, morality and health, every religious denomination or any section thereof shall have the right—

(a) to establish and maintain institutions for religious and charitable purposes;

(b) to manage its own affairs in matters of religion;

(c) to own and acquire movable and immovable property; and

(d) to administer such property in accordance with law.

27. No person shall be compelled to pay any taxes, the proceeds of which are specifically appropriated in payment of expenses for the promotion or maintenance of any particular religion or religious denomination.

28. (1) No religious instruction shall be provided in any educational institution wholly maintained out of State funds.

(2) Nothing in clause (1) shall apply to an educational institution recognized by the State or receiving aid out of State funds shall be required to take part in any religious instruction that may be imparted in such institution or to attend any religious worship that may be conducted in such institution or in any premises attached thereto unless such person or, if such person is a minor, his guardian has given his consent thereto.

CULTURAL AND EDUCATIONAL RIGHTS

29. (1) Any section of the citizens residing in the territory of India or any part thereof having a distinct language, script or culture of its own shall have the right to conserve the same.

(2) No citizen shall be denied admission into any educational institution maintained by the State or receiving aid out of State funds on grounds only of religion, race, caste, language or any of them.

30. (1) All minorities, whether based on religion or language, shall have the right to establish and administer educational institutions of their choice.

(2) The State shall not, in granting aid to educational institutions, discriminate against any educational institution on the ground that it is under the management of a minority, whether based on religion or language.

RIGHT TO PROPERTY

¹31. (1) No person shall be deprived of his property save by authority of law.

²(2) No property shall be compulsorily acquired or requisitioned save for a public purpose and save by authority of a law which provides for compensation for the property so acquired or requisitioned and either fixes the amount of the compensation or specifies the principles on which, and the manner in which, the compensation is to be determined and given; and no such law shall be called in question in any court on the ground that the compensation provided by that law is not adequate.

(2A) Where a law does not provide for the transfer of the ownership or right to possession of any property to the State or to a corporation owned or controlled by the State, it shall not be deemed to provide for the compulsory acquisition or requisitioning of property, notwithstanding that it deprives any person of his property.

(3) No such law as is referred to in clause (2) made by the Legislature of a State shall have effect unless such law, having been reserved for the consideration of the President, has received his assent.

(4) If any Bill pending at the commencement of this Constitution in the Legislature of a State has, after it has been passed by such Legislature, been reserved for the consideration of the President and has received his assent, then, notwithstanding anything in this Constitution, the law so assented to shall not be called in question in any court on the ground that it contravenes the provisions of clause (2).

---

¹ In its application to the State of Jammu and Kashmir, in art. 31, cls. (3), (4) and (6) shall be omitted and for cl. (5), the following clause shall be substituted, namely:—
"(5) Nothing in clause (2) shall affect—
    (a) the provisions of any existing law; or
    (b) the provisions of any law which the State may hereafter make—
        (i) for the purpose of imposing or levying any tax or penalty; or
        (ii) for the promotion of public health or the prevention of danger to life or property; or
        (iii) with respect to property declared by law to be evacuee property."
² Subs. by the Constitution (Fourth Amendment) Act, 1955, s. 2, for the original clause.

(5) Nothing in clause (2) shall affect—

(a) the provisions of any existing law other than a law to which the provisions of clause (6) apply, or

(b) the provisions of any law which the State may hereafter make—

(i) for the purpose of imposing or levying any tax or penalty, or

(ii) for the promotion of public health or the prevention of danger to live or property, or

(iii) in pursuance of any agreement entered into between the Government of the Dominion of India or the Government of India and the Government of any other country, or otherwise, with respect to property declared by law to be evacuee property.

(6) Any law of the State enacted not more than eighteen months before the commencement of this Constitution may within three months from such commencement be submitted to the President for his certification; and thereupon, if the President by public notification so certifies, it shall not be called in question in any court on the ground that it contravenes the provisions of clause (2) of this article or has contravened the provisions of sub-section (2) of section 299 of the Government of India Act, 1935.

¹31A. ²(1) Notwithstanding anything contained in article 13, no law providing for—

(a) the acquisition by the State of any estate or of any rights therein or the extinguishment or modification of any such rights, or

(b) the taking over of the management of any property by the State for a limited period either in the public interest or in order to secure the proper management of the property, or

(c) the amalgamation of two or more corporations either in the public interest or in order to secure the proper management of any of the corporation or

(d) the extinguishment or modification of any rights of managing agents, secretaries and treasurers, managing directors, directors or managers of corporations, or of any voting rights of shareholders thereof, or

(e) the extinguishment or modification of any rights accruing by virtue of any agreement, lease or license for the purpose of searching for, or winning, any mineral or mineral oil, or the premature termination or cancellation of any such agreement, lease or license.

---

¹ Ins. by the Constitution (First Amendment) Act, 1951, s. 4 (with retrospective effect).
² Subs. by the Constitution (Fourth Amendment) Act, 1955, s. 3. for the original clause (with retrospective effect).

shall be deemed to be void on the ground that it is inconsistent with, or takes away or abridges any of the rights conferred by article 14, article 19 or article 31:

¹Provided that where such law is a law made by the Legislature of a State, the provisions of this article shall not apply thereto unless such law, having been reserved for the consideration of the President, has received his assent:

²Provided further that where any law makes any provision for the acquisition by the State of any estate and where any land comprised therein is held by a person under his personal cultivation, it shall not be lawful for the State to acquire any portion of such land as is within the ceiling limit applicable to him under any law for the time being in force or any building or structure standing thereon or appurtenant thereto, unless the law relating to the acquisition of such land, building or structure, provides for payment of compensation at a rate which shall not be less than the market value thereof.

(2) In this article,—

³[⁴(a) the expression "estate" shall, in relation to any local area, have the same meaning as that expression or its local equivalent has in the existing law relating to land tenures in force in that area and shall also include—

> (i) any *jagir*, *inam* or *muafi* or other similar grant and in the States of Madras and Kerala, any *janmam* right;
> (ii) any land held under ryotwari settlement;

---

¹ In its application to the State of Jammu and Kashmir, the proviso to cl. (1) of art. 31A shall be omitted.

² Ins. by the Constitution (Seventeenth Amendment) Act, 1964, s. 2.

³ Subs. by the Constitution (Seventeenth Amendment) Act. 1964, s. 2, for sub-clause (a) (with retrospective effect).

⁴ In its application to the State of Jammu and Kashmir, for sub-clause (a) of cl. (2) of art. 31A, the following sub-clause shall be substituted, namely:—

"(a) 'estate' shall mean land which is occupied or has been let for agricultural purposes or for purposes subservient to agriculture, or for pasture, and includes—
> (i) sites of buildings and other structures on such land;
> (ii) trees standing on such land;
> (iii) forest land and wooded waste;
> (iv) area covered by or fields floating over water;
> (v) sites of *jandars* and *gharats;*
> (vi) any *jagir, inam, muafi* or *mukarrari* or other similar grant, but does not include—
> >   (i) the site of any building in any town, or town area or village *abadi* or any land appurtenant to any such building or site;
> >   (ii) any land which is occupied as the site of a town or village; or
> >   (iii) any land reserved for building purposes in a municipality or notified area or cantonment or town area or any area for which a town planning scheme is sanctioned."

(iii) any land held or let for purposes of agriculture or for purposes ancillary thereto, including waste land, forest land, land for pasture or sites of buildings and other structures occupied by cultivators of land, agricultural laborers and village artisans;

(b) the expression "rights," in relation to an estate, shall include any rights vesting in a proprietor, sub-proprietor, under-proprietor, tenure-holder, ¹[*raiyat, under-raiyat*] or other intermediary and any rights or privileges in respect of land revenue.

²31B. Without prejudice to the generality of the provisions contained in article 31A, none of the Acts and Regulations specified in the Ninth Schedule nor any of the provisions thereof shall be deemed to be void, or ever to have become void, on the ground that such Act, Regulation or provision is inconsistent with, or takes away or abridges any of the rights conferred by, any provisions of this Part, and notwithstanding any judgment, decree or order of any court or tribunal to the contrary, each of the said Acts and Regulations shall, subject to the power of any competent Legislature to repeal or amend it, continue in force.

RIGHT TO CONSTITUTIONAL REMEDIES

32. (1) The right to move the Supreme Court by appropriate proceedings for the enforcement of the rights conferred by this Part is guaranteed.

(2) The Supreme Court shall have power to issue directions or orders or writs, including writs in the nature of *habeas corpus, mandamus,* prohibition, *quo warranto* and *certiorari,* whichever may be appropriate, for the enforcement of any of the rights conferred by this Part.

³(3) Without prejudice to the powers conferred on the Supreme Court by clauses (1) and (2), Parliament may by law empower any other court to exercise within the local limits of its jurisdiction all or any of the powers exercisable by the Supreme Court under clause (2).

---

¹ Ins. by the Constitution (Fourth Amendment) Act, 1955, s. 3 (with retrospective effect).
² Ins. by the Constitution (First Amendment) Act, 1951, s. 5.
³ In its application to the State of Jammu and Kashmir, cl. (3) of art. 32, shall be omitted; and after cl. (2), the following new clause shall be inserted, namely:—

"(2A) Without prejudice to the powers conferred by clauses (1) and (2), the High Court shall have power throughout the territories in relation to which it exercises jurisdiction to issue to any person or authority, including in appropriate cases any Government within those territories, directions or orders or writs, including writs in the nature of *habeas corpus, mandamus,* prohibition, *quo warranto* and *certiorari,* or any of them, for the enforcement of any of the rights conferred by this Part."

(4) The right guaranteed by this article shall not be suspended except as otherwise provided for by this Constitution.

33. Parliament may by law determine to what extent any of the rights conferred by this Part shall, in their application to the members of the Armed Forces or the Forces charged with the maintenance of public order, be restricted or abrogated so as to ensure the proper discharge of their duties and the maintenance of discipline among them.

34. Notwithstanding anything in the foregoing provisions of this Part, Parliament may by law indemnify any person in the service of the Union or of a State or any other person in respect of any act done by him in connection with the maintenance or restoration of order in any area within the territory of India where martial law was in force or validate any sentence passed, punishment inflicted, forfeiture ordered or other act done under martial law in such area.

¹35. Notwithstanding anything in this Constitution,—

(a) Parliament shall have, and the Legislature of a State shall not have, power to make laws—

    (i) with respect to any of the matters which under clause (3) of article 16, clause (3) of article 32, article 33 and article 34 may be provided for by law made by Parliament; and

    (ii) for prescribing punishment for those acts which are declared to be offenses under this Part;

and Parliament shall, as soon as may be after the commencement of this Constitution, make laws for prescribing punishment for the acts referred to in sub-clause (ii);

(b) any law in force immediately before the commencement of this Constitution in the territory of India with respect to any of the matters referred to in sub-clause (i) of clause (a) or providing for punishment for any act referred to in sub-clause (ii) of that clause

---

₁ In its application to the State of Jammu and Kashmir, in art. 35,—

  (i) references to the commencement of the Constitution shall be construed as references to the commencement of the Constitution (Application to Jammu and Kashmir) Order, 1954 (14th May, 1954);

  (ii) in cl. (a) (i), the words, figures and brackets "clause (3) of article 16, clause (3) of article 32" shall be omitted; and

  (iii) after cl. (b), the following clause shall be added, namely:—

    "(c) no law with respect to preventive detention made by the Legislature of the State of Jammu and Kashmir, whether before or after the commencement of the Constitution (Application to Jammu and Kashmir) Order, 1954, shall be void on the ground that it is inconsistent with any of the provisions of this Part, but any such law shall, to the extent of such inconsistency, cease to have effect on the expiration of fifteen years from the commencement of the said Order, except as respects things done or omitted to be done before the expiration thereof."

shall, subject to the terms thereof and to any adaptations and modifications that may be made therein under article 372, continue in force until altered or repealed or amended by Parliament.

Explanation.—In this article, the expression "law in force" has the same meaning as in article 372. [1]

PART IV[2]

DIRECTIVE PRINCIPLES OF STATE POLICY

36. In this Part, unless the context otherwise requires, "the State" has the same meaning as in Part III.

37. The provisions contained in this Part shall not be enforceable by any court, but the principles therein laid down are nevertheless fundamental in the governance of the country and it shall be the duty of the State to apply these principles in making laws.

38. The State shall strive to promote the welfare of the people by securing and protecting as effectively as it may a social order in which justice, social, economic and political, shall inform all the institutions of the national life.

39. The State shall, in particular, direct its policy towards securing—

(a) that the citizens, men and women equally, have the right to an adequate means of livelihood;

(b) that the ownership and control of the material resources of the community are so distributed as best to subserve the common good;

(c) that the operation of the economic system does not result in the concentration of wealth and means of production to the common detriment;

---

[1] In its application to the State of Jammu and Kashmir, after art. 35, the following new article shall be added, namely:—

"35A. *Savings of laws with respect to permanent residents and their rights.*—Notwithstanding anything contained in this Constitution, no existing law in force in the State of Jammu and Kashmir, and no law hereafter enacted by the Legislature of the State,—

(a) defining the classes of persons who are, or shall be, permanent residents of the State of Jammu and Kashmir; or

(b) conferring on such permanent residents any special rights and privileges or imposing upon other persons any restrictions as respects—

(i) employment under the State Government;

(ii) acquisition of immovable property in the State;

(iii) settlement in the State; or

(iv) right to scholarships and such other forms of aid as the State Government may provide.

shall be void on the ground that it is inconsistent with or takes away or abridges any rights conferred on the other citizens of India by any provision of this Part."

[2] Not applicable to the State of Jammu and Kashmir.

(d) that there is equal pay for equal work for both men and women;

(e) that the health and strength of workers, men and women, and the tender age of children are not abused and that citizens are not forced by economic necessity to enter avocations unsuited to their age or strength.

(f) that childhood and youth are protected against exploitation and against moral and material abandonment.

40. The State shall take steps to organize village panchayats and endow them with such powers and authority as may be necessary to enable them to function as units of self-government.

41. The State shall, within the limits of its economic capacity and development, make effective provision for securing the right to work, to education and to public assistance in cases of unemployment, old age, sickness and disablement, and in other cases of undeserved want.

42. The State shall make provision for securing just and humane conditions of work and for maternity relief.

43. The State shall endeavor to secure, by suitable legislation or economic organization or in any other way, to all workers, agricultural, industrial or otherwise, work, a living wage, conditions of work ensuring a decent standard of life and full enjoyment of leisure and social and cultural opportunities and, in particular, the State will endeavor to promote cottage industries on an individual or co-operative basis in rural areas.

44. The State shall endeavor to secure for the citizens a uniform civil code throughout the territory of India.

45. The State shall endeavor to provide, within a period of ten years from the commencement of this Constitution, for free and compulsory education for all children until they complete the age of fourteen years.

46. The State shall promote with special care the educational and economic interests of the weaker sections of the people, and, in particular, of the Scheduled Castes and the Scheduled Tribes, and shall protect them from social injustice and all forms of exploitation.

47. The State shall regard the raising of the level of nutrition and the standard of living of its people and the improvement of public health as among its primary duties and, in particular, the State shall endeavor to bring about prohibition of the consumption except for medicinal purposes of intoxicating drinks and of drugs which are injurious to health.

48. The State shall endeavor to organize agriculture and animal

husbandry on modern and scientific lines and shall, in particular, take steps for preserving and improving the breeds, and prohibiting the slaughter of cows and calves and other milch and draught cattle.

49. It shall be the obligation of the State to protect every monument or place or object of artistic or historic interest, [declared by or under law made by Parliament] to be of national importance, from spoliation, disfigurement, destruction, removal, disposal or export, as the case may be.

50. The State shall take steps to separate the judiciary from the executive in the public services of the State.

51. The State shall endeavor to—
    (a) promote international peace and security;
    (b) maintain just and honorable relations between nations;
    (c) foster respect for international law and treaty obligations in the dealings of organized peoples with one another; and
    (d) encourage settlement of international disputes by arbitration.

PART V

THE UNION

CHAPTER I— THE EXECUTIVE

THE PRESIDENT AND VICE-PRESIDENT

52. There shall be a President of India.

53. (1) The Executive power of the Union shall be vested in the President and shall be exercised by him either directly or through officers subordinate to him in accordance with this Constitution.

(2) Without prejudice to the generality of the foregoing provision, the supreme command of the Defense Forces of the Union shall be vested in the President and the exercise thereof shall be regulated by law.

(3) Nothing in this article shall—
    (a) be deemed to transfer to the President any functions conferred by an existing law on the Government of any State or other authority; or
    (b) prevent Parliament from conferring by law functions on authorities other than the President.

---

[1] Subs. by the Constitution (Seventh Amendment) Act, 1956. s. 27, for "declared by Parliament by law."

APPENDIX G

THE ARREST AND TRIAL OF MAHATMA GANDHI

PRETRIAL STATEMENT

For months in 1922, the rumor of Mr. Gandhi's impending arrest was in the air. Expecting the inevitable, Mr. Gandhi had more than once written his final message. But in the first week of March, 1922, the rumor became more widespread and pronounced. The stiffening of public opinion in England, and Mr. Montagu's speech in defense of his Indian policy in the Commons, revealed the fact that the Secretary of State had already sanctioned Mr. Gandhi's prosecution. Realizing this, Mr. Gandhi wrote the following in his Gujarari weekly, *Nava Jiran:*

I have been constantly thinking of what the people would do in case I am arrested. My co-workers also have been putting this question to me. What would be the plight of India if the people took to the wrong path through love run mad? What would be my own plight in such a case?

Rivers of blood shed by the Government cannot frighten me, but I would be deeply pained even if the people did so much as abuse the Government for my sake or in my name. It would be disgracing me if the people lost their equilibrium on my arrest. The nation can achieve no progress merely by depending upon me. Progress is possible only by their understanding and following the path suggested by me. For this reason I desire that the people should maintain perfect self-control and consider the day of my arrest as a day of rejoicing. I desire that even the weakness existing today should disappear at that time.

What can be the motive of the Government in arresting me? The Government are not my enemy; for I have not a grain of enmity towards them. But they believe that I am the soul of all this agitation, that if I am removed, the ruled and the ruler would be left in peace, that the people are blindly following me. Not only the Government but some of our leaders also share this belief. How then can the Government put the people to the test? How can ghe Government ascertain whether the people do understand my advice or are simply dazzled by my utterances?

The only way left to them is to arrest me. Of course there still remains an alternative for them and that lies in the removal of the causes which have led me to offer this advice. But intoxicated as they are with power, the Government will not see their own fault and even if they do, they will not admit it. The only way then that remains for

234

them is to measure the strength of the people. They can do this by arresting me. If the people are thus terrorized into submission, they can be said to deserve the Punjab and the Khilafat wrongs.

If, on the other hand, the people resort to violence, they will merely be playing into the hands of the Government. Their airplanes will them bomb the people, their (General) Dyers will shoot them, and their (Governor) Smiths will uncover the veils of our women. There will be other officers to make the people rub their noses against the ground, crawl on their bellies and undergo the scourge of whipping. Both these results will be equally bad and unfortunate. They will not lead to *Swaraj*. In other countries Government have been overthrown by sheer brute force, but I have often shown that India cannot attain *Swaraj* by that force. What then should the people do if I am arrested?

The answer now is simple. The people 1) should preserve peace and calmness; 2) should not observe *Hartal;* 3) should not hold meetings, but 4) should be fully awake.

I should certainly expect 5) all the Government Schools to be vacated and shut down; 6) lawyers to withdraw from practice in greater numbers; 7) settlement by private arbitration of cases pending before the Courts; 8) opening of numerous national schools and colleges; 9) renunciation of all foreign cloth in favor of the exclusive use of hand-spun and hand-woven garments by lakhs of men and women, and selling or burning of any foreign cloth in stock; 10) none to enlist in the army or in any other Government service; 11) those able to earn their livelihood by other means to give up Government service; 12) contribution of as much as is wanted towards national funds; 13) title holders to surrender titles in greater numbers; 14) candidates to withdraw from elections, or if already elected, to resign their seats; 15) voters who have not yet made up their minds, to resolve that it is sin to send any representative to the Councils.

If the people resolve and carry this out, they would not have to wait for *Swaraj* even for a year. If they exhibit this much strength we shall have attained *Swaraj*.

I shall then be set free under the nation's seal. That will please me. My freedom today is like a prison to me.

It will only prove the peoples' incompetence if they use violence to release me and then depend upon my help to attain *Swaraj* for them. Neither I nor any one else can get *Swaraj* for the Nation. It will be got on the Nation proving its own fitness.

In conclusion, it is useless to find fault with the Government. We get what government we deserve. When we improve, the Government is also bound to improve. Only when we improve can we attain *Swaraj*. Noncooperation is the Nation's determination to improve.

Will the Nation abandon the resolve and begin to cooperate after my arrest? If the people become mad and take to violence and as a result of it crawl on their bellies, rub their noses on the ground, salute the Union Jack and walk eighteen miles to do it, what else is that but cooperation? It is better to die than to submit to crawling. In fine, consider it from any point of view, the course suggested by me is the right one for the people to take.

Gandhi's Plea

M. K. Gandhi, 53, farmer and weaver by profession, was arrested at the Satyagraha Ashram, Ahmedabad, on March 10, 1921, for certain articles published in his *Young India*. The Superintendent of Police, Ahmedabad, the first witness, produced the Bombay government's authority to lodge a complaint for four articles published in *Young India*, dated June 15, 1921, entitled "Disaffection: a Virtue"; dated September 29, "Tampering with Loyalty"; dated December 15, "The Puzzle and its Solution" and dated February 23, 1922, "Shaking the Manes." Two formal police witnesses were then produced. The accused declined to cross-examine the witnesses, but said:

I simply wish to state that when the proper time comes, I shall plead guilty so far as disaffection towards the Government is concerned. It is quite true that I am the Editor of the *Young India* and that the articles read in my presence were written by me, and the proprietors and publishers had permitted me to control the whole policy of the paper.

Gandhi's Courtroom Statement

Before I read this statement, I would like to state that I entirely endorse the learned Advocate-General's remarks in connection with my humble self. I think that he was entirely fair to me in all the statements that he has made, because it is very true and I have no desire whatsoever to conceal from this Court the fact that to preach disaffection towards the existing system of Government has become almost a passion with me. And the learned Advocate-General is also entirely in the right when he says that my preaching of disaffection did not commence with my connection with *Young India* but that it commenced much earlier, and in the statement that I am about to

The case then having been committed to the Sessions, Gandhi was taken to the Sabarmati Jail where he was detained until the hearing which was to come off on March 18. At that hearing Gandhi, who had no lawyer, pleaded guilty and said that he had a statement.

read it will be my painful duty to admit before this Court that it commenced much earlier than the period stated by the Advocate-General. It is the most painful duty with me, but I have to discharge that duty knowing the responsibility that rested upon my shoulders.

And I wish to endorse all the blame that the Advocate-General has thrown on my shoulders in connection with the Bombay occurrences, the Madras occurrences and the Chauri Chaura occurrences. Thinking over these things deeply and sleeping over them night after night and examining my heart, I have come to the conclusion that it is impossible for me to dissociate myself from the diabolical crime of Chauri Chaura or the mad outrages of Bombay. He is quite right when he says that as a man of responsibility, a man having received a fair share of education, having had a fair share of experience of this world, I should know the consequences of every one of my acts. I knew them. I knew that I was playing with fire. I ran the risk and if I was set free I would still do the same. I would be failing in my duty if I do not do so. I have felt it this morning that I would have failed in my duty if I did not say all what I said here just now. I wanted to avoid violence. Nonviolence is the first article of my faith. It is the last article of my faith. But I had to make my choice. I had either to submit to a system which I considered has done an irreparable harm to my country or incur the risk of the mad fury of my people bursting forth when they understood the truth from my lips. I know that my people have sometimes gone mad. I am deeply sorry for it; and I am therefore here to submit not to a light penalty but to the highest penalty. I do not ask for mercy. I do not plead any extenuating act. I am here therefore to invite and submit to the highest penalty that can be inflicted upon me for what in law is a deliberate crime and what appears to me to be the highest duty of a citizen. The only course open to you, Mr. Judge, is, as I am just going to say in my statement, either to resign your post or inflict on me the severest penalty if you believe that the system and law you are assisting to administer are good for the people. I do not expect that kind of conversion. But by the time I have finished with my statement, you will perhaps have a glimpse of what is raging within my breast to run this maddest risk which a sane man can run.

The following is the full text of the written statement which Gandhi made before the court:

I owe it perhaps to the Indian public and to the public in England to placate which this prosecution is mainly taken up that I should explain why from a staunch loyalist and cooperator I have become an uncompromising disaffectionist and noncooperator. To the Court too I should say why I plead guilty to the charge of promoting disaffection towards the Government established by law in India.

My public life began in 1893 in South Africa in troubled weather. My first contact with British authority in that country was not of a happy character. I discovered that as a man and as an Indian I had no rights. On the contrary I discovered that I had no rights as a man because I was an Indian.

But I was not baffled. I thought this treatment of Indians was an excrescence upon a system that was intrinsically and mainly good. I gave the Government my voluntary and hearty cooperation, criticizing it fully where I felt it was faulty, but never wishing its destruction.

Consequently when the existence of the Empire was threatened in 1899 by the Boer challenge, I offered my services to it, raised a volunteer ambulance corps and served at several actions that took place for the relief of Ladysmith. Similarly in 1906, at the time of the Zulu revolt, I raised a stretcher-bearer party and served till the end of the rebellion. On both these occasions I received medals and was even mentioned in despatches. For my work in South Africa I was given by Lord Hardinge a Kaiser-i-Hind Gold Medal. When the War broke out in 1914 between England and Germany, I raised a volunteer ambulance corps in London consisting of the then resident Indians in London, chiefly students. Its work was acknowledged by the authorities to be valuable. Lastly in India when a special appeal was made at the War Conference in Delhi in 1917 by Lord Chelmsford for recruits, I struggled at the cost of my health to raise a corps in Kheda and the response was being made when the hostilities ceased and orders were received that no more recruits were wanted. In all these efforts at service, I was actuated by the belief that it was possible by such services to gain a status of full equality in the Empire for my countrymen.

The first shock came in the shape of the Rowlatt Act, a law designed to rob the people of all real freedom. I felt called upon to lead an intensive agitation against it. Then followed the Punjab horrors beginning with the massacre at Jallianwala Bagh and culminating in crawling orders, public floggings and other indescribable humiliations. I discovered too that the plighted word of the prime Minister to the Mussulmans of India regarding the integrity of Turkey and the holy places of Islam was not likely to be fulfilled. But in spite of the foreboding and the grave warnings of friends at the Amritsar Congress in 1919, I fought for cooperation and working the Montagu-Chalmsford reforms, hoping that the Prime Minister would redeem his promise to the Indian Mussulmans, that the Punjab wound would be healed, and that the reforms, inadequate and unsatisfactory though they were, marked a new era of hope in the life of India.

But all that hope was shattered. The Khilafat promise was not to be redeemed. The Punjab crime was whitewashed, and most culprits went not only unpunished but remained in service and some continued to draw pensions from the Indian revenue and in some cases were even rewarded. I saw too that not only did the reforms not mark a change of heart, but they were only a method of further draining India of her wealth and of prolonging her servitude.

I came reluctantly to the conclusion that the British connection had made India more helpless than she ever was before, politically and economically. A disarmed India has no power of resistance against any aggressor if she wanted to engage in an armed conflict with him. So much is this the case that some of our best men consider that India must take generations before she can achieve the Dominion Status. She has become so poor that she has little power of resisting famines. Before the British advent, India spun and wove in her millions of cottages just the supplement she needed for adding to her meager agricultural resources. The cottage industry, so vital for India's existence, has been ruined by incredibly heartless and inhuman processes as described by English witnesses. Little do town-dwellers know how the semi-starved masses of Indians are slowly sinking to lifelessness. Little do they know that their miserable comfort represents the brokerage they get for the work they do for the foreign exploiter, that the profits and the brokerage are sucked from the masses. Little do they realize that the Government established by law in British India is carried on for this exploitation of the masses. No sophistry, no jugglery in figures can explain away the evidence the skeletons in many villages present to the naked eye. I have no doubt whatsoever that both England and the town-dwellers of India will have to answer, if there is a God above, for this crime against humanity which is perhaps unequalled in history. The law itself in this country has been used to serve the foreign exploiter. My unbiased examination of the Punjab Martial Law cases has led me to believe that at least ninety-five percent of convictions were wholly bad. My experience of political cases in India leads me to the conclusion that in nine out of every ten the condemned men were totally innocent. Their crime consisted in love of their country. In ninety-nine cases out of a hundred, justice has been denied to Indians as against Europeans in the Courts of India. This is not an exaggerated picture. It is the experience of almost every Indian who has had anything to do with such cases. In my opinion the administration of the law is thus prostituted consciously or unconsciously for the benefit of the exploiter.

The greatest misfortune is that Englishmen and their Indian associates in the administration of the country do not know that they are engaged in the crime I have attempted to describe. I am satisfied that many English and Indian officials honestly believe that they are administering one of the best systems devised in the world and that India is making steady though slow progress. They do not know that a subtle but effective system of terrorism and an organized display of force on the one hand, and the deprivation of all powers of retaliation or self-defense on the other, have emasculated the people and induced in them the habit of simulation. This awful habit has added to the ignorance and the self-deception of the administrators. Section 124-A under which I am happily charged is perhaps the prince among the political sections of the Indian Penal Code designed to suppress the liberty of the citizen. Affection cannot be manufactured or regulated by law. If one has no affection for a person or thing, one should be free to give the fullest expression to his disaffection so long as he does not contemplate, promote or incite to violence. But the Section under which Mr. Banker and I are charged is one under which mere promotion of disaffection is a crime. I have studied some of the cases tried under it and I know that some of the most loved of India's patriots have been convicted under it. I consider it a privilege therefore to be charged under it. I have endeavored to give in their briefest outline the reasons for my disaffection. I have no personal illwill against any single administrator, much less can I have any disaffection towards the King's person. But I hold it to be a virtue to be disaffected towards a Government which, in its totality, has done more harm to India than any previous system. India is less manly under the British rule than she ever was before. Holding such a belief I consider it to be a sin to have affection for the system. And it has been a precious privilege for me to be able to write what I have in the various articles tendered in evidence against me.

In fact I believe that I have rendered a service to India and England by showing in Noncooperation the way out of the unnatural state in which both are living. In my humble opinion, noncooperation with evil is as much a duty as is cooperation with good. But in the past, noncooperation has been deliberately expressed in violence to the evil doer. I am endeavoring to show to my countrymen that violent noncooperation only multiplies evil and that as evil can only be sustained by violence, withdrawal of support of evil requires complete abstention from violence. Nonviolence implies voluntary submission to the penalty for noncooperation with evil. I am here therefore to invite and submit cheerfully to the highest penalty that can be inflicted upon me for what in law is deliberate crime and what appears to me to be the highest duty of a citizen. The only course open to you, the Judge and the Assessors, is either to resign your posts and thus dissociate yourselves from evil, if you feel that the law you are called upon to administer is an evil and that in reality I am innocent, or to inflict on me the severest penalty if you believe that the system and the law you are assisting to administer are good for the people of this country and that any activity is therefore injurious to the public weal.

THE JUDGMENT

After Gandhi's statement, C. N. Broomfield, Session Judge, pronounced the following judgment:

"Mr. Gandhi, you have made my task easy one way by pleading guilty to the charge. Nevertheless what remains, namely, the determination of a just sentence is perhaps as difficult a proposition as a Judge in this country could have to face. The law is no respecter of persons. Nevertheless it will be impossible to ignore the fact that you are in a different category from any person I have ever tried or am likely to have to try. It would be impossible to ignore the fact that in the eyes of millions of your countrymen you are a great patriot and a great leader. Even those who differ from you in politics, look upon you as a man of high ideals and of noble and even saintly life. I have to deal with you in one character only. It is not my duty and I do not presume to judge or criticize you in any other character. It is my duty to judge you as a man subject to the law who has by his own admission broken the law and committed, what to an ordinary man must appear to be, grave offenses against the State. I do not forget that you have consistently preached against violence and that you have on many occasions, as I am willing to believe, done much to prevent violence. But having regard to the nature of political teaching and the nature of many of those to whom it was addressed how you could have continued to believe that violence would not be the inevitable consequence, it passes my capacity to understand. There are probably few people in India who do not sincerely regret that you should have made it impossible for any Government to leave you at liberty. But it is so. I am trying to balance what is due to you against what appears to me to be necessary in the interest of the public, and I propose in passing sentence to follow the precedent of a case in many respects similar to this case that was decided some twelve years ago. I mean the case against Mr. Bal Gangadhar Tilak under the same section. The sentence that was passed upon him as it finally stood was a sentence of simple imprisonment for six years. You will not consider it unreasonable I think that you should be classed with Mr. Tilak. That is a sentence of two years' simple imprisonment on each count of the charges, six years in all which I feel it my duty to pass upon you; and I should like to say in doing so that if the course of events in India should make it possible for the Government to reduce the period and release you no one will be better pleased than I."

APPENDIX H

NEHRU'S INDEPENDENCE SPEECH

Tryst With Destiny*

Long years ago we made a tryst with destiny, and now the time comes when we shall redeem our pledge, not wholly or in full measure, but very substantially. At the stroke of the midnight hour, when the world sleeps, India will awake to life and freedom. A moment comes, which comes but rarely in history, when we step out from the old to the new, when an age ends, and when the soul of a nation, long suppressed, finds utterance. It is fitting that at this solemn moment we take the pledge of dedication to the service of India and her people and to the still larger cause of humanity.

At the dawn of history India started on her unending quest, and trackless centuries are filled with her striving and the grandeur of her success and her failures. Through good and ill fortune alike she has never lost sight of that quest or forgotten the ideals which gave her strength. We end today a period of ill fortune and India discovers herself again. The achievement we celebrate today is but a step, an opening of opportunity, to the greater triumphs and achievements that await us. Are we brave enough and wise enough to grasp this opportunity and accept the challenge of the future?

Freedom and power bring responsibility. The responsibility rests upon this Assembly, a sovereign body representing the sovereign people of India. Before the birth of freedom we have endured all the pains of labor and our hearts are heavy with the memory of this sorrow. Some of those pains continue even now. Nevertheless, the past is over and it is the future that beckons to us now.

That future is not one of ease or resting but of incessant striving so that we may fulfill the pledges we have so often taken and the one we shall take today. The service of India means the service of the millions who suffer. It means the ending of poverty and ignorance and disease and inequality of opportunity. The ambition of the greatest man of our generation has been to wipe every tear from every eye. That may be beyond us, but as long as there are tears and suffering, so long our work will not be over.

*Speech delivered in the Constituent Assembly, New Delhi, August 14, 1947, on the eve of the attainment of Independence.

And so we have to labor and to work, and work hard, to give reality to our dreams. Those dreams are for India, but they are also for the world, for all the nations and peoples are too closely knit together today for any one of them to imagine that it can live apart. Peace has been said to be indivisible; so is freedom, so is prosperity now, and so also is disaster in this One World that can no longer be split into isolated fragments.

To the people of India, whose representatives we are, we make an appeal to join us with faith and confidence in this great adventure. This is no time for petty and destructive criticism, no time for ill will or blaming others. We have to build the noble mansion of free India where all her children may dwell.

I beg to move, Sir,
"That it be resolved that:

After the last stroke of midnight, all members of the Constituent Assembly present on this occasion do take the following pledge:

'At this solemn moment when the people of India, through suffering and sacrifice, have secured freedom, I........., a member of the Constituent Assembly of India do dedicate myself in all humility to the service of India and her people to the end that this ancient land attain her rightful place in the world and make her full and willing contribution to the promotion of world peace and the welfare of mankind' . . . .

APPENDIX I

NEHRU'S SPEECH ON THE DEATH OF GANDHI

The Light Has Gone Out*

Friends and comrades, the light has gone out of our lives, and there is darkness everywhere. I do not know what to tell you and how to say it. Our beloved leader, Bapu, as we called him, the Father of the Nation, is no more. Perhaps I am wrong to say that. Nevertheless, we will not see him again as we have seen him for these many years. We will not run to him for advice and seek solace from him, and that is a terrible blow, not to me only but to millions and millions in this country. And it is a little difficult to soften the blow by any other advice that I or anyone else can give you.

*Broadcast to the nation on the evening of January 30, 1948, after Gandhi's assassination.

The light has gone out, I said, and yet I was wrong. For the light that shone in this country was no ordinary light. The light that has illumined this country for these many many years will illumine this country for many more years, and a thousand years later, that light will still be seen in this country and the world will see it and it will give solace to innumerable hearts. For that light represented something more than the immediate present; it represented the living, the eternal truths, reminding us of the right path, drawing us from error, taking this ancient country to freedom.

All this has happened when there was so much more for him to do. We could never think that he was unnecessary or that he had done his task. But now, particularly, when we are faced with so many difficulties, his not being with us is a blow most terrible to bear.

A madman has put an end to his life, for I can only call him mad who did it and yet there has been enough of poison spread in this country during the past years and months, and this poison has had an effect on people's minds. We must face this poison, we must root out this poison, and we must face all the perils that encompass us, and face them not madly or badly, but rather in the way that our beloved teacher taught us to face them.

The first thing to remember now is that none of us dare misbehave because he is angry. We have to behave like strong and determined people, determined to face all the perils that surround us, determined to carry out the mandate that our great teacher and our great leader has given us, remembering always that if, as I believe, his spirit looks upon us and sees us, nothing would displease his soul so much as to see that we have indulged in any small behavior or any violence.

So we must not do that. But that does not mean that we should be weak, but rather that we should, in strength and in unity, face all the troubles that are in front of us. We must hold together, and all our petty troubles and difficulties and conflicts must be ended in the face of this great disaster. A great disaster is a symbol to us to remember all the big things of life and forget the small things of which we have thought too much. In his death he has reminded us of the big things of life, the living truth, and if we remember that, then it will be well with India. . . . *Jai Hind.*

APPENDIX J

INDIRA GANDHI'S PROGRAM*

Thirty-six years ago, on this very day, my voice was one of thousands repeating the historic and soul-stirring words of our Pledge of Independence.

In 1947 that pledge was fulfilled. The world acknowledged that a new progressive force, based on democracy and secularism, had emerged. In the seventeen years that Jawaharlal Nehru was Prime Minister, the unity of this country with its diversity of religion, community and language became a reality, and democracy was born and grew roots. We took the first step towards securing a better life for our people by planned economic development. India's voice was always raised in the cause of the liberation of oppressed peoples, bringing hope and courage to many. It was heard beyond her frontiers as the voice of peace and reason promoting friendship and harmony among nations.

During his brief but memorable stewardship, Shastriji enriched the Indian tradition in his own way. He has left our country united and determined to pursue our national objectives. Only yesterday we committed his mortal remains to the sacred rivers. The entire country sorrowed for the great loss. I feel his absence intensely and personally, for I worked closely with him for many years.

My own approach to the vast problems which confront us is one of humility. However, the tradition left by Gandhiji and my father, and my own unbounded faith in the people of India give me strength and confidence. Time and again, India has given evidence of an indomitable spirit. In recent years, as in the past, she has shown unmistakable courage and capacity for meeting new challenges. There is a firm base on Indianness which will withstand any trial.

The coming months bristle with difficulties. We have innumerable problems requiring urgent action. The rains have failed us, causing drought in many parts. As a result, agricultural production, which is still precariously dependent on weather and rainfall, has suffered a sharp decline. Economic aid from abroad and earnings from export have not come to us in the measure expected. The lack of foreign exchange has hurt industrial production. Let us not be dismayed or

---

*Speech to the nation on January 26, 1966.

discouraged by these unforeseen difficulties. Let us face them boldly. Let us learn from our mistakes and resolve not to let them recur. I hope to talk to you from time to time to explain the measures we take and to seek your support for them.

Above all else we must ensure food to our people in this year of scarcity. This is the first duty of Government. We shall give urgent attention to the management and equitable distribution of food grains, both imported and procured at home. We expect full cooperation from State Governments, and all sections of the people in implementing our plans for rationing, procurement and distribution. Areas like Kerala which are experiencing acute shortage will receive particular attention. We shall try especially to meet the nutritional needs of mothers and children in the scarcity-affected areas to prevent permanent damage to their health. We cannot afford to take risks where basic food is concerned. We propose, therefore, to import large enough quantities of food-grains to bridge this gap. We are grateful to the United States for her sympathetic understanding and prompt help.

Only greater production will solve our food problem. We have now a well thought-out plan to reach water and chemical fertilizers and new high-yielding varieties of seed as well as technical advice and credit to farmers. Nowhere is self-reliance more urgent than in agriculture, and it means higher production not only for meeting the domestic needs of a large and increasing population but also for growing more for exports. We have to devise more dynamic ways of drawing upon the time and energy of our rural people and engaging them in the tasks of construction. We must breath new life into the rural works program and see that the income of the rural laborer is increased.

Our strategy of economic advance assigns a prominent role in the public sector to the rapid expansion of basic industries, power and transport. In our circumstances, this is not only desirable but necessary. It also imposes an obligation to initiate, construct and manage public sector enterprises efficiently and to produce sufficient profits for further investments. Within the framework of our Plans, there-is no conflict between the public and private sectors. In our mixed economy, private enterprise has flourished and has received help and support from Government. We shall continue to encourage and assist it.

Recent events have compelled us to explore the fullest possibilities of technological self-reliance. How to replace, from domestic sources, the materials we import, the engineering services we purchase, and the know-how we acquire from abroad? Our progress is linked with our ability to invent, improvise, adopt and conserve. We have a reservoir of talented scientists, engineers and technicians. We must make better use of them. Given the opportunity, our scientists and engineers have demonstrated their capacity to achieve outstanding results. Take the shining example of Dr. Homi Bhabha and the achievements of the Atomic Energy Establishment. The path shown by Dr. Bhabha will remain an inspiration.

Our programs of economic and social development are encompassed in our Plans. The Third Five-Year-Plan is drawing to a close. We are on the threshold of the Fourth. The size and content of the Fourth Plan received general endorsement of the National Development Council last September even while we were preoccupied with the defense of our country. Its detailed formulation was interrupted due to many uncertainties, including that of foreign aid. We propose now to expedite this work. In the meantime an annual plan has been drawn up for 1966–67, the first year of the Fourth Plan. This takes into account the main elements of the Five-Year-Plan.

In economic development, as in other fields of national activity, there is a disconcerting gap between intention and action. To bridge this gap, we should boldly adopt whatever far-reaching changes in administration may be found necessary. We must introduce new organizational patterns and modern tools and techniques of management and administration. We shall instill into governmental machinery greater efficiency and a sense of urgency and make it more responsive to the needs of the people.

In keeping with our heritage, we have followed a policy of peace and friendship with all nations, yet reserved to ourselves the right to independent opinion. The principles which have guided our foreign policy are in keeping with the best traditions of our country, and are wholly consistent with our national interest, honor and dignity. They continue to remain valid. During my travels abroad, I have had the privilege of meeting leaders in government and outside and have always found friendship and an appreciation of our stand. The fundamental principles laid down by my father, to which he and Shastriji dedicated their lives, will continue to guide us. It will be my sincere endeavor to work for the strengthening of peace and international cooperation, so that people in all lands live in equality, free from domination and fear. We seek to maintain the friendliest relations with our neighbors and to resolve any disputes peacefully. The Tashkent Declaration is an expression of these sentiments. We shall fully implement it in letter and spirit.

Peace is our aim, but I am keenly aware of the responsibility of Government to preserve the freedom and territorial integrity of the country. We must, therefore, be alert and keep constant vigil, strengthening our defenses as necessary. The valor, the determination, the courage and sacrifice of our fighting forces have set a magnificent example. My thoughts go out today to the disabled and the families of those who gave their lives.

Peace we want because there is another war to fight—the war against poverty, disease and ignorance. We have promises to keep with our people—of work, food, clothing and shelter, health and education. The weaker and underprivileged sections of our people—all those who require special measures of social security—have always been and will remain uppermost in my mind.

Youth must have greater opportunity. The young people of India must recognize that they will get from their country tomorrow what they give her today. The nation expects them to aspire and to excel. The worlds of science and art, of thought and action beckon to them. There are new frontiers to cross, new horizons to reach and new goals to achieve.

No matter what our religion, language or State, we are one nation and one people. Let us all—farmers, and workers, teachers and students, scientists and technologists, industrialists, businessmen, politicians and public servants—put forth our best effort. Let us be strong, tolerant and disciplined, for tolerance and discipline are the very foundations of democracy. The dynamic and progressive society, the just social order which we wish to create, can be achieved only with unity of purpose and through hard work and cooperation.

Today I pledge myself anew to the ideals of the builders of our nation—to democracy and secularism, to planned economic and social advance, to peace and friendship among nations.

Citizens of India, let us revive our faith in the future. Let us affirm our ability to shape our destiny. We are comrades in a mighty adventure. Let us be worthy of it and of our great country. *Jai Hind.*

APPENDIX K

INDEX